To J. B. Angell, LL.D.
with the kindest
regards of the Author.
Feb. 13. 69.

THE BUDGET CLOSED.

BY

JANE ANTHONY EAMES,

AUTHOR OF "A BUDGET OF LETTERS," "ANOTHER BUDGET," &C.

BOSTON:
TICKNOR AND FIELDS.
MDCCCLX.

PRINTED BY WM. BUTTERFIELD,
PATRIOT OFFICE,
CONCORD, N. H.

TO HON. CARROLL SPENCE,

LATE UNITED STATES MINISTER TO THE SUBLIME PORTE,

THIS VOLUME IS, BY PERMISSION,

DEDICATED,

IN GRATITUDE FOR NUMEROUS ACTS OF KINDNESS AND ATTENTION,

WHILE IN CONSTANTINOPLE AND ITS ENVIRONS.

PREFACE.

I do not know as it is necessary for me to apologize to the public in general, and my own friends in particular, for so long delaying to bring before them THE BUDGET CLOSED. I will, therefore, pass over in silence the reasons I might give for this delay, and will merely say that those who followed us in our boat life, our journey across the Desert, and our sojourn in the Holy Land, will, I hope, find something to interest them in the present volume.

CONCORD, N. H., *Sept.*, 1860.

TABLE OF CONTENTS.

LETTER XLV.

LETTER XLVI.

LETTER XLVII.

LETTER XLVIII.

LETTER XLIX.

LETTER L.

LETTER LI.

LETTER LII.

LETTER LIII.

LETTER LIV.

LETTER LV.

LETTER LVI.

LETTER LVII.

LETTER LVIII.

LETTER LIX.

LETTER LX.

LETTER LXI.

LETTER LXII.

LETTER LXIII.

LETTER LXIV.

LETTER LXV.

LETTER LXVI.

LETTER LXVII.

LETTER LXVIII.

LETTER LXIX.

LETTER LXX.

LETTER LXXI.

LETTER LXXII.

LETTER LXXIII.

LETTER LXXIV.

LETTER LXXV.

LETTER LXXVI.

LETTER LXXVII.

LETTER LXXVIII.

LETTER LXXIX.

LETTER LXXX.

LETTER LXXXI.

LETTER LXXXII.

LETTER LXXXIII.

LETTER XCI.

LETTER XCII.

LETTERS.

LETTER XLV.

Departure from Smyrna.—Crowded Steamboat.—Gallipoli.—Arrival at Constantinople.—Geography of the place.—Wooden Houses.—Singular looking Carriages.—Streets of Pera.—Beautiful View.—Large Cemetery.

CONSTANTINOPLE, May 22d.

MY DEAR P.:

I am sure you will unite with us in gratitude to our Heavenly Father, for bringing us safely through our journey in Asia, and landing us once more on the shore of Europe. And as I say to myself, "we are again in Europe," it seems to me we are almost at home; and though months must elapse before we can see your dear faces once more, our steps are homeward turned, and that of itself has a peculiar charm.

We arrived here early on Monday morning, and having secured good accommodations (a difficult thing just now, when there are so many foreigners here,) at the "Hotel de Byzance," we at once commenced the duties of sight-seeing, which are doubly fatiguing here, from the heat of the weather and the wretched pavement of the streets.

I am sorry that I can give you no information concerning the voyage from Smyrna here, for I really know nothing of what there could have been seen outside the steamer. We left on Saturday afternoon, and, as I wrote you, the steamer was crowded with soldiers, which effectually prevented my going on deck, till after they had disembarked, on Sunday, at Gallipoli, and then the decks were so dreadfully dirty, I could not stay there with any degree of comfort. You can imagine somewhat the state of the upper deck, when I tell you six hundred soldiers had been quartered there for nine days, two or three of which had been very stormy, and there being two pipes to the steamer, a vast amount of cinders had collected on the deck, which there seemed to be no disposition to clean off, even after the troops had disembarked. I felt so very anxious, however, to see somewhat of the country, that I attempted two or three times to go on deck; and by standing on a camp-stool, and stretching out my neck, I made out to see a bit of blue sea and a hill, but except that, I literally saw nothing save soldiers and dirt. However, on our way to Athens, I believe the steamer will touch at Smyrna, when I shall hope to make amends for seeing nothing on my first voyage from there, for I am sure it must have been full of interest, coming, as we did, from the Gulf of Smyrna into the Archipelago, studded with islands, dear with their classical associations, and then entering the narrow Straits of Dardanelles, which connect the Archipelago with the Sea of Marmora.

At Gallipoli we stopped several hours, but I did not go on shore, as I could see the town from the steamer, and the encampment was too far from the harbor to walk there with comfort. I saw the hills that rise up back of Gallipoli, and at their feet the town, a mass of stone houses, interspersed with a few trees, and at a distance, the white tents of the troops, scattered along the valley and on the hillsides.

The cabin of the steamer was very comfortable, though we could not get a state-room together; in fact, the first night, Mr. E. slept on a narrow sofa, and the last, had a berth in a small cabin, with three other gentlemen. I was in the ladies' cabin, a small room, with five French ladies, who chattered like a parcel of magpies. The table was good, and we had every thing to satisfy our wants, as long as those wants were confined to the cabin, and as we did not have to pay any thing additional, we passed over the discomforts of the troops and the dirt as well as we could. As I wrote you from Beyroot, six francs extra a day are charged each passenger for board, but as Mr. E. had no bed the first night, the steward would not take the twenty-four francs due for our board. Liberal for him, and exceedingly gratifying to us.

As early this morning as I possibly could get ready in a small cabin with five other ladies, I dressed myself and went on deck, not a whit cleaner than it was the day before. But I thought not of the dirt, when I saw the view from the steamer, for Constantinople, "the magnificent," was before us. How queenly she looked, seated on her seven hills, her stupendous domes, and towering minarets, and slender cypresses seeming to pierce the sky! Was there ever a lovelier sight? Walls and towers, and palaces and mosques and gardens, passed all too quickly, and one exclamation of admiration had scarcely died away, when another broke forth. The Marmora stretched behind us, sparkling and blue, and before us, it narrowed off till it was fairly merged in the Straits of the Bosphorus, which connect it with the Black Sea. I was so absorbed in looking at the city, I scarcely saw the rock-girt isles in the Marmora, nor the Asiatic shore beyond.

At last the anchor was dropped, and we were surrounded by a crowd of boats and long, slender caiques, and after not a little confusion and jabbering in unknown tongues, ourselves and our luggage were safely deposited in a large boat, and we were rapidly rowed to the shore, and after an interval of more than seven months, found ourselves again in Europe.

And now, before I go farther, I will take the geographer's vocation, and describe more particularly the situation of Constântinople, for fear you may not have a good map on hand, and in order that you may form a clear conception of its numerous spots of interest, and its different localities.

On the south, Constantinople lies on the Sea of Marmora, while on the opposite side sweeps down the coast of Asia, backed, at a distance, by the lofty range of Taurus, whose summits glitter with snow. On the west, it lies on the Bosphorus, having opposite to it, on the Asiatic side, the town of Scutari in the foreground, its immense cemetery containing a forest of dark cypresses, and its stupendous barracks, and the background formed by rolling hills, studded with palaces and gardens.

Rounding the point on which Constantinople projects into the Bosphorus, an arm of the straits makes up, termed the "Golden Horn," and on the opposite side of this, and extending round to the Bosphorus, lie the suburbs of Constantinople, Galata, Pera and Tophana. These suburbs are mostly inhabited by what is termed the Christian population, a mixture of every nation, and almost of every religion, under the sun. Here the ambassadors from foreign courts reside; here the wealthy merchants and bankers transact their business, and a thousand petty traders and craftsmen attend to their various vocations. Constantinople, or as it is termed by the natives, Stamboul, is connected with its suburbs by three bridges thrown across the Golden Horn, and these, with their crowd of motley passengers, and the thousand little caiques darting hither and thither, present at all times an animating and ever varying sight.

Having now stirred up your memories in relation to the geographical position of Constantinople, in which general name I include Pera, Galata and Tophana, though here they are spoken of as quite distinct, I come back once more to the period of our arrival. Our keys were demanded, and our luggage slightly examined, nothing undergoing any scrutiny, except my worsted work. Our luggage, and that of the party with us, was strapped on the backs of porters, who, bending almost double under their load, staggered up the hill. And what a hill it was! Steep and crooked, and withal paved with such stones, that I defy any one to walk on them with any thing like grace or ease.

We were in a new world, for we saw, what we have not seen since we left home, wooden houses, but not such houses as we should see in the United States; for they all have more or less an oriental look, some being of fantastic architecture, and almost all having little balconies and narrow latticed windows, and large clumsy doors, with ungainly knockers. Then we met Turkish women, in their cloaks or mantles of various colors, and their faces concealed by their "yashmacks," formed by two pieces of muslin, the one covering the head, and reaching down to the eyebrows, the other being bound tight across the lower part of the face, covering even the nose and mouth, so that it is a mystery to me how they breathe. Their feet, often without stockings, are encased in overgrown boots of yellow morocco, thrust into slippers of the same color, without heel-pieces, so that there is nothing but the toe to keep the foot in its place, and the consequence is, they shuffle along when they walk, with the most awkward, ungainly gait imaginable. Their cloaks or mantles, or whatever they are called, are entirely different in their shape from any thing we have seen before; they are not very full, but have a long square cape hanging down behind, and as they wrap themselves closely in them, probably to keep from showing the dress beneath, they do not present the most elegant figures in the world. They seem to affect gay colors; for some of the cloaks (I declare I don't know what else to call them) are red and green, and pink and yellow, and as they are all bound with black, they really look quite fantastic. But as many of the faces are very pale, and unearthly looking, with their covering of thin white muslin, bound in such a manner around them, I am sure if they would shut their eyes, they would look like corpses prepared for burial.

Another strange thing we saw too—carriages in some of the streets; but although I have seen them more than once, I despair, as yet, of giving you a correct description of them, so utterly unlike are they to any thing of the vehicle kind ever before seen. At first sight, I should say they were antique specimens, as they look somewhat like that old carriage that was paraded through our streets on July 4th, 1853, which doubtless you all remember, as it excited much attention at the time; but when I saw the elaborate carving and gilding which adorned them, I concluded they must be of more modern date.

At last, after much toil, and turning many corners, and walking through an abundance of narrow streets, some of them not over and above fragrant, we arrived at that part of Pera where our hotel is situated, and after a little brushing up and prinking, we were once more in the street, on our way to see the "lions." Mr. F. hearing of our arrival, came at once to see us, and he, with two other Americans and an English gentleman whom we met on the steamer, joined with us in forming a party, and engaging a guide to go around with us. The guide is a Greek, and as he speaks French and Italian very well, and English in a perfectly incomprehensible manner, he generally speaks to us in French.

As it was late in the morning before we went out, we confined ourselves to Pera and its immediate environs, and found a good many things in our long walk to interest us, though I do not know as the recital of them will prove as interesting to you. We walked through the principal street of Pera, which looks more like a street in an European than in an Eastern town; for on both sides we saw shops displaying European goods in such a variety that I, long deprived of seeing any thing of "the fashions," had to stop a great many times to stare at bonnets, and muslins, and laces, and ribbons, and materials for dresses, and at ladies and gentlemen in European costume.

We walked on and on, till we passed the houses and shops, and came to large barracks and a parade ground, and beyond, on a hill, stopped at a café, from the garden of which we had a magnificent view of the Bosphorus. We were tired and warm, and as we could not get any ices, we thought we would try some of the far-famed Turkish sherbets. We were asked what kind we would take, as they had different syrups from which the drink was made. I chose cherry, for I fancied that would be particularly nice; but it was well I was told it was cherry, for otherwise I should never have been able to form even a conjecture of what I was drinking.

But no description can do justice to the view from this height; and although in my different travels I have seen many fine views, I don't know when one has pleased me more than this. Below us lay palaces and mosques, and villages with their oriental looking houses; beyond, was the blue Bosphorus, with ships from all nations lying there, and hundreds of little caiques darting hither and thither, while on the Asiatic side were other palaces and mosques and villages, and behind them, hills dotted with sunny fields, and beautiful gardens, and handsome little summer houses and chateaus. A little way beyond us, on the shore of the Bosphorus, we saw the new palace of the Sultan, an immense edifice of white stone, not yet completed. Around us were large palaces, used for different purposes, some for barracks, some for colleges, and others for hospitals.

But perhaps as striking a feature as any, was the extensive cemetery on our right, where the thick grove of cypress trees made an almost impervious shade. I cannot say that these Turkish cemeteries throw me into such ecstasies of delight as some travellers have indulged in, for, with the exception of the tall, dark cypress, there is nothing beautiful about them. They all look sadly neglected, and the white head-stones, surmounted by the gilded turban or the red tarboosh, and adorned with

Turkish inscriptions, are often leaning on one side, and many of them are entirely prostrate.

For my first letter from Constantinople, written at intervals hastily snatched amid the confusion incidental on arriving at a strange place, I flatter myself I have done pretty well, in quantity, at least, if not in quality. I dated this letter "Constantinople" purposely, although we are in Pera; and I suppose I have no more real right to date Constantinople than I should have to commence a letter "New York," when I was in fact in Brooklyn. But I thought if I commenced this "Pera," you might not at first sight imagine where we were, so I used the more familiar name of Constantinople.

And now good bye.

LETTER XLVI.

Over to Constantinople.—Bridge.—Varied Scene.—Thousand and one Columns.—Hippodrome.—Janizaries.—Burnt Pillar.—Bazaars.—Return to Pera.—Sunset Scene.

PERA, May 23d.

MY DEAR F.:

Another day of sight-seeing in this land so full of fascinating wonders. To-day we went over to Constantinople, and as we were gone more than six hours, during which time we scarcely sat down, you may be sure we came home well tired. There are three ways of going through the streets here, on foot, in a carriage, or on horseback. In a carriage, over such wretched pavements, through crowded streets, you can readily imagine our progress would be neither easy nor rapid; and I should be still more unwilling to take a horse, as really

I cannot see how one could get safely over such stones; so our only alternative is to walk, though walking on these round stones is attended with its inconveniences.

Going through a part of Pera, we came to a gateway, which separates Pera from Galata, and then we went down the narrow, steep streets of the latter, by offices and warehouses, and fish and vegetable markets, jostling against crowds of people, representing all nations, as I judged from their costumes, till we came to the first bridge over the Golden Horn. This is a bridge of boats, with two draws, through which vessels pass going up the Horn. More than once, in crossing this bridge, which is over a quarter of a mile in length, we stopped to gaze at the different objects around. Before us rose the city, swelling up gradually, its palaces and mosques and countless roofs varied with trees of every shade of green; behind us, the motley houses of Pera and Galata crowned the heights; on our right, wound the Golden Horn, and on our left, where it opened into the Bosphorus, were innumerable ships and steamers, and hundreds of caiques, flitting like birds across the water. On the bridge, the gay horseman dashed by us, and the gilded carriage, filled with Turkish women peeping out from their "yashmacks," rumbled along, the beggar, lame, blind, deformed, followed us or sat beneath the railing, the vender of cold water, or sherbet, or cakes, or a very watery looking ice cream, screamed after us, and the crowd jostled against us; the Turk, the Armenian, the Greek, the Italian, the Frenchman, the English officer in his bright uniform, the Scotch soldier with his bare legs, the American tar, rolling his quid from side to side, the Jew, all were there, each in his own distinguishing costume, and each speaking his own language.

What a fantastic medley of colors, and what a Babel of sounds!

High above the buildings of Stamboul, rose the gilded dome and graceful minarets of St. Sophia, and farther on, the equally beautiful dome and six minarets of the mosque of Sultan Achmet; but as we are intending to make a visit to these mosques, on Saturday, I shall reserve a farther account of them till that time.

After we got through the fish and meat and vegetable bazaars, we found the streets both wider and cleaner than we expected to see them, but they seemed apparently deserted, for we met but very few in them. The houses were all of wood, many of them painted with gay colors, none but Turks being allowed to paint their houses a cheerful color; but their closely latticed windows give them a prison-like look.

Our first object was to find the cistern of the "thousand and one" columns, and after a long walk through all kinds of streets, we came to a little hut, where our guide had quite a squabble with a man, the most prominent word being "buksheesh"; so you see we hear that familiar sound even in Europe. We went down a flight of tottering wooden stairs, till we reached the bottom, and then we found ourselves in an immense vault, the roof of which was supported by tall, slender pillars, with richly carved capitals. This cistern was once filled with water, brought by an aqueduct from the mountains, but it is now quite dry, and is used by a company of silk-reelers, who flitted around in the dim light like beings of another world. I did not attempt to count the pillars, but I am told that instead of being a "thousand and one," there are not three hundred. There is still another at a little distance, which is said to have a larger number of columns, but the entrance to it is through a house, to which, by some informality or other, we failed to get access. The one we visited is said to be of size sufficient, if in good repair, to hold water to supply the whole Turkish capital for sixty days.

Our next walk was to the Hippodrome, the great public square of the ancient Byzantium, where once under triumphal arches triumphant processions marched, where games and sports were celebrated in the presence of the emperors themselves, and around which, in the days of former glory, were arranged seats of marble capable of accommodating hundreds of thousands. Behind these seats were porticoes, adorned with masterpieces of art, brought from all the cities of the empire, to adorn this public square of the capital. Alas! for human greatness, these have all disappeared; the statues and many of the pillars have been demolished or carried away by the conquerers, and vast numbers of the columns have been taken by the Mohammedans to adorn their mosques. Only three monuments remain as proofs of former greatness; one is an Egyptian obelisk, between fifty and sixty feet high, covered with hieroglyphics, which looked to us like old familiar friends. The next is called by some the most venerable relic of the ancient pagan world. It is a brass column, formed by the bodies of three serpents twisted together, tapering off towards the neck, where the three heads, with open mouths, branched off, and supported a golden tripod, on which the priestess of Delphi sat when she uttered the oracles which told the fate of empires and nations; but the tripod and the heads are gone, like many other things of old Byzantium. The third is a column of hewn stone, formerly covered with brass plates, which have been stripped off by the Turks, and the column left naked and broken, and almost ready to fall. The area of the Hippodrome is about one thousand feet by four hundred, and it is now surrounded by common looking houses, except on one side, where stands the mosque of Sultan Achmet.

Near here once stood the barracks of the powerful Janizaries, and from close beside the mosque the cannon were levelled upon them, as they rushed out from the conflagration. The Janizaries were a military corps, composed at first of Greek captives, who were compelled to adopt the Moslem faith, and were afterwards blessed by a Dervish, who gave them the title of "Yeni Seri," (new soldiers,) which has since been corrupted into Janizary. Like the Mamelukes of Egypt, they became so powerful a body, their monarch decided to destroy them, and after they had become the terror and the scourge of Turkey, they were murdered in cold blood, by the orders of the late Sultan Mahmoud.

Still passing on, where the upper story of the houses projects far over the narrow, crooked streets, and the latticed windows allow the inmates to see what is going on below them, without risk of being seen themselves, we came to a mosque of white marble, with barred windows facing the street, and on the sill of the window were bright metal cups, filled with clear cold water, one of which I eagerly drained. The cup was instantly drawn inside by an invisible hand, filled and put back in its place, without a word being spoken, not even that so common every where, "buksheesh." By endowment, a fountain is constantly kept in order at this mosque, and a man stationed there, whose business it is to keep the cups filled, ready for any thirsty traveller, be he pacha or slave, Turk or Christian. I need not say how wise a provision this is, and how acceptable it often proves to a stranger, who otherwise might suffer for "a cup of cold water."

In other places in the city there are fountains and a cup always attached by a chain, and the water of these fountains is clear and cold, which, in these hot climates, is a great luxury, and you may be sure one of my thirsty propensities does not often pass by without stopping to drink. As we were walking on, we were struck by a singular looking pillar, rising above the roofs of the houses beyond us. It is called the "burnt pillar," from the fact that it has been repeatedly scathed and cracked, by the frequent conflagrations that have swept over it. It is bound around by copper hoops, and is so blackened by smoke as to render it difficult to ascertain of what material it is composed, or to read the inscriptions upon it. It is said to have been brought from the temple of Apollo at Rome, and to have been surmounted by a statue. The shaft is ninety feet in height, and the pedestal measures thirty feet at its base, and is said to enclose several pieces of the true cross.

Still on and on we went, not feeling so much fatigued as we otherwise would have done, had we been less interested in all we saw; for after all, that is the greatest preventive against fatigue, At last we reached the bazaars, and here, you may be sure, I was on the alert. These bazaars form a labyrinth of avenues, of more or less size and richness, and are all covered, many of them having lofty arched ceilings, the roofs being a succession of small domes, through which the light is admitted. I have, at different times, dwelt so much upon bazaars, that perhaps you will think a repetition of the subject somewhat of a bore; but I should do violence to my feminine propensity of admiring fine things and picturesque sights, to pass by the bazaars of Constantinople, without bestowing upon them more than a few ordinary remarks.

As in other cities of the East, each kind of goods has its own particular compartment, or, more properly speaking, is a bazaar by itself; and if I should attempt to tell you half I saw, it would be like an enumeration of the different articles mentioned in a catalogue, so I shall merely dwell upon those that mostly attracted my attention.

What makes the bazaars of Constantinople more brilliant than those in any other city, is that they are larger, and their goods are displayed in a more artistic manner. True, silks and embroidered muslins, and delicate goods, that would be injured by too constant exposure, are generally kept out of sight, folded up neatly in paper, and laid upon a shelf; but often when the shop-keeper (particularly if he is a lively Greek or Armenian) sees a foreigner approaching, he dexterously unfolds some beautiful fabric, and temptingly holds it up to view. Nor is he satisfied by merely holding it up in full sight, but he calls out to the passer by, "Capitain," (for he thinks every man who looks like an Englishman must be an officer,) "Madama," "Signora," which he flatters himself is very good English. If he can, you may be sure he adds a few words in French or Italian, which often exhausts all the stores of foreign languages he possesses. But the Turk disdains to call to his aid any factitious circumstances to help his trade. He sits cross-legged on the counter front of his goods, and even though you stop and point at something which attracts your attention, it is ten chances to one if he offers to take it down, unless he is decidedly requested so to do.

In the gold and silver bazaar, though I saw many curious and antique things, there was nothing which, for richness or skill in workmanship, could compare with what you would see at home, in the establishments of some of our workers in the precious metals; and in those bazaars where European goods were exposed, of course there was not half the variety or splendor as could be found in a large "dry goods" store in our own city; therefore, I did not stop to look at them, but confined my attention exclusively to such things as might decidedly be called oriental. And here, I assure you, there is enough to feed the most vivid imagination. Come, for instance, to the shoe bazaar. Look down that avenue, bordered on both sides with open shops, the shelves of which display slippers of every hue, embroidered in the most beautiful manner, with gold and silver, and many of them with pearls, on real cachemere. Here you may find slippers of every price, from ten piastres to one thousand. Could I pass by so tempting an array, without stopping often to look, and occasionally to buy?

In the silk bazaar, we saw the far famed Broussa silks; and though there is not a great variety in the patterns, yet the material is good, and what will interest some purchasers, it is said they "will wear forever." I tried to make a bargain for a dress; for you must know it is customary here to name one price, and take another; but either the Greek merchant was too shrewd for me, or I did not set a sufficiently high price on his goods, so I came away, hoping he would call me back, but he didn't, and I suppose I must come to his terms, and return for the dress some time.

In embroideries, I saw shawls and scarfs of muslin, splendidly wrought in gold and silver threads and silks of different colors; small table cloths of crimson and purple velvet, actually covered with gold and silver embroidery; veils and handkerchiefs of gauze, spotted with gold; pocket handkerchiefs of muslin, with borders of divers colors; bags and tobacco pouches of cachemere, prettily wrought with gold; in short, I don't think I could enumerate half the beautiful things which kept my eyes constantly dilated. If I had shut my eyes, another sense would have told me what bazaar I was next approaching, for the air was loaded with fragrance. Who that has been to Constantinople, has not heard of Mustapha, "perfumer to the Sultan"? We stopped in front to look at some perfumery, but we were politely invited inside, to a room in the rear of the little shop, where we found a perfect cabinet of curiosities, shawls, daggers, pipes, coffee cups, and perfumeries of the choicest kind. While we were selecting some ottar of rose, we were regaled with cool lemon sherbet, and the gentlemen who manifested a tendency that way, were furnished with pipes, all as an act of politeness from Mustapha to his customers, though I doubt not he put on an extra price to the articles we bought, to cover the cost of thus refreshing us.

In the fur bazaar, we saw coats and robes lined and trimmed with costly furs, and a number of men at work making up such coats, while the furs were piled all around them. Although the weather is very hot here, we constantly meet men in the streets with such coats on; for my part, it actually makes me warm to see them, and I don't know what would be the effect, if I should venture to wear one.

Pipes we saw in great abundance and variety, from the plain stick of cherry, to those gaudily covered with gay colors and decked out with a profusion of tassels and gold cord. We saw them making the long tubes for the nargeelehs, the favorite pipe of many Turks, the smoke passing through water, which is said to purify it and make it less injurious to the smoker.

In the saddlery bazaar, we saw the most beautiful saddle cloths of velvet, gorgeously adorned with gold and silver work. In short, during our saunter through the various bazaars, we saw much to interest and amuse us, and, I may add, to tempt us; and not one of us left them without carrying away some little token of interest.

Nor must I forget the drug bazaar, where venerable looking Turks, with white beards, and clouds of smoke rolling above their heads, sat in attitudes the most picturesque, each face and figure and dress being a fit subject for a painter. The drugs are arranged in the most attractive manner, on the receding shelves of the stalls, the baskets and jars containing them being turned over with rich colored paper, a peculiar color for every species. The odor, too, is delightful, for here are gathered the most costly drugs of the Orient.

I thought I had done; but I forgot the candy bazaar, where confectionary of every shape and hue is arranged in heaps and masses, sufficient, I should think, to satisfy every candy-loving child in the whole of New England.

Nor was this variety, great as it was, all we saw to interest us. The groups of people in various costumes, the jabber of strange tongues, mingled, now and then, with a few words in English, the cries of the venders of sherbet, ices, cakes and fruit, the porters, bent double under enormous loads, the occasional clatter on the stones of horses' hoofs, which sent the crowds scattering in different directions, the Turkish women stopping full before us, to stare at us with their great black eyes, the beggars following us with beseeching cries and gestures, the eagerness of some of the shopkeepers, and the phlegmatic indifference of others, the lights and shades thrown over the whole, these and a thousand like things, render a walk in the bazaars of Constantinople one of stirring and constantly changing interest.

At last, it was time to turn our faces homeward, and tired though we all were, we stopped often on the bridge to look down into the water, and watch the caiques as they darted rapidly by. Up the steep streets of Galata and Pera we toiled, till at length we found ourselves once more in our hotel, and after going up three flights of stairs, in our pleasant chamber, that commands an extensive view of the Golden Horn, with Stamboul before us, seated on her seven hills, her countless domes and minarets standing out clear against the blue sky.

As twilight came on, I laid aside my pen, and looked abroad over the beautiful scene. Across the placid water glided countless caiques, with so little apparent motion, they did not leave the slightest wake behind. The setting sun lighted up the crescents on the domes of the mosques, and brought out clear and distinct the fretted galleries around the minarets. And hark! from each gallery rings forth the muezzin's cry, "There is but one God, and Mohammed is his prophet; come to prayers, come to salvation," and a thousand obedient children of the Prophet obey the call, and throng to the mosques, while others in the streets, or in their houses, unroll their prayer carpets, and turning their faces towards Mecca, go through their evening devotions.

Once more good bye.

LETTER XLVII.

Queen's Birthday.—Dogs.—Marvellous Story.—Caiques.—Scutari.—Disappointment.—Tophana.—Review of English Troops.—Araba.—Another Carriage.—Chrysopolis.—Cemetery.—Lovely Country.—Bulghurlhu.—Extensive View.—Adventure.—Return to Pera.

PERA, May 25th.

MY DEAR ——:

The almanac will tell you this is the birthday of Queen Victoria; and we heard from some English officers at our table that there was to be a grand review of the troops early this morning, in honor of the day. Averse as I am to an early start, I could not think of letting such an event go by without making some exertions to witness it; and the consequence was, I slept but little last night, partly owing to fear lest I should oversleep myself, but more, I must confess, to the incessant barking of some "forty-leven" dogs beneath our windows. I thought Egypt was a great place for dogs, but they are not to be mentioned in the same breath with the dogs of Constantinople. By day, I believe they never attack strangers, but at night they are not so forbearing; and our guide told us that not long since, an English soldier was attacked by some dogs, and entirely eaten up, except his boots! But, as an offset to this marvellous story, I must admit his narratives are not always to be depended upon.

To get a party of six together, early in the morning,

is no slight job; but at last we were all mustered in the vestibule of the hotel, and in a few minutes were on our way to Tophana, to take caiques for Scutari, where the troops are quartered. I had been told so much of the ease with which these little boats are upset, I was quite afraid to get into one; however, as the only danger is in stepping on the side, I made a great effort, and leaped directly into the middle. These caiques are narrow, graceful looking little boats, the smallest ones rowed by one man, (who puffs and blows like a porpoise,) and you seat yourself, like a Turk, on a cushion in the bottom of the boat. Only two can go in one of the smaller caiques, so our party, dividing themselves into twos, were soon on their way across the Bosphorus. The row over was delightful, as we wound in and out among the shipping, bearing the flags of nearly every nation.

Landing at Scutari, we made our way up the steep hill, (for all the hills in this neighborhood are steep,) to the immense barracks, capable, it is said, of accommodating eighteen thousand soldiers. We saw nothing that indicated any extraordinary event going on, so we went to the English encampment, a little farther off. The ground was white with the tents spread over it, but nothing was to be seen of officers or soldiers. At last we succeeded in finding out that the review was to be at eleven o'clock. Here was a nice "mess." Should we lounge around there, breakfastless, or come home for our breakfast, and return in season for the review? Some of the party were for staying, and trusting to fortune, in the shape of a poor restaurant, for breakfast; but I preferred to come back, so we turned back to the caiques, and in due time were landed at Tophana.

Here is another of those exquisite fountains, which form one of the peculiar beauties of Constantinople. It is of white marble, of Saracenic style of architecture, elaborately adorned with carvings and fretwork, and letters of gold. On the four sides, the water runs out into a little basin; and here, young and old, rich and poor, may stop to quaff the cool drink. I never pass it by without stopping to look with renewed admiration at this perfect little gem.

Breakfast over, we started once more for Scutari; and now we saw the vessels in the harbor decked out with flags and streamers, and some with wreaths of evergreen. The St. Louis, in addition to her "stars and stripes," carried English and Turkish flags, while some of the English men-of-war bore American as well as Turkish colors. But we heard no firing. "How is this?" we asked. "Why, they were all saving their powder to use it on the Russians!" Economical, truly.

The review had commenced when we reached the ground, and to my eye, so totally unaccustomed to lines of soldiers, the number of troops seemed enormous. I believe there were about twenty thousand on the ground, which you must admit was quite an army. I shall not dwell upon their manœuvres, nor the skill and discipline they manifested, for I am too ignorant on such subjects to do them justice. At one time, the band struck up "God save the Queen," and after playing a few notes, stopped, and then the signal was given for "three cheers for the Queen, God bless her Majesty," and immediately every head was uncovered, every hat and cap waved in the air, and three prolonged cheers rung out. Even the spectators paid this mark of respect to the Queen of Great Britain, and French, Americans, Italians, Spaniards, all of whatever nation, except Turkish, (and they have no hats to take off,) uncovered, and united their cheers with those of the soldiers. Do not laugh at me, when I say it was a sublime sight; but republican as I am, and glorying, too, in my republicanism, I was moved almost to tears.

The review over, our party gathered together to decide what we should do the remainder of the day. Constantine (no relation to the Emperor of that name, but our Greek guide,) told us there was a delightful drive to Bulghurlhu, (an unpronounceable name, I admit, but not more difficult to pronounce than to spell,) and a magnificent view after we got there. We wanted to see as much of Turkey in Asia as possible, so at once we decided to go there, (I do not think I can spell that again;) but how to go? was the question.

In Syria and Palestine, there was no other way to get about but on horseback, for such a thing as a carriage is never seen in those countries, for the best of all reasons, there are no roads; but here were both carriages and roads, so "my voice" was for the carriage; and being the only lady's voice in the party, was listened to with attention, probably more from that fact than from its intrinsic merits. But even here, we could not come to a harmonious decision, for we had two different kinds of carriages to choose from. Let me describe them to you, though I am confident no description can do them justice, they are so totally unlike any thing you ever saw.

One is called an "araba," and looks more like the fantastic vehicles in which fairy queens come upon the stage, than any thing in real, every day life. It is a long wagon, of a peculiar shape, and if it were not for comparing it with too common things, I should say it somewhat resembled what we, at home, call a "meat wagon;" but it is covered with a crimson cloth, rolled up at the sides, displaying three or four seats inside. The body of the carriage, and even the wheels, are elaborately adorned with gilded carvings, which help to add to its fantastic appearance. Nor is the carriage all that is peculiar, for it is drawn by two oxen, their tails tied to a hoop, bent back from the front of the pole, their heads and horns, and the long curve of the hoop, decked with a profusion of red or yellow tassels. Beside the carriage walks an eunuch or old Turk, while a slave runs along by the side of the oxen; and in vehicles like this many of the Moslem ladies take an airing. But from there being no springs to the carriage, I should fancy it could not be very easy, particularly over paved streets; still, for the very fun of the thing, I was willing to brave all inconveniences, for I thought it would be very "jolly," as the English say, riding all together in that vehicle, though some of my companions thought it would terminate more in "jelly" than in "jolly."

Turn we now to the other carriage, for as I do not know the Turkish name for it, I can designate it by no other term than the general one of carriage. This is smaller than the "araba," and has two immense wheels behind, and two as proportionably small before. It has no windows like our carriages, but the sides are cut out in a peculiar manner, and decked with white muslin curtains. There is no door, but after getting upon the step, you are forced to climb over the side, not an easy or agreeable performance. Like the "araba," it is adorned with a profusion of carving and gilding, and though it has a seat for the driver, I think he never mounts, but walks by the side of his horse, for this is drawn by a horse, not by oxen.

Four of us took possession of this vehicle, while two of the gentlemen, and Constantine, mounted donkeys, and though the first start almost sent us off the seats, and the jostling over the pavements was far from being easy, I believed we all enjoyed the ride very much, though I strongly suspect the springs of the carriage were not after the most improved pattern. The three gentlemen, probably from their early rising this morning, were soon nodding, though the jolts and jerks of the carriage prevented them from enjoying any very long naps.

Scutari was called by the ancients Chrysopolis, "the golden city," because here, during wars, and in troublous times, the Persians deposited their treasures and paid their tribute; and although generally considered a part of Constantinople, it is in itself a large and populous city, containing, I believe, more than eighty thousand inhabitants. It is situated on a hill, very steep upon the side washed by the Marmora, but gracefully leaning towards the Seraglio on the opposite shore, like an Asiatic lady bowing to her European partner, (an old figure of speech, not at all original.) The cemetery at Scutari covers as much ground as some cities, and it is said that on no other spot on the earth, are so many of the human race gathered together. Its immense pall of cypress stretches far away over the hill, and through the valley, till it terminates, at last, in a long point projecting into the Marmora, as though it were pouring its contents into the sea.

I must say I was glad when we left the paved streets, and once more had the ground beneath our feet. How like it seemed to a scene at home, the wide road bordered with stone walls, or wooden houses, though houses like these, with the upper story projecting over the lower, and with closely latticed windows, are unlike any we would see in our land. The country was very pretty, with its sloping hills looking smiling and fertile, and we caught snatches of the Bosphorus, which only made us long for more. I should think we rode quite six miles, and some part of the way the hills were so very steep, the gentlemen got out and walked, leaving me in undisputed possession of the carriage.

At last, we reached the village, and there leaving the carriage, we walked to the top of the hill, and sat down to rest and to enjoy the prospect. Come and sit with me on this rocky seat, and let your eye take in the whole scene. Is it not lovely? See, we are on the hill Bulghurlhu, which is a link in the Bythynian chain, and below us, embowered in trees, lie villages and palaces and kiosks, while beyond is Scutari, with its forest of cypresses, and opposite to it, Constantinople, "the magnificent;" and does she not well deserve her title? The light falls upon St. Sophia's "gleaming dome," and the seven towers loom up against the clear sky. You look far over the glittering Propontis, and along the winding, village-covered shores of the Bosphorus, and up even into the Golden Horn; the ancient walls of Byzantium, and the new palace of the Sultan, all are before you, and if you turn slightly round, the islands of the Marmora lie beneath you, while far in the distance rises the snow-crested Olympus, looking down upon the fertile plain of Broussa, at its feet. Have I brought it before you, so that you can see it distinctly with your mind's eye? My eyes never rested upon a fairer scene, and you may readily imagine we were loath to leave it. But the sun was getting lower, and we must follow his example, so we descended the hill, climbed up into our clumsy vehicle, and soon were rumbling on towards Scutari.

We passed another large cemetery on our way back by a different road, and the tall white tombstones, and the lofty cypresses, planted so closely together as to form an almost impervious shade, gave it a picturesque appearance.

While Constantine was trying to get a caique large enough to take us all across, I sat down to rest, (for my ride had jounced me to an uncomfortable degree,) on a block of pure white marble, forming two steps, and scarcely was I seated, when a soldier came up to me, and said "*non bono*," (not good;) but I did not agree with him, for I thought it a very nice seat indeed, and very soon I had quite a crowd around me. But as I am by this time accustomed to being stared at, it produced no effect upon me, so I sat still, jotting down in my note-book the proceedings of the day. Presently one of my companions came to me, and asked me what I had been saying to that soldier, for he saw him go back to his commanding officer, and evidently tell him something about me, as he pointed to me while he was talking, and then the officer seemed to wish him to come again, but the man demurred, whereupon the officer then pushed him, and finally struck him with the hilt of his sword, all to no effect, for the man shook his head and walked away. I could not imagine what it all meant, so I called Constantine to my aid. He turned to some of the crowd and asked what was the matter. At least a dozen voices clamored forth a reply, but at last I succeeded in getting his interpretation. It seems I was sitting upon steps put there for his "Imperial Majesty the Sultan" to stand upon, when he was about to mount his horse to ride to any of his palaces near Scutari; and it was not deemed proper for a Christian to sit upon the Sultan's horse-block! When I first refused to get up, the soldier had returned to his officer with the account of the non-success of his mission; he was then bidden to come again and command me to leave my seat, and he refused to obey, on the ground that I was "English," and not to be dictated to, for some of the people here think they must put up with a great many things from the English, because they have come to fight for them.

So much for this day.

LETTER XLVIII.

Buyukdere.—Unquiet Nights.—Ramazan.—Night Scene.—Galata.—Walls of the City.—Seven Towers.—Costumes.—Palace of the Seraskier.—Extensive View.

BUYUKDERE, May 30th.

MY DEAR S.:

After an interval of nearly a week, I take up my pen once more to give you an account of our further rambles in and around Constantinople, and as from the name at the head of this letter, you may wonder where we are, I hasten to tell you that Buyukdere is a small town on the Bosphorus, about fifteen miles from Constantinople, and five or six from the Black Sea. The weather was getting so hot, we found it very fatiguing to go about, and after six days spent in sight-seeing, being out nearly every day from ten o'clock till six, and attempting to write each evening, and early every morning, I found my health and strength too severely taxed, so we came up here to recruit, and to bring up my writing, which as is often the case, is sadly in arrears. Besides, the nights in Pera were very unquiet, for the dogs kept up a constant barking, and at intervals, an unearthly howl rung out upon the air, which was repeated from post to post. For a long time we could not make out what it was, but after asking a great many people, we were finally told it was the cry of the night watch. I should think they might have fixed upon a more musical sound for their signals.

Last Saturday too, the Ramazan commenced, the yearly fast of the Turks, which lasts a lunar month. During the day, from sunrise to sunset, the devout Mussulman eats nothing, neither does he drink, not a drop of cold water even, touching his lips. His dearly beloved pipe too, is laid aside, but to pay for all the self-denial by day, the moment the sunset gun booms forth, they give themselves up to feasting and revelry, to noise and merriment. In order to get along still easier, many of them sleep the greater part of the day, and stay up three-fourths of the night, and the dogs too follow their example, for they lie dozing in the streets all day, and bark incessantly at night. Drums and trumpets and bugles were sounding in the streets, the whole night long; in short it was a repetition on a mammoth scale of the scene which invariably takes place at home, on the night before the fourth of July. We really could not sleep, and you may imagine, after such a night, how poorly we were prepared for a day of sight-seeing. But the appearance of Constantinople at night, was perfectly lovely, for the whole city is brilliantly illuminated every night during the Ramazan. Before that commenced, we could scarcely see a light twinkling across the Golden Horn, for we have not yet arrived in the regions of gas lights, and Constantinople, immense, as it is, is as unfit for a person to walk about in, after dark, as a little town in Nubia.

But now the scene is changed, and the city looks like a picture in magic land. Each dome, each tapering minaret, almost every house, are lighted, and the little lamps, far up in the domes, arranged so as to form Turkish characters, and the bright lights, twinkling out of the fretted gallery of each minaret, like lustrous stars in the sky, make the city, enthroned on her seven hills, shine forth with almost unearthly beauty, and when I could not sleep, I would get up and stand by the window, and gaze forth upon the unrivalled scene, till I grew too sleepy to look longer.

And now we are here in quiet, and I sit by my window opening out upon the Bosphorus, which is here so hemmed in, as to look like a lake, and my paper is spread out upon the table, and I am ready to recall and record past scenes. Let me see, where did I leave off! Oh, on the night of the Queen's birth-day; so I will take up the thread of my narrative from that time.

On Thursday morning, we went down to Galata to take a caique for a row down the Sea of Marmora. The lower streets of Galata would not give you a favorable idea of the cleanliness of the town, for I must say I have walked in much cleaner streets, even in some towns in the East. I like to know the meaning of names, and perhaps you have a tendency that way yourself, so I will tell you, that to the best of my knowledge, Galata means "milk," that suburb having originally been the milk market of the neighborhood, and Pera, is taken from the Greek preposition signifying "beyond," because it lies beyond Galata.

Having delivered myself of this piece of wisdom and information, I will proceed, in a less didactic manner, to say, that having procured a large caique, with three men and six oars, we were soon speeding down the Bosphorus into the Sea of Marmora, round the point on which is seated the Seraglio, the palace where the former Sultans lived in state, by gardens and kiosks, and under the windows through the lattices of which Sultanas and slaves peeped down on the sea beneath them, and near the little door whence unfaithful mistresses were thrown into the Marmora, till we left the Imperial palace behind, and came in front of the wall, which hems in that part of the city that lies beyond the Palace. For more than six miles, we kept along the wall, which is high and strengthened with bastions. It does not rise directly out of the water, but has a narrow terrace at its base, thus affording a pleasant walk the whole length of the city. In different parts of the wall, we saw inserted marble and columns, remains of the former glory of Byzantium. The houses are all dark colored, tumble-down-looking affairs, but still they have a picturesque aspect.

As I told you once before, the city of Constantinople is situated on a triangular promontory, watered on the one side by the Marmora, and on the other by the Bosphorus, and both on the sea and land side, it is surrounded by a wall, in some places in rather a dilapidated state.

At the south-west angle of the city, where the land

wall meets that on the Marmora, stand the celebrated seven towers. These are a cluster of fortresses, some of them dating back to the days of Theodosius; others are of a later origin, having been added by some of the Greek emperors, and one was built more recently still, by Mohammed the second. They were originally lofty octagonal towers, and when they all frowned at once upon the Propontis, must have presented a formidable aspect. Three of them are now in ruins, and only five of them rise above the massive battlements, while but one bears the crescent. These towers, could they speak, would a gloomy tale unfold, for they have witnessed many a scene of horror and bloodshed; but though it is said "walls have ears," we are no where told they have tongues. Fortunately, the voice of history is not always silenced, and she gives forth many a dark record of the seven towers of Constantinople. They have served as a castle for tyrants, a prison for offenders against the state, and a treasury for the spoils of the imperial conqueror. In despite of the law of nations, an ambassador, offending the Sublime Porte, was shut up in one of these gloomy dungeons; and an instance is given of a Russian count, who was confined there three years, on account of some little misunderstanding between the court of the Sultan and the Czarina Catharine. Within the enclosure of the walls is shown a spot called "the place of heads," from the great number of heads once piled here, one upon another, and there was once a "well of blood," from which the blood of the slain flowed over the pavement into the sea.

These towers are now used as a magazine for powder and arms, and the Turks, guarding the entrance, refused to let us go in, without a "firman" from government;

and for one, I was not sorry to be spared seeing the spots where such dark deeds were perpetrated.

We walked through some of the streets of the Greek quarter, and found them clean, comparatively speaking, but many of the houses were entirely shut up, so many of the Greeks being recently banished from the empire. The Greek women here dress as in Smyrna, their hair braided across their red caps, and some of their faces are very handsome. The children are many of them lovely, with their classical features and their large, lustrous eyes.

Once more we were in our caique, and our boatmen were puffing and blowing with all their might. Their dress is very pretty; large, full Turkish trousers of white cotton, and shirts with loose flowing sleeves of thin striped stuff, made, I think, of silk and linen, or linen and cotton, I don't know which.

We dismissed our caique, just beyond Seraglio point, and made our way through streets crowded with motley groups. I am now learning to tell different nations and classes, by some peculiar feature of their dress; for instance, the Dervish, (the Moslem monk,) wears a conical cap of drab-colored felt; the Persian, a tall black cap of skin, finished off at the top somewhat like a Bishop's mitre, while the Circassian, with his round, ruddy face, wears a high cap of cloth, with a border of sheepskin around it, the long wool arranged in curls.

Arriving at the palace of the Seraskier, or commander-in-chief of the army, we went up into a high tower, which is used for giving the signals, when there is a fire in any part of the city. We ascended to the top, by a flight of one hundred and seventy-nine steps, and as they are very high, they are not at all easy to ascend.

But the view from the top is superb. The city and its suburbs, from the numerous cemeteries scattered through them, and the courts of many of the houses being planted with trees and vines, look like one immense garden, with clusters of houses nestled down among the trees. Directly beneath us lay the palace, a long range of grated prisons, and the dome and minarets of the mosque of Bajazet.

From this elevation, I saw the great extent of the bazaars, for the succession of low domes, pierced with small windows, indicated their different locations; and I suppose this is really the only point where one could form a just estimate of the world-famed bazaars of Constantinople. In fact the whole city is here spread out like a map, and if you had the time, it is said you could count one thousand domes and five thousand minarets. But the distant view surpasses all. Far to the south, spreads the Sea of Marmora, studded with lovely isles; on the east, the continent of Asia presents a long range of mountains, every one of which is known to the world for some deed of blood and heroism, and among which lie Bithynia, Phrygia and Cappadocia, dear to the Christian heart, as the scene of many of the labors of the great Apostle of the Gentiles. Far above them all, towers Olympus, its summit crowned with a diadem of eternal snow.

Like a deep chasm in the hills, the Bosphorus opens, and as far as you can follow its course, you see jutting promontories and deeply indented bays, so that it is said if the water could be drawn out of the straits, and the opposite shores be brought together, they would fit into each other perfectly. Along the promontories, and around the bays, you see palaces and mosques, castles and forts, backed by gentle hills, bright and green.

On the north, the Golden Horn winds away, till it tapers off into a narrow stream, and is lost among the overhanging trees and encircling hills of the "Valley of Sweet Waters." Far to the left, amid domes and slender minarets, and palaces and trees, are the picturesque remains of an old Roman aqueduct, its double row of arches overgrown with ivy and clustering vines.

What a view it was! I was almost tempted to say it was the loveliest, the most extensive I ever saw. And while we walked from window to window, and returned again and again to some favorite spot, a company of soldiers gathered in the court beneath, and the band struck up an animating quickstep. As a general thing, the Turkish music we have heard has been nothing to boast of, but this was really very good.

We took a stroll through some of the bazaars, and once more the purse strings were unloosed, and the silk dress was bought, and another pair of embroidered slippers.

But this certainly is enough for one day.

LETTER XLIX.

The Sultan.—Dervishes.—Valley of Sweet Waters.—Attractive Scene.—Cemetery.—Mosque of Eyoub.

BUYUKDERE, May 31st.

MY DEAR F.:

Without any "preliminary remarks," I proceed with my record of the past week. On Friday, we hired a caique by the day, and started off soon after breakfast, on another "exploring expedition." Our first destination was a little way up the Bosphorus, our object, to see the Sultan go to a mosque for the noonday prayers, for every Friday, (which you know is the Mohammedan Sunday,) this orthodox Mussulman goes to some mosque, and it is always announced early in the morning what mosque he will attend, which is a very good thing for those who like to see royal personages. We passed by the new palace of the Sultan, an extensive edifice, not yet finished, and came to that in which he now resides. Here we landed, and going up into the town, got a good situation, on a little bank under the shade of a tree, and there we waited a half hour for the approach of the brother of the sun! Lines of soldiers were stationed along the street through which the royal train was to pass, and bands of music at little intervals. The middle of the street was watered, so that no dust should sully the feet of the Arabian charger which bore the "illustrious descendant of a long line of kings." At last, the report of a cannon told that the Sultan had left his palace; the bands struck up, and every head was turned towards the upper end of the street. I can't tell who came first, for there was no one near me whom I could ask, but immediately preceding the Sultan, came the Minister of War, the Minister of Police, and the Minister of Finance, and then, mounted on a splendid black horse, appeared Abdel Medjib, the head of the Ottoman empire, which some predict is now tottering to its fall. As he rode slowly by, I had a good opportunity to see him, and a more inanimate face, or eyes from which all life and soul seemed to have departed, I never saw. He was dressed very plainly, in European style, though the collar and cuffs of his coat were studded with diamonds. He wore a red tarboosh, and the long blue tassel was fastened to the cap with an immense diamond. His saddle cloth was of velvet, embroidered with gold, and the horse was perfect.

Each band stopped as he passed by it, and not a cheer was given or a head uncovered, except those of our own party, nor the slightest symptom of enthusiasm or affection manifested. Just as he passed us, a woman who stood near me, waved a petition, (at least, I supposed it was one,) and immediately an officer, walking behind the Sultan, stepped up, and taking it from her, placed it in a large portfolio which he carried.

Once more in our caique, we went back to Tophana, and landing, walked to a small mosque of the Dervishes, where we hoped to see one of their dancing performances, but contrary to the usual custom, none took place that day, and we were told there would be none till the next Sunday; but as we did not want to go then, we have not yet seen them.

It was Friday, and "all the world" goes to the "sweet waters" on that day of the week, so we, not to be behind the times, went too. Passing through the immense shipping in the harbor, we went under the bridge, and were soon darting away towards the tip of the Golden Horn, through a large fleet of ships and vessels of different sizes, Constantinople lying on our left, Pera, Galata and smaller suburbs on our right. Indeed, I scarcely knew when the cities ended, for almost a continued line of villages extended for several miles up the Horn. Barracks and hospitals, and a marine college, and the arsenal, and Turkish men-of-war, and Jews' and Armenian quarters, all were passed, and then we came to green fields coming down to the water's edge, and now and then a café, or an imperial kiosk, which is a small summer palace. And then the Horn narrowed, and we found ourselves soon after almost hemmed in by the banks, and shaded by large trees, and we knew we were on the little river that runs into the Golden Horn. It is this river of fresh water that gives the name to this valley, of the "sweet water," "sweet" being always used in the East in contradistinction to salt. Judging from the thick, muddy looking stream, I should call the water any thing but "sweet."

Long before we reached our stopping place, we passed caiques in countless numbers, moored to the banks, while along the shore were scattered groups of men and women, some walking, some standing, and some seated on carpets and matting under the trees. We passed a beautiful little palace, directly on the bank, and a number of horses standing near, Constantine told us the Sultan had come up, and was undoubtedly looking out through the blinds, and recommended us to lower our umbrellas, as we passed, as a token of respect to his Majesty, but before we could possibly have closed the umbrellas, our caique had darted by.

I had heard this valley so much praised, I must confess my first impression fell far below the idea I had conceived of it; but as we went farther up the valley, it became more and more lovely, till I was forced to confess its beauties had not been overrated. The stream flowed quickly on, through willow shaded banks, and the valley was thickly studded with large trees, and the hills swept down and then rolled away, revealing picturesque glens, and wooded dells, and romantic ravines.

But no words can describe the gay scene this valley presented. We did not then know, that during the

Ramazan, the Turks do not visit this lovely spot, else we might, in a measure, have accounted for the excessive brilliancy and animation of the whole, as this would be the last visit for a month. Families sitting on the grass, enjoying a pic-nic, carriages rolling by, filled with Turkish women, many of whom seemed to have no idea of any thing but looking at themselves in a little hand mirror, Europeans dashing by on horseback, and staring at the faces covered with the "yashmacks," strolling bands of musicians playing various airs, a company of Gipsies dancing an Arab dance, accompanying it with their voices, (carrying us back at once to the Nile,) beggars, uttering in doleful notes their petitions for charity, sellers of fruit and pastry and confectionary, and sherbet, and so-called ice cream, these and a thousand other things, kept our attention constantly alive. The diligence with which the black slaves guarded the mistresses confided to their care, the coquettish airs which the young Turkish women practiced when they saw a foreigner approaching, the "arabas" and other carriages decked with gilding, the endless variety of costumes, the children playing on the grass, all formed pictures exceedingly attractive to the eye.

We noticed that the plain and old women wore yashmacks made of thick muslin, while those of the younger and more beautiful class were so transparent as to allow every feature of the face to be distinctly seen, and instead of concealing charms, I am sure they added to them. It is a well-known fact, that the Turkish women (the handsome ones, I mean,) paint, and this artificial complexion is seen to much better advantage, through a thin covering of white muslin than without such a veil. They not only paint red and white, but black also, that is, they dye the rims of their eyes with kohl, which serves to give a peculiarly beautiful appearance to the eyes themselves. Without doubt, the eyes of many of the Turkish women, are among the finest in the world, but it is the beauty of form and color, while that of the mind, the heart, the soul, seems wanting.

No! let Turkish women look to it; the day they leave off their "yashmacks," they will find their beauty has lost half its charms. The women here almost universally have bad figures, and without any exception, they are the worst walkers I ever saw. It is almost impossible to find of what materials their dress is composed, so closely do they keep those hideous cloaks wrapped around them, but on standing near a group that day, when no gentlemen were by, one of them put back her cloak to arrange some part of her dress, or perhaps from a pardonable vanity to show me it was not from necessity the cloak was so carefully kept around her, and I found she wore a figured muslin gown, exceedingly short-waisted, very open in front, displaying her neck and chest, and full trousers gathered around the ankle. Their feet always look clumsy, for I scarcely think the foot of a fairy would look well in those ungainly boots and slip-shod shoes.

We tried to form some idea of the numbers of the people upon the ground, though of course there was no way by which we could come to any accurate conclusion, but Yankee-like, we could guess, and our guesses varied from five to eight thousand. Our return down the Golden Horn was like a procession of boats, for the water was actually covered with caiques. We passed a café surrounded by a garden, and there we saw a large number of Greek and Armenian women. These, we are told, flock to the "sweet waters" on Sunday, not mingling there with the Turks on Friday.

About half way down the Horn, we stopped to visit the cemetery near the mosque of Eyoub, not that there was any thing particularly interesting about the cemetery itself, but the view from the top of the hill was very fine, commanding the whole length of the Horn, and far up the "Valley of Sweet Waters." What a contrast was this cemetery, with its tall cypress trees, and turbaned head stones, to that of the Jews, upon the opposite side of the Horn, which looks like a barren, stony field, the grave-stones being laid upon the surface of the earth, without any regularity, and without a tree, or shrub or flower to soften the scene. Alas! for the poor Jews; outcasts in life, from all the human race, they are not allowed, in death to lie near a Christian or Mussulman! The mosque of Eyoub is large and handsome, but within its courts no Christian foot is ever permitted to tread, for in addition to its other points of sacredness, every Sultan, on his accession to the throne, is here invested with the sword of sovereignty. Within the enclosure of the mosque, is the most beautiful place of burial, I have yet seen in Turkey, for besides the cypress, roses cluster over every grave, and almost conceal every head-stone. White and fresh too, the stones look, and gay withal, many of them having inscriptions in gold. Here too, none but those of distinguished birth in the empire are buried, and of course, we were not allowed to step upon the hallowed ground, but through the bars of the windows in the wall around the outer court, we looked, and saw many a pretty little picture. I believe I told you before, the turban or tarboosh indicates the grave of a man, while a plain stone, or one with a sculptured rose branch upon it, points out that of a woman. The turban varies in form and size, according to the rank of the deceased, but as all the inscriptions are in Turkish characters, we are no judges how applicable to the Turks is the proverb, that "tombstones lie."

As we were coming down the hill, we met the gay arabas, full of Turkish women, coming home from the "sweet waters." They were riding in more silence than would have been known, I dare say, among a like party of Americans or English; but whether the Turkish women are no great talkers, ("unlike the rest of the sex," perhaps you say,) or whether their yashmacks, bound so tightly around their noses and mouths, prevent their talking, I cannot say.

We came home very hungry and tired, but as we never dined at the Hotel de Byzance till seven o'clock, I had time to rest a little before dinner.

And now I think I have given you enough for one letter, so I will reserve the remainder of our excursions about Constantinople till another time.

LETTER L.

The Seraglio.—Sublime Porte.—Church of St. Irene.—Visit to the Mosques.—St. Sophia.—Sultan Achmet.—Sultan Mahmoud.—Sultan Sulyman.

BUYUKDERE, June 3d.

MY DEAR FRIENDS:

We are still here in our quiet retreat, and are becoming daily more and more delighted with it. Here, calmly and quietly, I have passed a few days, writing several hours a day, trying to bring up that tardy journal of mine. And now I will finish my record of sight-seeing in Constantinople. Last Saturday, a party of about twenty, French, English and Americans, went to visit the mosques of Stamboul, for which it is necessary to have a firman from government. The French party attended to getting the firman, so we had nothing to do, but to pay our share of the expenses, which was fifteen francs apiece, (three dollars,) rather an expensive excursion for one day.

Knowing we should not be allowed to wear in the mosques the boots or shoes we had been walking in, and as it is no easy thing to lace and unlace boots a half dozen times in a few hours, I wore shoes that I could put on and off easily, and took a pair of slippers to wear in the mosques, marble floors not being very agreeable to feet encased merely in stockings.

To avoid the long walk over the bridge, we rowed over to Seraglio Point, which juts out into the Marmora on the one side, and the Bosphorus on the other. We walked through a labyrinth of courts and gardens and rooms, and I must confess in all, except the gardens, I was disappointed. With the exception of a corridor running round one of the courts, paved with marble, and supported by rare pillars, and a bath room, an exquisite gem, lined with rich marble, I saw but little marble, the staircases being of wood, and the floors also, or at least, all that we saw, a few rooms being covered with straw matting. Divans and chairs covered with satin, silk or damask, were in all the rooms, but neither the furniture nor the palace itself could begin to compare with palaces we saw in Egypt. We passed through a long gallery, with closely latticed windows, through which the ladies of the palace formerly looked down upon a court below, to witness games and feats of strength. In one of the courts we saw a marble column, about seventy feet high, with a beautiful Corinthian capital, and in this court, or another one, I have forgotten which, a magnificent sycamore tree, measuring thirty-seven feet around the trunk.

The buildings and grounds of the Seraglio cover about three miles, and the palace, or rather succession of palaces, is sufficiently large to accommodate four thousand retainers, besides the women, the last by no means an unimportant item in the palace of the Sultan. The kitchens occupy one side of a court, and are immense rooms, surmounted by ten domes. Report says the Turks are exceedingly fond of good living, and that the women consume unheard-of quantities of candies and sweetmeats, more than two thousand pounds of sugar being daily used in the kitchen of the womens' apartments belonging to the royal family.

The gate leading to the first court from the city, is called the imperial gate, or the Sublime Porte, which gives name to the Ottoman court. Over it is an inscription in Arabic, and as I never before saw a translation of it, and you may be in equal ignorance, I copy this from an excellent work on Turkey, by Admiral Slade. "By the assistance of God, and his good pleasure, the lord of the two continents and seas, the shadow of God among men and among angels; the favorite of God in the East and in the West; the monarch of the terraqueous globe; the conqueror of the city of Constantinople, that is, the victorious Emperor Mehemet, son of the Emperor Amurath, and grandson of the Emperor Mehemet, laid the foundation of this august building, united the parts solidly together, for the preservation of quiet and tranquility. May the Almighty perpetuate his empire, and exalt it above the lucid stars of the firmament."

The charm of the Seraglio, to me, was its terraced gardens, and the lovely views of the Marmora, the Bosphorus, and the Golden Horn. I am never wearied with looking out upon this varying scene, and I eagerly seize every opportunity of viewing it to the best advantage. The ancient church of St. Irene, just beyond the Seraglio, is now used as a place of deposit for arms, and here we found specimens of almost every date and kind, from a full suit of armor, down to a gun, sword and pistol. Above the great altar, in a glass case, are the keys of every town in Turkey, and on the walls hang the swords of vanquished kings and princes. The massive arches and heavy galleries, the small semicircular windows, high up in the thick walls, give you a good idea of ancient Byzantine architecture.

Not far from the Seraglio, is the venerable pile of St. Sophia, whose "gleaming dome" and gilded crescent, and "sky-piercing minarets," make it a conspicuous object from any part of Constantinople and its environs. It was the hour for the midday prayers, and as, for some reason or other, we were obliged to wait some time before the entrance to the mosque, I sat down upon a stone seat, and saw the bearded Turk, and the young boy, stop at the fountain opposite to me, and wash their face and neck and feet, before going into the temple of their God, and then, tired of looking and waiting, I opened my note book, and was soon absorbed in my writing. Suddenly the light was obscured, and on looking up, I saw a crowd of men and boys around me, gazing in wonder at the closely written page before me. As I knew not one of them could read what I was writing, I wrote on, not at all disturbed by their presence, till the summons came for us to go into the mosque. As the Ramazan had just commenced, the mosque was more than usually full, and from different parts the priests were expounding the Koran. Quite a crowd assembled round some favorite preacher, while another at a little distance seemed to be speaking in vain, so few listeners had he. Here, a number of men were prostrating themselves, and going through their stated devotions, and there a knot of boys were rocking themselves backward and forward, reciting passages of the Koran in a sing-song tone, while here and there a group of merry little children were playing and bounding about, and even turning somersets on the floor. Women are rarely seen in a mosque, but perhaps they pray at home. Men may traffic and gossip in the mosques, and even pursue their different vocations, for I saw several sewing, making a "comforter" for a bed, and children may play and gambol round; but the presence of a Christian pollutes the sanctuary!

We were led at first to the wide gallery that runs around the interior of the mosque, and there we stood a long time, gazing at the groups below, or looking round upon the vast edifice in which we were. I cannot say St. Sophia struck me so very forcibly with the idea of its magnificence or vastness, for in this respect its effect is nothing compared with St. Peter's, at Rome, the Cathedral at Milan, or the venerable Minster at York; but the associations of St. Sophia render it deeply and painfully interesting, for consecrated once to the worship of the living God, it now bears aloft the crescent instead of the cross.

It was built by Justinian, and consecrated on Christmas eve, 538, to the "Divine Wisdom," the second Person in the ever adorable Trinity. Sixteen years were occupied in its erection, and its consecration was accompanied with the slaughter of one thousand oxen, one thousand sheep, one thousand pigs, six hundred deer, ten thousand chickens, and a distribution of thirty thousand measures of corn to the poor. When every thing was in readiness for the consecration, the Emperor, accompanied by the Patriarch Eutychius, came to the great door of the church, where suddenly leaving the venerable priest, he ran to the altar, and eagerly embracing it, exclaimed, "God be praised, who hath esteemed me worthy to complete such a work! Oh, Solomon, I have surpassed thee!"

All that was venerable in the old religions of the world was brought here to do honor to this magnificent temple, porphyry pillars from the great temple of the Sun, columns of verd-antique from the celebrated temple of Diana of the Ephesians, and pillars from the Acropolis in Athens, from the temple of Osiris and Isis in Egypt, and from that of Apollo at Delos.

For nearly a thousand years, Santa Sophia was used for the worship of the Most High God, but then a change came. Upon the fall of Constantinople, in 1453, thousands of Christians took refuge in the church. There they were pursued by the conquering Moslems, who were commencing a general massacre, intending afterwards to demolish the sacred edifice, when Mohammed the Second entered on horseback, rode up to the great altar, and there dismounted. Ascending the steps of the altar, he proclaimed that the church of Jesus Christ should henceforth be sacred to the Prophet. The pictures were torn from the walls, the pulpit was overthrown, the altar removed, and the rich mosaics that lined the dome daubed over with paint or with gilding. Over the altar, there was an image of Christ in mosaic, with a halo around the head, and even now, by gazing very intently, one can distinctly trace the whole figure through the gilding that covers it.

The dome rises up two hundred feet from the pavement, and the effect is very fine, as you stand in one of the galleries, looking up to the very top of the dome, and then down upon the area below, over which the light, falling through stained glass, plays beautifully. We afterwards walked through the lower part of the edifice, between groups of men still on the floor at their devotions, or reading very rapidly and monotonously from the Koran, while the preaching was going on in a half dozen different parts of the mosque. Not the least striking feature of the scene, was the man following us, who carried the boots and shoes of the whole party slung over his shoulder, looking precisely like a peddler of second-hand boots and shoes.

Our next visit was to the mosque of Sultan Achmet, which stands, as I told you before, on one side of the Hippodrome. The only thing to break the interior of this large mosque, is four immense pillars of white marble, that support the dome. White pillars, white floor, white walls, varied here and there with characters inscribed in gold on them, give an impression of purity and grandeur that a mosque of itself is not calculated to inspire, for beautiful as the building may be, you cannot divest your mind of the fact it is erected to a false religion.

The principal characteristic of the mosque of Sultan Achmet is its six minarets, no other mosque in the empire having more than four. He wished to build a mosque that would excel all others in beauty, and to effect this, he intended to give it six minarets. But the mufti, whose consent was necessary for the completion of this design, refused to sanction it, on the plea that the most holy of all the mosques, that at Mecca, had but four minarets. The Sultan maintained there were six, and the mufti then proposed that a caravan of pilgrims should be dispatched immediately to Mecca, to settle the question. The Sultan joyfully agreed, taking the precaution to send a swift courier before to order two extra minarets to be immediately erected, so when the pilgrims arrived, behold six minarets adorned the holy mosque. Achmet was no longer denied permission to erect the six minarets, and when his mosque was completed, orders were sent to Mecca to take down the two new minarets, and the mosque of Sultan Achmet stands, therefore, without a rival in the Ottoman empire, in its number of minarets.

Willis, in his sprightly narrative of a "Summer Cruise in the Mediterranean," compares a minaret to an ever-pointed pencil-case, the bands around it answering to the encircling galleries, one above another, from which the muezzin calls out the hour of prayer. The minarets are always of a dazzling white, the galleries encircling them are richly cut in fretwork, and rising to a height often of two or three hundred feet, they seem to pierce the very sky. Each of the seven hills on which Constantinople is built, is crowned with a mosque, each having one large dome and a number of small ones, and from two to six minarets. Elevated above the mass of the surrounding houses, the gilded crescents flashing in the sun, the domes swelling out in their perfect proportions, the slender minarets rising up so gracefully, these mosques form the most prominent feature of Constantinople, and are seen from every point of view.

Once more we put off our shoes, and entered the mosque, or mausoleum of the late Sultan Mahmoud, an exquisite little gem of white marble, adorned with elaborate carvings and fretwork. Here repose the remains of Mahmoud himself, and several members of his family, each tomb made somewhat in the shape of an ark, higher and larger at the head than the foot, and having a steep roof, and over these were thrown rich cachemere shawls, the possession of any one of which would have thrown a New York belle into ecstasies. Stands of precious woods, inlaid with pearl and shell, silver and gold, support beautifully written and decorated copies of the Koran, and these are scattered in profusion around the tombs.

By the time we had finished our survey of this mosque, we were very tired, and finding the mosque of Sultan Sulyman was a long distance off, we voted to give up seeing it, as one mosque, in architectural design and finish, differs but little from another. I have since regretted this decision, for I have been told that was the most magnificent of all the mosques.

A few words on mosques in general, and then I will have done with the subject. As I have said more than once, each mosque is distinguished by a principal centre dome, and this is generally supported by two or more semi-domes at its base, and a greater or less number of small domes or cupolas over the angles of the building, and the arches of the corridors running around the court. Thus an imperial mosque is a vast edifice, two or three hundred feet square, having a mountain of cupolas and domes, varying in size, the centre one, like a large half globe, crowning the whole. These are relieved by round or narrow windows, adorned by delicate tracery and fretwork, cut in stone, and these windows, illuminated now in the Ramazan, present a beautiful sight, gleaming with myriads of lamps, arranged to form Turkish characters. To give you some idea of the number of these domes and cupolas, I will just say the mosque of Sultan Achmet alone has more than thirty.

Adjoining every mosque, is a large court, several hundred feet square, around the sides of which in the interior, run open arcades, supported often by pillars of precious marbles, the remains of the former glory and beauty of the ancient city, many of them having been taken from Christian temples. In the centre of the court, is a marble fountain, with a beautiful stone canopy; and here the Moslem stops to wash before entering the mosque to pray. Sometimes beautiful trees adorn these courts, and hundreds of pigeons flutter around the branches, fed at stated times each day by private bounty, a sum having been left for this purpose by some pious individuals.

Tired as I was, I could not resist the temptation of strolling through some of the bazaars, but I found their aspect very different during the Ramazan from what it was before. Many of the Turkish bazaars were closed, and the Turks we saw were no longer smoking, but lounging on their little counters, most of them asleep.

I really cannot write another word except "good bye."

LETTER LI.

English Church.—Beauties of the Bosphorus.—Castles of Asia and Europe.—Black Sea.—The Sultan.—American Minister.—Life at Buyukdere.—Sweet Waters of Asia.—Letters from Home.

BUYUKDERE, June 4th.

MY DEAREST FRIENDS:

Still in our delightful retreat and beautiful valley, for the meaning of the long word at the beginning of my letter, (pronounced Bu-yuk-de-re,) is "great valley." I have not yet finished my record of the past, so I once more go back. Last Sunday, we enjoyed the rare privilege of going to church twice, a pleasure we have not known since we were in Alexandria. The services are held in a chapel in the palace of the English ambassador in Pera, the church having been recently burnt to the ground. Owing to the great number of English at present here, on account of the war, the chapel was crowded, and to an eye accustomed to the every day attire of sober citizens, the officers in their scarlet uniforms presented rather a strange sight. "The panoply of war," and the service of the Prince of Peace, how incongruous it seems, and yet may not good Christians be good soldiers, and *vice versa?*

On Monday, Mr. F., J. and myself took a four-oared caique, and came to Buyukdere, to complete our arrangements about coming here for an interval of rest. Every body has heard of the beauties of the Bosphorus, and although I had formed a high idea of them, I am ready to confess I was not at all disappointed. In fact, I do not see how the lover of the picturesque and beautiful can be, for from Constantinople up the whole length of the Bosphorus, there is every thing to feast the eye. Twenty-six villages skirt the banks of these charming straits, ten on the Asiatic side, sixteen on the European. In Asia, they are scattering, green fields and wooded dells often coming down to the very water's edge. On the European side, the villages lie closer together; in fact, it is difficult to tell where one leaves off and another begins. On both sides, the hills come down very near the water, so that the villages lie in a narrow valley, and stretch up the hillside. With the exception of a few palaces, and the mosques, the houses are of wood, but totally unlike what you would find in any other quarter of the globe. Fantastic in shape, picturesque in coloring, many of them set in a framework of green trees and brilliant flowers, backed by rolling hills, they present a constant succession of charming pictures. Palaces innumerable, belonging to the Sultan and different members of the Imperial family, to Pashas and Beys and other dignitaries of state, their closely latticed windows, telling of treasures within, not to be seen by every eye, mosques, with their graceful minarets, forts, with their formidable looking cannon, cemeteries, with their tall cypresses and white stones, gardens, with their rich foliage and beautiful flowers, ships and steamers lying almost under the projecting roofs of some of the palaces and houses, caiques darting along under the shade of balconies and lattices, the hills, some wooded, some covered with waving grass and ripening grain, many of them crowned with a kiosk, (summer palace,) a castle, or a fort, or a country seat, luxuriant valleys opening up through the hills, sunny glades, wooded dells, wild ravines, these, and a hundred similar objects of interest, keep one's attention alive, every time the passage of the Bosphorus is made.

On the European side, are two of the most beautiful mosques I have ever seen. They are built of marble of a dazzling whiteness, and are adorned with carvings and fretwork. The swelling dome, the two slender minarets, the dazzling brilliancy of the marble, make them perfect little gems; indeed, I call them "the two gems of the Bosphorus."

And then the winding of the Bosphorus, its beautiful little curves and graceful bends, give it a peculiar charm. Tiny bays and projecting promontories chase each other in quick succession. There is no tide, and often the houses rise directly from the water, while in other places a wide foot-path runs along in front. The current is rapid, and sets swiftly down from the Black Sea, so that in three places the caique was pulled up by a man, who ran along the bank, with a large rope fastened around one of the benches for the rowers, and the other end thrown over his shoulder, and his efforts to stem the powerful current, called in one place "the devil's current," were so great as to make him almost bend double. For this immense physical exertion, he demanded not quite two cents of our money.

About half way between Constantinople and Buyukdere, on opposite points of the Bosphorus, stand the castles of Asia and Europe, the former built by Bajazet, to control the navigation of the straits, the latter by his grandson, Mahomet, to impede it. The latter occupies much the most ground, and is said to represent, in shape, the name of Mohammed in Arabic characters. I have not much of an eye for military fortifications, but I should say these were by no means the strongest in the world.

A very pretty feature to me, in coming up the Bosphorus, is to see the little graves nestling beneath a tree in some quiet, secluded garden, in sight of the windows of the house to which the garden belongs, thus making the living and the dead seem side by side.

At a sudden turn, the Black Sea opens before you, and beyond Buyukdere, the villages become more scattering, the hills seem higher, and the remains of one or two ancient castles are seen on some of the most prominent summits. Every hill and every vale have a romantic or a historic legend connected with them, and as, in coming up, we rowed along the European side, and in returning, the Asiatic, we had a good opportunity to see every point, every bay, every palace and garden, to the best advantage.

Just before we reached Pera, we saw the Sultan's caique going down the Bosphorus. It is painted white, and adorned with gilding and carving to a magnificent extent. The Sultan reclined on the bottom of the caique, under a red umbrella, held over him by one of the high dignitaries, and we could not, therefore, see his face. Soldiers were drawn up on the shore to receive him, the imperial flag was flying, the officers bowed themselves to the ground as he landed, a salute was fired, and he almost immediately disappeared from our sight, going into a mosque for evening prayers.

We spent all the morning of Tuesday in the bazaars at Constantinople, in search of a shawl, but I found none to suit, not in quality, but in price. That day we bade farewell to Mr. and Mrs. R. and Mr. F., who have gone to Greece, and now, for the first time since entering Egypt, we are without companions. But we are not without kind friends, however, for our Minister to the Ottoman Porte, Hon. Carroll Spence, and his family, are at this hotel, and they are as kind and polite to us as though they had known us all our lives.

Our rooms open upon a wide balcony or terrace, and when I am tired of writing, I step out and gaze upon the view around me. In front, the Bosphorus spreads out like a lake, so encircled is it by mountains; on the right, the lower part of the bay of Buyukdere sweeps round, and on the left, at a little distance, is the entrance to the Black Sea, while along the shore, stretches the town, a wide street running along the water's edge. The evenings are delicious; the moon shedding a flood of light on bay and shore and verdant hill, and I say a hundred times a day, "I never saw a lovelier sight."

Last Tuesday afternoon we arrived here, and took up our abode for the present, and already the breeze from the Euxine, and the still nights, have begun to restore my strength and spirits. We breakfast at ten, and dine at seven, and the meals are good, and our rooms clean and nice. Indeed, we have not been more comfortable since we left home, and if any one knows how to prize that word "comfortable," it is travellers, particularly those in the East. Yesterday, we took a caique and rowed down to the "Valley of Sweet Waters," just below the castle of Asia; but, contrary to our expectations, we found no one there. However, we took a long walk up the valley, which, although beautiful, will not compare with the "sweet waters" of Europe. The trees are large, the little river winds gracefully on, spanned by several bridges, but the grass is crisp and dried, and looks as though a shower would refresh it.

We went down to Pera this morning, in a steamboat, attended church twice, and reached home about seven o'clock. And what a feast awaited us on our return! A package of ten letters! Ever since we arrived at Pera, we had been expecting letters, and I began to fear the banker in London had not received the directions to send them here. But all suspense is now at an end; the letters have arrived; all at home are well, and we are happy.

LETTER LII.

Sir Stephen Lakeman.—Mr. E.'s departure for Schumla.—Kindness of American Minister.—Bebec.—American Missionaries.—Annual Meeting of Bible Society.—Large Sycamores.—Fine Ride.—Bendt.—Forest of Belgrade.—Cottage of Lady Montague.—Giant's Mountain.—Legends.—Genoese Castle.—Shopping in Pera.—Symplegades.

Buyukdere, June 16th.

To you, my mother, I have chosen to address this letter, and to write to you on this day, rather than any other, because it is your birthday, and afar off, over land and sea, I send you my greetings, and hearty wishes for many happy returns of the day. You may be surprised to find I am still here, and more surprised to see that I say "I" instead of "we," but I am alone just now, J—— having gone "to the wars." Soon after our arrival here, we made the acquaintance of an officer in the English army, Sir Stephen Lakeman, and every day when he rode out, he invited J—— to go with him, as he had a number of fine horses here, and if I had not been such a coward, I might have gone too, but his horses looked quite too gay and spirited for me.

A few days after the acquaintance was formed, he kindly invited J—— to go with him to Schumla, as he was going with his own horses, tents, cook, &c. Such an opportunity to see the country, the army and the great men, might not occur again in a lifetime, and for a week, to go or not to go, that was the question. The only obstacles were, that our journey would be retarded three weeks at least, and that I must be left behind and almost alone in a strange land. The first objection grew less and less formidable, for I had been taking a fatiguing journey, and a long rest would not be amiss. Besides, my heap of notes, to be enlarged and copied out, had not decreased according to my wishes, and a little more leisure would help me on quite wonderfully. The last objection speedily vanished, for our Minister, hearing of J.'s wishes to go, kindly offered to take care of me in his absence, and nobly has he thus far redeemed his promise. I no longer dine at the public table, but in their own room, at five o'clock, thus giving me an opportunity to row or walk with them every evening. You need no assurances from me, to know that these acts of kindness do not fall on an ungrateful heart, but are dearly cherished as tokens of a kind interest in my welfare, that knows no bounds. The "pros and cons" being duly discussed, and thus satisfactorily decided, on the morning of the 14th, the travellers set forth, and I have in prospect a period of rest of three weeks duration.

And now I will go back a few days, and tell you what else has transpired since my last letter. On Monday, the 5th, Mr. S. invited us to row to Bebec with them, but J—— was engaged to ride with Sir S., so I went, and enjoyed the excursion very much. They have a large caique with six oars, and instead of carrying a flag, to show that it is the boat of the American Minister, it is painted on the outside in red and white stripes, with a border of blue, spotted with stars.

Bebec is a beautiful village, encircling a little bay, just below the Castle of Europe. We landed under the shade of large sycamore trees, and went to the house of one of the American missionaries living there, where we had the pleasure of meeting some eight or ten clergymen, from different parts of the East, who are holding their annual meeting at present at Pera. Some of these missionaries have been thirty years from their native land, and in that long period have been home but once. I can only say they are made of different stuff from what I am, to be able to stay away so long. But they are doing their Master's work, and cannot easily leave, to their honor be it said.

The next day we went down to Pera, with Mr. and Mrs. S. and the children, it being the anniversary of a Bible Society, of which his Excellency has been chosen President. At the opening of the meeting, he made an address, which was received with great applause, and was followed by speakers from all parts of the world, English chaplains in the army and navy, American missionaries from the far East, and even a surgeon in the army, relating his experience of the benefits of a free circulation of the Bible. It was an occasion of great interest, from the fact that the speakers were thus of different professions, and from different quarters of the globe. It was Whitsun-Tuesday, too, and it seemed to me almost a Pentecostal scene, for there were assembled "dwellers in Mesopotamia, and in Judea and Cappadocia, in Pontus and Asia, Phrygia and Pamphylia, Jews and proselytes," to say nothing of those distant countries, England and America, unknown to the Christian world, when the Holy Ghost miraculously conferred the gift of tongues.

Though I have now been on the Bosphorus more than a half dozen times, I constantly see new beauties to admire. The picturesque houses, the rich coloring, the rolling hills, the lights and shades, the transparent water, the glorious hues of the clouds, the gorgeous palaces, the magnificent gardens, the groups sitting here and there under the trees, at the close of the day, the soldiers standing at their posts, the caique gliding quickly through the water, these are a few of the far-famed charms of the Bosphorus, charms, I believe, that never pall upon the sight.

Before we arrived here, that afternoon, the sun went down in a flood of brilliant hues, the Ramazan gun boomed out, and echoed and re-echoed from the hills, and from the minarets came forth the call to evening prayer. And then beyond the mountain top, the moon suddenly beamed forth, and a new beauty was added to the lovely scene.

On Wednesday, I overcame my timidity so far as to be persuaded to mount a beautiful Arabian pony belonging to Sir S. L., and although he was a spirited little creature, he was gentle and easily managed. But I rode in constant terror, though I tried to enjoy the scene, for it was a lovely country through which we were passing.

Just after leaving Buyukdere, we turned a little aside to see the immense trees under which Godfrey of

Bouillon and Raymond of Toulouse encamped on their way to Palestine. One of these trees measures forty feet around the trunk. We rode along a paved road for some little distance, our horses slipping over the large stones, for it had rained that morning, but soon we left the stones behind us, and then we entered upon a road so good that if I had seen it in Palestine or Syria, I should have thought it had lost its way. Under the o'erspreading branches of large trees, a murmuring rivulet running by our side, and gleaming here and there among the grass and leaves, our way laid, and then we passed under the arches of an aqueduct built by Valens and Justinian, and soon after came to a large reservoir of water, enclosed in solid masonry, and surrounded by trees and shrubs. This is called a "bendt," and here the water is collected to supply the aqueduct which extends to Constantinople. We saw three of these "bendts," the last two adorned with marble balustrades, and here and there a little sculpture. And then the magnificent trees that throw their shadow over the water, and the grass below, so free from underbrush, and the little red strawberries peeping here and there from their leafy bed, and the blue sky above, seen through the many boughs, what a scene it all was!

Reclining on the grass, beside a rippling, gushing fountain, we ate our lunch, while the horses fed with much apparent relish on the luxuriant grass. This was the forest of Belgrade, and near here is a cottage, in which the witty Lady Montague dwelt for some time, and where she wrote many of her interesting letters.

As we came back into the village, it began to rain, so we sought shelter in a house till the shower was over, but before we were half way home, the rain came on again, and I got nicely wet. Last Thursday, his Excellency went down to Pera in his caique, and invited us to go with him, and we once more enjoyed the delights of the Bosphorus, and again spent several hours in the bazaars of Constantinople. They do not seem like the same places they were before the Ramazan commenced, so many of the little stalls are closed, while their owners are at home, sleeping away the effects of the last night's excess. Still, the bazaars present an animating sight, and I do not think I should soon grow weary of them.

The next three days I spent very quietly, scarcely going out of my room, except to my meals. Diligently I labored with my pen, and when my mind and my body grew weary, I went upon the terrace, and looked abroad on the Bosphorus. And when night came with its quiet, and rest from labor, and the bright stars shone out, and the full moon appeared in all her glory, then care and labor were forgotten, and the delicious scene brought peace and repose to the weary spirit.

On Monday, we rowed across the Bosphorus, and ascended the Giant's Mountain. It was a long walk, but not a very fatiguing one, for we stopped a half dozen times to feast our eyes upon the exquisite view around us. Byron says,

> "'Tis a good sight from off the Giant's cave,
> To watch the progress of these rolling seas,
> Between the Bosphorus, as they lash and lave
> Asia and Europe."

I have already said so much of the Bosphorus, I am afraid you will grow weary of the subject, and yet I feel I have not done it justice. The theme of the historian, the novelist, the traveller and the poet, it has been described a thousand times, and for one, I am ready to say I do not think it has ever been overdrawn.

The Giant who gave his name to this mountain, showed his taste for beautiful scenery, by selecting such a spot for his abiding place. Mussulman tradition says he was a Dervish, and that his sanctity was equal to his stature, which makes him a very holy man indeed, inasmuch as it is affirmed he sat on the summit of the mountain, and bathed his feet in the limpid waters of the Bosphorus, far, far down below. The legend of the Christian is, that he was a man of immense stature and ferocious nature, to whom the Symplegades were vassals, and who, from his lofty station on the mountain top, watched the approach of every ship that ventured to brave the rough waters of the Euxine.

From this elevated spot, we had a magnificent view of the undulating banks of the Bosphorus, its castled rocks, smiling valleys, and beautiful bays, across which the little caiques were skimming like birds. Hill and dale and wooded glade intervened between us and the Black Sea, which swept far away, till sea and sky were blended in one deep and heavenly blue.

On the summit of a hill, a little distance beyond us, were the remains of an old castle, known by the name of "the Genoese Castle." It is said this castle was once defended by a fair young girl, the daughter of the governor, who was killed in its defence, and that for three days after her father fell, she boldly held out against the enemy, her little garrison growing weaker and more dispirited every day, till at last she fell, a victim to her bravery and stout resistance.

Once more I have been up and down the Bosphorus,

for J—— found it necessary to go to Pera, to make some preparations for his departure. We made another attempt to see the dancing Dervishes, but without success. The remainder of the day was devoted to shopping, a transaction not always attended by pleasant circumstances, particularly in Pera, where different articles are scattered in the most unlooked-for places, the nicest boots and shoes being often found in a candy shop, and ready-made coats and vests in a furniture store! Day before yesterday, Sir S. L. and his party set out, and I need not say what my feelings were, when I returned to my solitary room, after seeing them off. But the consciousness that both I and mine are in the hands of One who never slumbers or sleeps, and that He can watch over all, whether separated or together, buoys me up, and I go about my accustomed duties and pleasures with unabated cheerfulness and alacrity.

Yesterday morning, Mr. S. and his family and myself went up to the Black Sea, about six or seven miles from here. As we approached the sea, the villages grew more and more scattering along the shore of the Bosphorus, and the hills more steep and rugged. The current was very strong, but our three boatmen pulled well, and the caique danced over the waters "like a thing of life." Huge porpoises leaped about us, and white gulls floated lazily on the water, while myriads of little birds sped by us, almost touching the water with their wings. These birds go from the Black Sea down the Bosphorus, and back, and are never seen to alight, and they are said by the Turks to be the spirits of the wicked, doomed to roam up and down the straits, knowing no rest.

At the entrance of the Bosphorus into the Black Sea,

on the left hand, is a cluster of rocks, called the Symplegades. We climbed, with some difficulty, to the top of these rocks, and the boatmen, bringing up our provisions, we hoisted the American flag, and we ate our lunch there, sitting around a column of white marble, about six feet in height and three in circumference. When this pillar was erected, no one seems to know; some say it was put up there in honor of Pompey, others of Apollo. There we sat, with the Black Sea before us, not looking black, as in my childhood I thought it must, to deserve its name, but calm and clear and blue, its fair surface dotted here and there with a white sail. Our hunger being appeased, and our eyes tired of looking on the dazzling sea, we clambered down, not without a few slippings on the rock, and with merry laughter at our awkwardness. We rowed a little way up the sea, but calm and smooth as it looked from the rocks, we found it quite boisterous, when once upon its bosom, and the waves dashed over our prow quite merrily, so we were content to turn back.

And thus, in a dry and journal-like manner, I have told you of our doings the last two weeks; but uninteresting as the manner is, I hope the matter will not prove utterly devoid of interest to you.

My mother, adieu.

LETTER LIII.

Daily Routine.—Adventure.—Feast of the Beiram.—Close of the Ramazan.—Night Scene on the Bosphorus.—Mr. Brown.—Scene at Dawn.—Seraglio.—Kissing the Feet.—The Sultan.

BUYUKDERE, June 25th.

MY DEAR GIRLS:

It is Sunday afternoon, and nearly all day I have sat alone in my room, while my thoughts have wandered a hundred times to my far distant home, and to all I love there; and as I know a letter sent from such a distance would give you much pleasure, I thought I would write this time to you. Since I last wrote home, my days have passed in a quiet, pleasant routine, reading, writing, sewing, walking or rowing, but I am sorry to say my nights have not been at all tranquil, for I have now a room that opens upon the street, and night after night, dogs are barking, and cats are howling, fiddles are squeaking, and men are roaring, till long after midnight, and I must say I think that a queer religion that leads people to fast all day and revel all night, and for one, I shall be glad when the Ramazan is over, and, by the way, it ends to-day.

The rooms we had before your uncle went away, were double rooms, but, of course, I did not want to be at the expense of keeping them, when I need but one room, so now I have a room that looks down upon the street, and abroad upon a high and beautifully wooded hill, while on the right I have a view of the Bosphorus, almost to its entrance into the Black Sea.

Sometimes in the morning we walk out, going to the large trees about a mile from here, and Mrs. S. and I sit with our work under their grateful shade, while the children take turns in riding on their donkey. At other times, we row several miles down the Bosphorus, and landing near a spring, regale ourselves with cold water, a luxury unknown at this hotel. Over on the Asiatic side, are lovely valleys, and several of these we have visited, strolling along under magnificent trees, or sitting upon the grass, with books and work. After dinner, we invariably go out, one evening walking along the quay, meeting half of the inhabitants of the town, either sitting at their doors, or sauntering along the streets, and the next evening, going in the caique. Most of all, I enjoy a row on the Bosphorus at that hour. Groups of people sitting under trees in front of a rural café, sipping coffee or sherbet, the soft light upon the hills, and the lengthened shadows in the valleys, the white minarets rising from clusters of trees, and glittering with the last rays of the sun, the delicate coloring of the clouds, and the soft tints spread over the water, the caiques darting hither and thither, the little birds speeding rapidly on, the bustling steamer, the stately ship, with all sails spread, the delicious air, all have their peculiar charms. Often as I now have been on the Bosphorus, I am never weary of it, but every day I seem to see it under a new aspect.

Last Thursday, I was obliged to go down to Pera to see my dress-maker, who, by the way, belongs to the sterner sex, and who had disappointed me, a habit by no means confined to dress-makers in the East, and as Mrs. S. wanted some shopping done, she sent her nurse down with me, to attend to it. Having but little to do, I thought I should have ample time to leave here at twelve o'clock, and return at half past five, but I had forgotten how difficult it was to accomplish shopping with ease in Pera, and we found ourselves very much hurried towards the last. Then I lost my way going to the bridge, from which the steamers up the Bosphorus start, and that hindered us, so that the hour for leaving had passed before we reached the bridge, but knowing that Turkish punctuality is always to be behind the time, I did not feel very uneasy. When we had traversed half the bridge, a new difficulty appeared, for the draw was open, to let a steamship pass through. The whistles of the steamers sounded, and I could look ahead and see the black smoke issuing from the pipes, and then I knew we had not a minute to lose, so calling out "caique," a dozen of them instantly came alongside the bridge, and a dozen voices clamored out. But not a word of Turkish could we understand or speak, but "yes" and "no," so I selected the foremost caique. But how to get down to the crazy little egg-shell was a question. No time was to be lost, and we crawled under the railing of the bridge, and prepared to jump down, when another new difficulty made its appearance. A man and a woman, I cannot call them a gentleman and a lady, though they were nicely and fashionably dressed, were sitting on the railing, gazing at the steamship going through the draw, and on the bridge stood an oblong sort of a bundle, tied up in a colored handkerchief. In my haste to get under the railing, my dress swept the bundle over, and immediately I heard a crash. Down leaped the man and the woman; one grabbed me by one wrist and the other by the other, demanding, in furious tones, reparation of the grievous wrong I had done them in breaking a bottle of wine. I asked pardon in the choicest French and Italian I could muster, but they did not seem to understand much of either language, so I suppose they were Greeks or Armenians. At last, (how long it seemed,) I made them understand I was willing to pay, and wanted to know how much would satisfy them. "Twenty piastres." I venture to say the wine did not cost five, but I suppose it is not every day they have a bottle of wine broken, and they wished to make the most of it. I was in haste, else I would have gone with them to the embassy and had it settled, so I opened my purse and handed him a bill, (for they have paper money here, and villainous looking stuff it is, too, like the "shinplasters" we once had in the United States,) and went on my way. Unfortunately, it proved to be ten piastres, instead of twenty, and once more he flew at me, catching a book from my hand, which he intimated he should keep till I gave him the money. The book was not mine, or I would have given it up and walked on, so I tried to get the book back, but the wretch caught me by the wrist, and once more demanded his money. Margaret, having no intention of letting the book go, (it belonged to Mr. Spence,) now came to my rescue, and being mistress of no other tongue than her own, treated the man to a good, sound American scolding.

A crowd gathered round, the whistles shrieked, I must either go then, or stay in Pera all night, so throwing him a note for twenty piastres, and springing down into the caique, I bade the man row quickly to the Buyukdere steamer. But which one? for there were three. "I do not care which, only put us on board one," I cried, but before we went many steps, two of them started. The man, screaming for them to stop, rowed into a narrow space directly between the two, while the signal was given for the engines to be stopped, to take us in. Already in danger from the paddles, I would not have mounted either of those little ladders thrown over the side, for the half of Buyukdere, so I motioned to the man to row to the next steamer, which was just ready to start. More dead than alive, I was hauled up the ladder, and we were half way up the Bosphorus, before I recovered strength or composure, while my wrist actually showed for hours the marks of that brute's violence. So much for being in a hurry!

To-morrow is a great festival at Constantinople, the feast of the Beiram, when all the grandees of the empire are permitted to kiss the Sultan's feet! Mr. and Mrs. S—, to give me an opportunity of witnessing the ceremony, had most kindly prepared to go down, and as it takes place early in the morning, we are to leave here by four o'clock. To be sure it will be something of a trial to get up so early, but I am certain the Bosphorus must look lovely at that hour.

Tuesday Evening. While we were at dinner on Sunday, we ascertained that the ceremony of the Beiram commenced much earlier Monday morning, than we had imagined, and that it would be impossible to arrive at Constantinople in season to witness it, unless we left here in the night, so we concluded to go down to Pera that evening. The caique was ordered, our arrangements were speedily made, and at half past six, we were on the Bosphorus. Shall I ever forget that night? The current took us out into the middle of the straits, and we therefore had an excellent view of both banks. Never did the Bosphorus seem more lovely. The softened light threw a mellow tint over hill and grove, palace and mosque, house and garden; the tall cypress looked more dark and stately than ever, and the white headstones beneath them, more unearthly and mysterious. Under every clump of trees, sat a group of persons in their holiday attire, and Armenian and Turk, Greek and English, were seen sauntering along the shore. Soldiers stood at their guns, saluting the Minister as we passed, the Greek Priest walked from village to village, his thin veil of black crape floating back upon the breeze.

And then the sun went down, and the groups upon the shore became shadowy and indistinct. Hark! from the castles of Europe and Asia, boom forth the sunset guns, and peal after peal reverberates through the air, each hill sending back a separate echo. The Ramazan is over, and the guns from every fort, up and down the Bosphorus, send abroad the joyful news.

We are passing a mosque, its white minaret standing out distinctly in the faint light. A dark form appears in one of the galleries, the hands are raised, and forth upon the evening air, came the sonorous sounds, "There is but one God, and Mohammet is his prophet, come to prayers." Minaret after minaret sends forth a like cry, and thousands of Mohammedans, obeying the call, prostrate themselves before their God.

The soft and dreamy twilight comes on, hill and grove, palace and mosque, house and garden are mingled mysteriously together in dim outline, till suddenly light flashes forth. Every dome is lit up, every gallery shows fantastic characters, the palace of the Sultan has a line of lights in front, and the city, we are rapidly approaching, gleams forth like a scene in fairy land. What painter could do justice to the glorious hues of the evening sky, reflected back in the smooth sea! Oh!

gorgeous Eastern land! oh! magnificent Constantinople! How queenly she sat that night on her seven hills, every summit crowned by a vast mosque, whose proudly swelling dome and towering minarets sent forth a blaze of light!

Landing at Tophana, we passed the beautiful fountain, arrayed in fantastic splendor, from the little lamps around on the stands where fruit and candy, and crisp cakes, and sherbet and ices, were ready to tempt the passer-by. Slowly we toiled up the steep hills, treading very daintily on the round stones, the Kavass, (a Turkish officer) with his sword, ahead to clear the way for his excellency, no foreign minister ever walking out, without such an attendant.

Arriving at the Hotel de Byzance, we found it full, not a bed to be had, though lodging could be obtained out. But the minister sent a note to Mr. Brown, dragoman of the embassy, stating our dilemma, and in a short time, an answer came back, that he had rooms for all. I felt delicate about intruding myself on private hospitality, but there was no alternative, for, as we should be obliged to go out early the next morning, it was necessary for me to keep with my party. Kindly we were received, and kindly we were entertained. What American that has ever visited Constantinople, has not received kindness at the hands of Mr. Brown? A scholar, a gentleman, perfectly acquainted with the Turkish language and habits, and history, which his long residence at the Ottoman court, has given him rare facilities for acquiring, he is ever ready to impart information to the traveller, eager to know somewhat about the interesting people among whom he finds himself.

We were to be called at four o'clock the next morning, but afraid of oversleeping myself, I awoke at half past three. I opened the window to get more light to look at my watch, and I did not close it again very soon, for such a scene burst upon me, as I have not often witnessed. Dawn was breaking, and sea and land were awakening to new life and loveliness. Below me, down the hills of Tophana, was a mass of red roofs; beyond, gleamed the Golden Horn, across whose smooth surface, even at that early hour, were speeding the little caiques, and still farther on, rose the seven-hilled city, her magnificent domes and towering minarets and gilded crescents, standing out in full relief against the blushing sky. Away in the distance lay the sheeny sea, a rock-girt island looking dark and frowning, in contrast to the placid waters. "Lovely, lovely scene!" I exclaimed a half dozen times. All my objections to early rising, vanished before a view like that, and I am sure if I lived near Constantinople, I would often get up early to feast my senses on a scene so exquisite.

Brighter and brighter dawned the day, and more and more distinctly came out each beautiful object. Now I saw the old Seraglio, peeping out from its leafy covert; now the waters of the Golden Horn shone out more brightly, and now the gilded crescents flashed in the increasing light.

A tap at my door aroused me from my meditation, and I turned from the window to make my toilet, which I accomplished in great haste, that I might have the more leisure for gazing at the glorious scene without.

The party was soon assembled in the parlor; we partook of a slight repast, and then went out. Even at that early hour, every one was stirring, for it was a great festival among the Turks. Turbaned men and shrouded women and noisy children filled the streets. Around every café sat groups of men in picturesque attire, with coffee and pipes beside them, and every moment we jostled against man or boy with tray on their heads, in which (the tray, not the heads I mean) were cakes or bread for sale.

Down the steep streets, and over the rough stones we went till we reached Tophana, and then getting into the caique, were speedily rowed across the Bosphorus to Seraglio Point. Dozens of caiques were moored at the wharf, and we found the ceremony had already commenced, for the Sultan had gone to the mosque. Up the shaded paths of the Seraglio grounds, through court after court, and gate after gate our way led, till we reached the large court, where the ceremony of "kissing the feet" was to take place. Here we found a crowd of people, though not a thousandth part of what we might have expected such a scene to call forth. I did not see a Turkish woman among them, and excepting the soldiers and kavasses, hardly a Turk, but French and English, and Armenian and Greek, were well represented, and we heard more than a half dozen different languages around us.

We had a good place under the shade of a tree, where we could command the whole view. I think we waited more than half an hour, and then a signal announced that the Sultan was leaving the mosque. A company of soldiers came first, and then followed the horses belonging to the Sultan, ten in number. What splendid animals these were too! Each one had a saddle cloth of velvet, embroidered with gold, and stepped on as proudly, as though he was conscious of carrying royalty on his back. Next came the body guard, in an uniform of red and white, and caps surmounted by a knot of feathers, of every color of the rainbow.

And now came Sultan Abdel Medjib, "the servant of the all-glorious, the refuge of the world," mounted on a grey horse, the saddle cloth covered with rich embroidery, and the bridle decorated with diamonds. The Sultan wore white pantaloons, embroidered with gold up and down the sides, and a loose frock coat of blue cloth, the collar and cuffs studded with diamonds. A small cap of red velvet, with a feather fastened in with a diamond clasp, completed his attire. He rode slowly on, his eyes fixed on vacancy, and never turned his head to the right or the left. The gentlemen, (at least those who wore hats,) uncovered as he passed, but no cheers were given. He entered the Palace, and then another long interval of waiting was passed, while he "reposed," that is, smoked a pipe, and drank some coffee, and if report says true, took something a little stronger.

I wondered no larger cavalcade followed him from the mosque, but I was told they came in by a more private entrance, and were awaiting their turn to be presented to his Imperial Majesty.

Under an arch, in front of the Seraglio, the ceremony of kissing the feet of the Sultan was to take place, and the tediousness of waiting was lightened a little by witnessing the preparations made for the great event. A rich carpet was brought out, glittering with gold, and laid upon the ground, and on it was placed a gilded sofa, and, that no dust should alight where his Majesty was to sit, a heavy cloth of gold was thrown over the entire sofa.

At length, (and an interminable length it seemed)

symptoms of the Sultan's approach appeared. The body guard ranged themselves in a semi-circle, around the gilded throne, their heads so heavy with their plumed caps, that they seemed to be moving very cautiously, for fear of becoming top-heavy. The band of music was stationed at a distance in front of the arch, and the soldiers were drawn up in lines, in the avenue. A gun boomed forth; the music struck up, the cloth of gold was flourished from the sofa, and the Sultan appeared, and took his seat. Then one loud cheer rent the air, and distinctly were pronounced the words by hundreds of voices, "Sultan Abdel Medjib, may he live a thousand years;" (not in English as I have given them, but in Turkish.)

The Sultan stood up; a venerable Mufti, clothed in flowing white robes, stood before him, and raising his hands in one of the prescribed postures of the Moslem form, uttered a short prayer, the Sultan raising his hands, and every Turk and soldier on the ground, doing the same. The "amen" was another cheer, and a repetition of the wish that the Sultan might live a thousand years, (rather too long I should think for comfort.)

Then followed the presentation, and my eyes were dazzled with the rich array of gold embroideries before me. First came the Grand Vizier, then the ex-Grand Viziers, the Ministers of State and leading dignitaries, each dressed in military costume, literally covered with embroidery. The Sultan stood upon a footstool, and each one as he came up, bowed to the ground, waving his hand, seeming to touch the earth with it, approached the throne, bowed again, then throwing himself on his knees, before the Sultan, humbly kissed, not his feet as I expected, but the border of his coat, pressing it afterwards to his breast and his forehead. Rising then from his knees, he once more bowed to the ground, retreated to the edge of the carpet, with his face towards the Sultan, bowed again, and then took his place in a semi-circle on the right of his Imperial Majesty. What a ceremony this was to go through! I am sure much practice must have been necessary, before all the bowing, and bending, and kneeling could be performed with ease and grace. To be sure, in backing out from the Sultan's immediate presence, one Pasha, tripped and fell full length on the ground, quickly rising up however, covered with confusion, and I might add, with dust.

The Sultan then sat down, the Grand Vizier standing on his right, and those who had had the honor of kissing the Sultan's coat, in a semi-circle beyond, and every time the Sultan spoke to the Grand Vizier, which was quite often, he bowed to the ground, at the commencement and end of every sentence.

On the left of the Sultan, stood an officer holding the imperial scarf, once belonging to the Prophet himself, and then the inferior Pachas, Beys, and other officers went through a process of bowing and kissing the scarf, each one pressing it afterwards to his forehead and breast, but none of these were permitted the honor of kissing the hem of the Sultan's garment. Hundreds approached to kiss the scarf, and after a little, I grew weary, so I watched the Sultan. He looked bored, and actually seemed as though he did not know what to do with his hands, like many an awkward man at home. At last, he rolled them up in his coat sleeves, and seemed delighted with such a cosy place for them. All this while, the band was "discoursing most eloquent music," and I recognized one or two familar Italian airs. The leader of this band is Donizetti, brother to the far famed composer.

At last there came a change; the Sultan stood up, the cheers burst forth, and a line of muftis and imaums came up clothed in long flowing robes, of white and green and purple and grey, decked with gold embroidery, and immense turbans of white and green with a broad gold band around them, (the descendants of the prophets only being permitted to wear the green turbans). Each one of these had the honor of kissing the hem of the coat, and I wondered how those old men, for some of them had venerable grey beards, ever got through that maze of bowing and kneeling, but I suppose they are used to it.

The scarf-kissing commenced again, the music pealed forth a joyous strain, and then a flourish of drums and trumpets announced that the ceremony was over. The Sultan made a speedy exit, the sofa was dragged away, the gorgeous carpet was snatched up, and the crowd began to disperse. Cannons were fired in quick succession, announcing that the Sultan had entered the palace of his fathers.

It was not seven o'clock when we left the Seraglio grounds, and I sighed at the thought of the long day before me. I should have been glad to have gone again into the bazaars, but I was told the Turkish bazaar would be closed. The row back to Tophana was exceedingly refreshing to me, after standing so long, for I had not sat down once while I was on the ground, but the walk up to Mr. Brown's was not so easy.

Till breakfast time, which was between ten and eleven

o'clock, I regaled myself with reading papers from the United States, but they were so full of murders and riots, I more than once blushed for my country. After breakfast, I had some shopping to do, of course, and that being duly attended to, I had ample time to rest before dinner.

We left at six, and though I was wearied with having been up so long, I enjoyed the row here very much. Before we reached Buyukdere, the night came on, solemn and grand, and thousands of little fire-flies danced among the leaves on the banks.

I was not in my room many minutes, before I was in bed, for I had been up more than eighteen hours; rather a long day. Again we were on the Bosphorus this evening, and stopping at one of our favorite haunts, sat for a long time under the trees, coming home in the delicious twilight.

I have now, my dear girls, written you a long letter, and I hope it is one that will interest you. Last Saturday being dear little J.'s birthday, I thought a great deal of you all, and longed to be once more in your midst.

LETTER LIV.

Garden of the Russian Embassy.—Sweet Waters of Asia.—Return from the Wars.—Fourth of July.—Turkish Bath.

BUYUKDERE, July 2d.

MY DEAR P.:

As I cannot go to church to-day, there being none nearer than Pera, I have chosen to devote a part of this day to communing with you at home. I have, to be sure, but little to write, as I am leading a very quiet, though agreeable life, for such a long period of rest I do not often enjoy when travelling. I generally go out twice a day, early in the morning, and after dinner. Twice I have walked in the garden of the Russian embassy, not often visited by strangers, especially now that the ambassador is away, and the palace closed. This garden is very extensive, stretching along the shore of the Bosphorus, and reaching to the summit of the mountain in the rear. Winding walks, shaded by trees, through whose thick foliage the sun rarely penetrates, fountains, whose rippling sound delights the ear, glimpses of the blue Bosphorus below and green hills beyond, these are some of the charms of this garden. Farther up the hillside, is a large vineyard, the vine planted in rows along the ground, and beyond, an orchard of fig and apricot and peach trees.

Almost at the summit of the hill, we sat down one day, under the spreading branches of a venerable tree, and there we had a fine view of the Bosphorus. Encircled by mountains, it lay like a lake before us, its blue surface broken here and there by a noble looking ship. The Turkish fleet is at present at anchor in the bay of Buyukdere, and the red flag, with a white crescent, is waving from nearly every mast-head in sight. From my elevated seat that day, I counted forty-seven different vessels, not all of them Turkish, a few being French and English. Down the Bosphorus, I saw the houses of Therapia and Yenicue, and on the opposite shore of Asia, the new palace which either Abbas Pacha is building for the Sultan, or the Sultan for Abbas Pacha, I don't exactly know which. The hills that border the Bosphorus are beautifully shaped, not sharp and prominent, but gently rolling, with green, round tops, and often with wooded sides.

Opposite to us, rose the Giant's mountain, and just beyond, the ruins of the Genoese castle, while still farther on, the Black Sea opened. What a beautiful scene it was! And the little caiques flew hither and thither like birds over the water, and the gallant ship sailed majestically by, and the noisy steamer puffed and wheezed, and notwithstanding all this life and activity, the blue waters looked as calm and motionless, as though never stirred by a breeze. Again I repeat, what lovely scenes the Bosphorus constantly presents.

Last Friday, we went down to the valley of "sweet waters" on the Asiatic side, about half way between this and Constantinople. It is a lovely valley, but the grass now is crisp and yellow, as though suffering from drought. Along the "sweet waters," dozens of caiques were moored, and under every tree, and in every little glade, sat groups of people, their gay colors in pretty contrast with the foliage above them. Rich carpets and cushions were spread on the ground, carriages decked with gilded carvings were drawn up under the trees, while the horses quietly grazed around; strolling bands of musicians showed off their skill, jugglers played their wonderful tricks, handsome children gambolled on the grass and ran from tree to tree, and groups of women, in their white yashmacks and their cloaks of gay colors, reclined on their cushions or sauntered among the trees.

A little hammock was hung between two trees, and there a mother left her babe asleep, while she went down to a rivulet that murmured near, and washed out some clothes, leaving them on the grass to dry; so she combined work and pleasure together. Delicious apricots, cherries, green gages and other fruits were carried about for sale, immense cucumbers were seen in piles on the ground, ices, flavored with cherry, but looking as though colored with beets, were handed round in minute tumblers, and a great variety of so-called sherbets were displayed on every side.

Families assembled in groups under the trees, and the baskets of provisions were opened, cucumbers, bread and fruit being the principal contents, and every one seemed to be happy and contented. How many times we said to each other, "Why cannot our people at home oftener give themselves up to such innocent pleasures and recreation?" The Americans, as a nation, know little of what people in the East consider the enjoyment of life, and they really seem to look upon time spent away from business and duty, as time lost. Yet how much happier, how much healthier would they be, if they would but pass a little more time in the open air, away from the cares of the counting-house and the shop, and the drudgery of every day life in the house.

July 4th. Our national jubilee was ushered in this morning by the news of the safe arrival of the wanderer from the wars, and if any salutes had been fired, it might have been a matter of dispute whether they were in honor of the day, or of his return. The Americans residing in Pera and its environs, intended having a pic-nic to-day, near "the sweet waters" of Asia, but quite contrary to the usual custom on the Fourth of July, the rain poured down in such torrents during the whole morning, as to effectually wash away all ideas of a pic-nic. There have been several showers since our arrival here, but this is the only real pouring rain we have seen since we were at Jerusalem, nearly three months, which is certainly a long interval of pleasant weather.

Sunday Evening, 9*th*. This is our last day at Buyukdere, for to-morrow we leave for Athens, and after a sojourn of nearly six weeks among the lovely scenes of the Bosphorus, you may be sure I feel quite sadly at bidding them adieu, doubtful, as it is, if I shall ever see them more.

Independent of the pleasure I have experienced from visiting so many beautiful spots about here, my long stay has not been altogether in vain, for by laboring diligently three or four hours a day, I have been enabled to bring up that tardy journal of mine, and to arrange my notes and memoranda in a business-like way, so that I go away from here lightened of the heavy load of care that a journal, deplorably in arrears, brings upon one.

Since my last entry in this lengthened out epistle, I have taken a long walk to the top of the mountain in rear of our hotel, and enjoyed another extensive view of the windings of the Bosphorus, even getting a glimpse of some of the minarets of Constantinople. I have been again to the Black Sea, and again landed upon the Symplegades. And more than all else, I have been on the Bosphorus by moonlight, when its beauties seemed more enchanting and picturesque than ever.

I have once more braved the steamings and sousings and scrubbings of a Turkish bath, bearing up under all, with the hope that some of the traces of the sun of Arabia and Syria might be washed and steamed away, but no such favorable consequence seems to have ensued.

This morning, at the request of Lady G., Mr. E. read

prayers in her drawing room, and though the congregation was small, it was a select one, consisting of Lord and Lady G., the wives of two officers in the English army, Mr. M. and his wife, occupying for many years a prominent station in the British possessions in North America, the family of the American Ambassador, and our fellow traveller in the Desert, Mr. R., son of General R. A more pleasant circle than this, it has not often been our lot to meet while travelling, and it is one of my sources of regret at leaving this place, that I must say good bye to so many agreeable acquaintances.

And this is my last letter from Buyukdere, and I go to the window and take one more view of the dark mountain rising beyond, and to the terrace, and gaze once more upon the Bosphorus, shining "beneath the moon's soft gleam," and for the thousandth time I say, "How lovely it is!"

LETTER LV.

Departure from Buyukdere.—Austrian Steamer.—Scene on Board.—Beautiful Girl.—Dardanelles.—Mitylene.—Isles of Greece.—Smyrna.—Austrian Officer.—Delos.—Syra.—Quarantine.—Discomfort.—Arrival at Athens.—Palace.—Hotel des Etrangeres.

ATHENS, July 14th.

MY DEAR S.:

If there is one time more than another when a traveller feels especially uncomfortable, it is the first few hours after arriving at a strange place. This has been especially our case this morning, because the rooms we are to occupy are not yet vacant, and I can't begin to unpack, because trunks and boxes and portmanteaus must all be moved in a little time. I can't read, for two reasons; I am not in a mood for it, and if I were, I have nothing to read, and at last I have unlocked my desk, to spend my dullness on you, which I hope you will receive as a great compliment, imputing to you, as it does, the power to chase away my unquiet spirit.

We left Buyukdere Monday morning, J. in the steamboat, with the luggage, and I in the caique belonging to Mr. Spence. It was excessively hot, the usual cool breeze from the Black Sea not having made its appearance; but in despite of the scorching sun, I looked long and well at all my favorite views on the Bosphorus. We were only two hours in rowing down, and we found in the harbor of Constantinople, what we failed to find higher up, a good breeze. I spent two or three hours in the bazaars, making my last purchases, and taking my last look, and I can assure you it was with quite a heavy heart and a languid step I went from place to place, often whispering sadly to myself, "It is the last time!"

With our usual punctuality, we were early on board the Austrian Steamer L'Imperatrice, though this time, the merit was not due to our punctuality, but because we had nothing particular to keep us on shore. We were anchored in front of Seraglio Point, and for a long time I amused myself with looking at the old Palace peeping out from her gardens, and the domes and minarets of St. Sophia and Sultan Achmet, rising up in the rear. Then I looked up and down the Bosphorus as far as I could see, and up the Golden Horn, and over to Scutari, the cypress crowned city, and saw the busy steamers, and the countless little caiques go by, and then my eyes grew weary with looking abroad, and I turned my attention to the motley groups on the decks. Near me was a fat Turk, making his bed comfortable for the night, (for second class passengers are admitted to the quarter deck in these countries,) and in immediate proximity to him was a devout Mussulman, going through his stated forms of prayer. On one side, was a party of Greek and Italian gentlemen bidding adieu to each other, with a multitude of embraces and loud smacking kisses, and on the other, was a number of veiled Turkish women, in great grief at parting from some of their companions, while a pretty little child in the company amused me with her fruitless attempts to squeeze a few tears from her eyes. A beautiful Turkish girl, followed by an old nurse, and two or three male servants, threw the whole deck in a bustle, by her numerous attendants arranging cushions, chairs and various etceteras for the comfort of the youthful beauty, one handing her a glass of water, one a smelling bottle, and a third a golden lemon, which she occasionally held to her nose, in her slender fingers, delicately tipped with henna. She politely offered me her smelling bottle, which I found filled with a delicious perfume, and motioned for me to put some on my handkerchief. I had not looked at her long, for as she took the liberty of staring at me, I had no hesitation in gazing at her, before I was satisfied that young as she was, her sun would soon be set. Beneath the pure folds of her yashmack, I saw the hectic flush grow deeper and deeper, while the quick heaving of the purple cloak in which she was closely wrapped, showed with what difficulty she breathed, and as if these symptoms were not sufficient to betray her doom, a hollow cough often shook convulsively her slender figure. So many persons on board seemed to show her attentions, that I was curious to know who she was, and I soon found out she belonged to the harem of Redschid Pacha, who was sending her to "Scio's rocky isle," for her health.

The clatter of tongues was as confusing to the ear, as the medley of strange figures to the eye. At one moment I caught a familiar sentence in French or Italian, the next I heard nought but German or Greek, which in their turn, were quickly displaced by Turkish or mayhap English. Hour after hour passed, and there seemed no prospect of departing. The lengthened shadows fell, and still "St. Sophia's gleaming dome" was before us. In answer to inquiries concerning the delay, we were told the steamer was waiting for despatches. I grew impatient, not that I thought the despatches would prove of any importance to me, but having eaten nothing since eight o'clock, my appetite was becoming more and more ravenous, till I had serious thoughts of snatching at a cucumber and piece of bread I saw beside the fat Turk in front of me. A sleep too of less than five hours the night before, owing to the persevering songs of my Arab "roarer," added to the fatigue and heat of the day, did not contribute much to the buoyancy of my frame, and it would not have taken many drops more, to have made my cup run over with a discomforting draught. But fortunately at that critical moment, an officer appeared with a bundle of papers, elaborately dotted with red seals, the mate and helmsman took their station at the wheel, the word was given to "make ready," and in the same breath dinner was announced. While dinner was progressing however, so was not the boat, for after turning round, she once more stopped beneath the shadows of the walls.

and trees of Seraglio Point, and just as we came up from dinner, the mighty mass was again put in motion, and towers, and walls, and domes, and minarets began to fade away in the evening light. The seven hilled city was soon far in the rear, and Constantinople, "the magnificent" disappeared, I fear, forever from our gaze.

Four nights and three days, we spent in that steamer, and although we had a good state-room, and a table, amply spread, though wanting in many of the delicacies, which had been our portion while in the French steamers, I rarely passed more uncomfortable nights and days. The weather was intensely hot, and though at times there was a good breeze on deck, the cabin was intolerable, and sleep almost entirely out of the question. I would gladly have slept on deck, but it was not deemed prudent to brave the night air, and I bowed to the stern demands of prudence, and yielded my comfort, and what is sometimes as dear to me, my will.

We passed so many interesting spots during the day, that I could always manage to get along quite comfortably, but the nights were insupportable. Tormented by fleas, with the additional help of a few bed-bugs, exhausted with the heat, consumed by a raging thirst, that could not be quenched by the lukewarm water on board, I knew no peace or rest, and was glad when I could go on deck and snuff the fresh air.

When I got up on Tuesday morning, we were at Gallipoli, but no one was allowed to land on account of cholera there. Then, we entered the Dardanelles, or Hellespont, a narrow strait, which connects the Sea of Marmora with the Archipelago. The scenery along the shores of the Dardanelles cannot begin to compare in beauty to that of the Bosphorus; the hills are bold and grand in their outline, but they look rocky and bare, though I am told a month earlier, they were covered with verdure, but around those hills many a stirring scene has taken place. The Scamander, in whose limpid waters Venus bathed before contending for the prize of beauty, Mount Ida, famous in classic lore, the plains of Troy, the place across the Hellespont, where the invader Xerxes threw his bridge, the spot where once stood the "torch-lit tower" of Abydos, the story of Leander, who nightly swam across the straits that separated him from his lady love, the islands that are set like gems at the entrance of the Dardanelles into the sea, these and many other objects of interest, kept our attention alive the whole day.

As we entered the sea, Imbros was on our right, Tenedos on the left, and Lemnos rising up before us. These islands all look sere and brown now, though in many places I saw the hills terraced to their very summits, where the vine had been planted. In fact Tenedos has, for a long time, been celebrated for its wines.

Later, we were skirting Mitylene, one of the largest islands in the Archipelago, which carries on an extensive commerce with the neighboring ports. Its principal charm to me, was its being the birth-place of Sappho, "burning Sappho," as Byron calls her, and from its having been visited by St. Paul.

As we glided in and out among these islands, rising abruptly from the blue sea, I repeated more than a hundred times,

"The Isles of Greece, the Isles of Greece!
Where burning Sappho loved and sung,
Where grew the arts of war and peace,
Where Delos rose and Phœbus sprung!
Eternal summer gilds them yet,
But all, except their sun, is set."

Every island has its tale of love and poesy and song, and each, alas! has its own bloody record of Turkish ravage and Mohammedan fanaticism.

Late that night we anchored in the Gulf of Smyrna, directly before the town, and as I came on deck the next morning, I started at the change eight short weeks had made, for the hills we had left green and bright, were now parched and brown, and when I went down to breakfast I had still more convincing proofs that the season had advanced with rapid strides, for on the table, were large clusters of rich, purple grapes! Grateful sight to parched lips and feverish frames!

We went on shore, and walked in the bazaars, looking tame and dull after those of Constantinople, and more especially so that day, as all those kept by the Greeks were closed on account of some festival. And this reminds me that the day before, being that observed by the Greeks in honor of St. Peter, though his festival was kept by the rest of the christian church twelve days before, two Greek gentlemen on board both having the name of Peter, treated all at table, at breakfast and dinner with champagne, and I dare say some on board would gladly have had St. Peter's day come again, if they could have thus observed it.

Passing through the ladies' cabin that evening, I found the young Turkish girl asleep on a sofa, and as she was without her yashmack, I stopped to look at her unveiled charms. Fair and delicate as a lily, her jetty eyebrows and long silken lashes, were in charming contrast to the delicate skin, and the henna-tipped nails set off the white fingers, to good advantage. A short skirt and loose trousers of thin muslin, enveloped, as in a cloud, her slender figure, and her long black hair was negligently gathered under an embroidered handkerchief. How lovely she was! Perhaps she had been the light and joy of the harem, the favored one of the master, the despised by the mistress because she enjoyed the favor of her lord, but now she is for a while shut out from the smiles of the one, and the frowns of the other.

All day we were anchored off Smyrna, but towards evening the anchor was up, and we were once more on our way. Down the gulf of Smyrna we went, cleaving the transparent waters, the mountains rising around us, the white houses of Smyrna behind, the deep blue sea before.

But here a new occurence arose, that for a time effectually interfered with our quiet contemplation of the scene around us. A company of Austrian officers, from a ship in the harbor, had come on board, accompanied by a number of their companions. Much wine was drunk, and perhaps something stronger, and a great deal of kissing followed, and then a part went back to the ship, while the remainder, it seemed, was going to Trieste. The first lieutenant was ingloriously drunk, and staggered about our deck, singing snatches of songs, and then stopping to cheer the ship as we passed her. At last, to the great annoyance of the ladies, he climbed up into one of the boats, and commenced a succession of cheers, and this he repeated several times, each time at the imminent risk of pitching overboard. Our Captain seeing the annoyance of the ladies, tried to prevail upon him to desist, but he swore at the Captain, and again staggered up into the boat. Soon after, he went down into the cabin, in a violent rage, and on some one approaching him, he drew his sword, and thrusting right and left, made sad havoc among the dishes on the table, frightening a Greek lady into hysterics, and clearing the cabin of those who had ventured to oppose him. All at once, as though he feared he might do violence, he went up to J—— who was standing near, and giving him his sword, begged him to keep it for the sake of his honor, but just then, some one appearing at the door, against whom he had some fancied repugnance, he flew at his supposed enemy, threatening to kill him, wrestling for his sword with J—— who refused to give it up. Some of his brother officers stood by, but they were afraid to intermeddle, as he was of a higher grade than they were, and I don't know what would have been the end of the conflict, if the engineer of the boat had not gone to J's assistance. The sword was locked up in our state-room, and the officer dragged off to bed, and in a few hours he came upon the deck, and walked about as though nothing had happened. The Captain takes no notice of him, but he vows he will report the case to the proper authorities, and the lieutenant may have to pay dear for his glass too much, at bidding adieu to his ship-mates.

That night I was awakened by the stopping of the boat, and the sound of voices along side. I peeped out of the port-hole, and saw "Scio's rocky isle" looming up before us. The dash of oars followed, and a boat pulled off from the steamer, bearing the Turkish girl and her attendants to the shore. May the soft breezes of the sea-girt isle, bring health and strength to that lovely, drooping flower!

Still among "the isles of Greece," for on going on deck yesterday morning, a cluster of them was around us, Tenos on the right, Mycenos and Delos on the left, and Syra, rising up from the sea, far ahead. The town of St. Nicholas in the island of Tenos, presented a picturesque appearance from the sea. The houses are all of white stone, and are scattered over the hills, clusters of them peeping out from green trees, while to the right and left of the town, the hills are terraced off for the culture of the vine. These hills must present a beautiful appearance in the early summer, when vegetation is at its height, but now the most of them look brown and bare.

Delos is a small island, but celebrated in classic lore, as the birth-place of Apollo, and the seat of an oracle, second only in sanctity to that of Delphi, but now its ancient glories have passed away, and but few remains are left of its former magnificence.

About ten o'clock we arrived in the harbor of Syra, and there we lay twelve hours, not that there was any thing for us to do, but because it is the quarantine ground for the Levant, and never did I experience such heat as we felt that day. The scorching sun of Nubia, the arid plains and hills of the Desert, were cool compared to the close, sultry air in the bay of Syra. The live-long day, not a breeze ruffled the blue waters, not a breath fanned our hot faces. Once we were called to pass before the Doctor of the port, and as we had to go to the other end of the steamer, turn round and come back, that he might judge of the state of health of all on board, I really thought I should get a sun-stroke in that slow march around the ship, but I held up my head very bravely, and walked as firmly, as though I feared nothing, because I was afraid if I looked at all drooping, he might pounce upon me as a patient, which would have been more formidable to me than the heat.

The harbor of Syra is almost shut in by hills, and at the entrance, is a rocky island, on which stands a tall light-house. In front of us, rose the town, the white houses glaring down upon us in the fierce sun. A conical hill, looking like an immense sugar-loaf, rises up in the very centre of the town, covered all up its sides with white houses, and terminating at the very summit in a palace-like looking edifice. On either side of this hill, the town extends like two huge wings, and amid all the mass of white houses, I could scarcely see a tree, or anything to break the glare of light. At little distances from the town, however, I saw villas peeping out from verdant groves, and then the white houses looked pretty, contrasted with the green around them.

On one side of the town is a large Lazaretto, for those who are obliged to perform quarantine on shore, and hot as it was on board, I was sure it was far more comfortable, than being on that rocky hill, totally devoid as it seemed of all vegetation. A great deal of shipping was in the harbor, for independent of all vessels being obliged to stop here twelve hours for quarantine, Syra is a place of great commercial importance, and ships from all nations trade here. It is celebrated for its schools too, there being more than two thousand scholars in the different schools.

Towards evening, a delicious breeze sprung up, and it came to our exhausted frames like a gale from Paradise. Faint with the heat of the day, I spread my shawl upon the deck, and taking a rock-like cushion for my pillow, I gave myself up to meditation. Like the sun, every evening I flee to the west, and as twilight comes on, I am duly in my far-distant home, seeing loved faces, and listening to familiar voices. But that night, shall I confess it! I was not thinking so much of the dear ones at home, as of one of the comforts and luxuries of that home, and as plainly as I now see the paper before me, did I see a large wagon with "ICE," on it in great letters, stop before our door and leave its cold, white burden. I reached out my hand to take a piece, and carry it, to my fervent lips, and then I found it was all a delusion! I was no longer at home, but in the far-off East, the white houses of Syra gleaming in the misty light, and a few bright stars looking down from the clear sky.

How rough it was last night! The steamer rose with one wave, only to plunge down with another; she rolled to the right, only to return back with renewed violence to the left, and then withal, the air was so hot and suffocating, that rest and comfort were not to be thought of, excepting as things we sometimes "read about."

At last the morning dawned, and with it came a lull of the sea, and soon we entered the harbor of Piræus, the port of Athens. In a few minutes, we were ready to come on shore, but we were not allowed to land so easily, for an abundance of formalities had to be encountered, before we could leave the ship, bills of health signed, and I don't know what else, but at length all was in readiness, our baggage was stowed away in a small boat, which we entered, and in a few minutes our feet pressed the soil of Greece!

A small sum of money, placed in the hands of the custom house officers, prevented the delay of having the luggage examined, and when trunk and box, saddle and saddle-bag, carpet-bag and portmanteau were duly arranged, we jumped into a carriage, a luxury almost unknown to us for months, and were soon rolling towards Athens. The road was good, bordered in many places by vineyards, and groves of fig and olive trees, and after a ride of about five miles, we entered the streets of Athens, and in a few minutes were at the Hotel des Etrangeres, which had been previously recommended to us. It is situated on the square, at the head of which stands the Palace, a handsome building of white stone, ornamented with porticoes, window frames and cornices of Pentelican marble. In front, it is separated from the street, by a pretty garden surrounded by a hedge of oleander and cactus. Near by the garden, is a large and handsome house, occupied by the French ambassador, while on the right is our hotel, with two or three houses. The other end of the square is adorned with fine houses, all of stone, stuccoed, and painted white or yellow, with steps and window frames of white marble. Each house has little balconies in the second and third stories, and thus far I find modern Athens a much better looking town than I had any idea of seeing. But I must leave a further description of it to future acquaintance.

LETTER LVI.

Situation of Athens.—Stadium.—Fountain of Callirrhoe.—Thyme.—Temple of Jupiter Olympus.—Ruins of Greece.—Arch of Hadrian.—Monument of Lysicrates.—Acropolis.—Parthenon.—Temple of Victory without wings.—The Erectheum.—View from the Acropolis.—Tomb of Miller.—Garden of Plato.—Sunset.

ATHENS, July 15th.

MY DEAR FRIENDS:

I begin my description of Athens by giving you a short sketch of its locality, that you may better understand my account of it. It is situated about five miles from the sea, in the central plain of Attica, which is bounded on the north-west by Mount Parnes, on the north-east by Mount Pentelicus, on the south-east by Mount Hymettus, and on the west by Mount Ægaleos; on the south it opens on the Gulf of Salamis. The most prominent eminence in the whole plain is a conical hill, rocky at the top, and surmounted by a church, and this is Mount Lycabettus. From its summit, the view is said to be delightful, but I have not yet been tempted to judge for myself. The weather is so very hot here, we are warned against being out in the heat of the day, and thus far, we have only been out early in the morning, and after dinner, which is served at five o'clock. For the comfort of travellers wishing to come to Athens in the Summer, however, I must say the heat is not so intense, as from the accounts I heard I expected to find it, and generally there has been a delicious breeze, even while the sun has been very hot.

But to return to the boundaries of Athens. South-west of Lycabettus, are four hills, all included within the ancient city; the first is the Acropolis, a craggy rock rising several hundred feet above the plain, its summit crowned with the world-famed Parthenon. Beyond the Acropolis, is a smaller rocky hill, called the Areopagus, known also to Scripture readers as Mars Hill, identified, as it is, with the stirring address of St. Paul to the "men of Athens." Still farther on, are the hills known by the names of the Pnyx and the Museum, and of all of these I shall probably have a little to say hereafter. On the southeast of the city runs the Ilissus, and on the west the Cephissus, but both of these rivers are nearly dry at this season of the year. Now that I have had patience to write this long geographical description, and you to read it, I will pass to other things.

Our first business, after being comfortably settled in our rooms, (which open on the square, and are airy and clean,) was to engage a guide, and then commence the arduous duty of sight-seeing. A fat Greek, Stratis by name, armed with a book full of credentials from English and American travellers, was selected to be our guide, to the great disappointment of the one connected with this hotel, who speaks only French and Italian; but in this hot weather, it is too much of an effort to listen to long descriptions in a foreign tongue, so we preferred one who could speak English.

By the time these arrangements were duly made, it was too late to do more than to take a little stroll through the streets, which we found quite wide and clean, and adorned with comfortable houses. We ended the day by calling on the families of the American missionaries, well known to all our fellow-countrymen for their kind and hospitable attentions.

This morning, we rose before five o'clock, and after

drinking a cup of tea, and munching a piece of bread, (for it is said to be unhealthy to go out without previously eating and drinking something,) we started to see the lions of Athens. Willis says "admiration is the most exhausting thing in the world," and I may add, it is particularly so, when a full dose is taken on an almost empty stomach; and by the time we had been out four hours, I, for one, was glad to come home and get some breakfast.

But now let me recall, in a consecutive manner, the places of interest we have visited to-day. Leaving the Palace on the left, we walked over some brown hills, till we came to the spot where once stood the Stadium of Athens. It covered a semicircular hill rising from the Ilissus, and formerly had rows of seats of white marble, which were taken away by the barbaric Turks. Here the races took place, and the striver for the victory, starting from the lower extremity, ran one course in a straight line, and turning round at the farther end, ran back to the goal. The Stadium now presents the appearance of a long and grass-grown hollow, and a traveller might pass it many times, without imagining that here occurred some of the most stirring scenes of Athens.

Crossing the bed of the Ilissus, almost dried up, on the banks of which some nymphs, far from classical looking, were washing clothes, we came to a cave running under a hill. Through this cave we walked, and I could soon have wished it a great way off, for in it we made intimate acquaintance with a family of fleas, which liked our company so well that they were unwilling to leave us, and after pestering us almost to intolerance the remainder of our walk, we waged such mortal warfare with them, on our return home, that in a little while forty lay drowning in a bowl of water!

A little farther on, we came to the fountain of Callirrhoe, which, gushing from a rock, forms a little basin in a shady recess in the hill. From this fountain, the water was formerly conveyed to Athens by nine large pipes of stone, some of which remain to this day.

The hills and the plains over which we walked were covered with thyme, and the fragrance of it loaded the air with rich perfume. All up the sides of the Hymettus, these beds of thyme "the long, long summer gild," and from them the bees gather the sweets, which give the honey of Athens such a peculiarly delicious flavor.

Very soon after leaving our hotel, we came in sight of a ruined temple, and I eagerly asked what it was. "The temple of Jupiter Olympus," answered Strattis; and so picturesque looked its tall columns, standing out against the sky, that I would gladly have gone immediately to examine them more thoroughly, but the guide had his usual routine, and he did not like to depart from it, but now, as we turned from the fountain of Callirrhoe, and recrossed the Ilissus, the temple stood out in its beauty before us, and I was glad to see our steps now directed towards it.

Of the one hundred and twenty-four columns that once adorned the various parts of this temple, but fifteen are now standing, and these are composed of blocks of white marble, fluted, and having capitals richly carved. They are about sixty feet in height and twenty-five in circumference. Part of the frieze over some of the columns is yet standing, and here, seventy feet in the air, was once the cell of a monk. How he got up there, I know not, but every morning he lowered a little basket from his lofty dwelling, and some pious friends were always ready to load it with the necessaries, and even with some of the comforts of life.

We are told that travellers, coming here from the West, are delighted with these and other ruins of Greece, but those coming from the East are invariably disappointed. Thus far, the ruins we have seen here are certainly wanting in the grandeur and majesty and far-reaching antiquity that throw such a halo over the mighty ruins of Egypt, and nought that the whole world beside can present, can compare with them in these points; but for beauty of sculpture and design, for harmony in proportion and detail, for exquisite finish in all its parts, the ruins of Greece must ever stand out unrivalled. So far back do the temples and monuments of Egypt carry us, that, to the unlearned, they are lost in the obscurity of ages, but the ruins of Greece are of so modern a date, comparatively speaking, that they are associated with our every day studies and reading. The inspiration of the poet and the orator, the theme of the historian and student, the subject of schoolboy speeches at examinations and exhibitions, and of college graduates at Commencement, Greece, with her heroes of olden time, her stirring scenes, her hard fought battles and glorious victories, seems a part of our own life, our own history, and he who can walk among her ruins, her remains of former greatness and power, he who can press the soil once trodden by Pericles, and Themistocles, and Demosthenes, and Plato, and Socrates, and a host of other worthies, and not be moved, not feel high and noble thoughts within him, must be made of unenviable materials. The very name of Greece brings a charm, and the sight of her ancient monuments, many of them overthrown and lying in the dust, must fill every eye and touch every heart, even though the eye be sated with seeing the wonders of the world beside, and the heart be wearied with emotions oft excited by the thrilling records of the past.

The temple of Jupiter Olympus, from which I have strayed, occupied seven hundred years in its construction, from the time of Pisistratus to that of the Emperor Hadrian, and it has suffered more from the hand of the destroyer than almost any other temple in Greece, most of its marbles having been removed, at different times, for building purposes. After the Christian era, many of the temples were converted into churches, and this doubtless contributed much to their preservation, but the temple of Jupiter Olympus was too immense for such an use, and, therefore, block after block was borne away. Then came the Turks, foes alike to beauty and to Christianity, and pagan temple and Christian church were equally despoiled. One whole column of the Olympeum was thrown down, and its marbles carried away for one of their mosques, and night after night, it was said the wind moaned and sighed among the other columns, as though they were lamenting the loss of their sister! Is it not a pretty idea, and worthy of the poetical country of the Greeks?

The pavement of this temple is now used as a threshing floor, and here the country people bring their grain, and have it trod out by horses. At that early hour in the morning, it presented an animating sight, the men and the women and the children in their picturesque costumes, the bundles of sheaves on the one hand, and the heaps of grain on the other, while stretching far up into the clear sky, stood the pillars of the once beautiful temple.

Next we came to the Arch of Hadrian, built in the second century of the Christian era. The archway is twenty feet wide, and the whole height of the structure is about fifty-six feet. Above the centre of the arch is an inscription, purporting that it divides "Athens, the city of Theseus," from the "city of Hadrian."

Passing through a corner of the city, where the houses are small, and built of rough stone, or of clay, we reached the "Monument of Lysicrates," known for years to the modern world as the "Lantern of Demosthenes." It was built nearly four hundred years before the Christian era, and is said to be the "earliest authentic instance of Corinthian architecture." It is a small building, circular in form, adorned with pillars, having richly sculptured capitals, and a frieze, in which are bas-reliefs, representing the destruction of the Tyrrhenian pirates by Bacchus. It is surmounted by an urn, and from being built in this form, or from some other trifling cause, it was a long time called the "Lantern of Demosthenes." Some say the great orator was accustomed to shut himself up there for a month, to practice his orations, but as there is no access to the interior, and indeed in a building only eight feet in diameter, outside the columns, there could be no great interior, this must have been a difficult operation.

Near the monument, are the remains of a Franciscan convent, where Lord Byron once resided, and where, it is said, his name is still seen on a marble slab on the wall, written by his own hand, but I had not reverence enough either for the man or the poet to go out of my way to see it.

And now we began to climb the rugged hill, or rather rock, of the Acropolis, and as in different parts of the ascent, Strattis stopped to point out various objects of interest, I was glad of an excuse to rest every few minutes. This hill rises about three hundred and fifty feet above the level of the plain beneath it, and presents the appearance of a rocky platform exceedingly irregular in shape, its greatest length being eleven hundred feet, and its extreme breadth about four hundred and fifty. In some places it rises up very abruptly from the plain, and its ascent on a hot morning, and before breakfast, too, is not so very easily accomplished.

On the summit of the Acropolis are the finest ruins in Greece; indeed, there is such a labyrinth of ruins, that I really don't know whether to describe them in a mass, or give each one a separate description. Either would take more time and paper than I have at command at present, and I must therefore give a hasty account of what particularly struck my attention.

Since writing the above sentence, I have sat a half hour, my pen in hand, my eyes fixed on the opposite wall of my room, thinking where I should begin my account of the ruins of the Acropolis, and what I should say of them. If the hand could describe, as easily as the eye can take in, the prominent points of a scene, how easy would be the task of the traveller who keeps a journal, (and, in a parenthesis, I must once more say, "Blessed be they who carry about no such appendages.") I cannot tell what a load there is often upon my heart, when in the midst of intense observation of some interesting object, the thought suddenly comes to me, "And of all this I must give a description," and I walk round in a kind of mental maze, not seeing clearly my way out of the labyrinth by which I am surrounded. Often I am tempted to throw down my pen in despair, and say "the work is too hard for me," but then I remember the loved ones at home, who watch eagerly for my letters, and read them over and over again, not for their intrinsic merit, but because I wrote them, and this thought nerves me to renewed exertion, and I ply the pen with unwonted diligence, till I have said all I have to say.

As I have said more than once, I think, (for I know no more than "the man in the moon" what I have written in my countless letters to you,) I cannot go into detail, statistical, historical or architectural, concerning the various wonders I see in these foreign lands, for I am not fitted for such a work, either by nature or education, and if I were, I doubt whether such details would be appreciated by all of you. I try always to keep in mind that these letters are addressed to an assembled household, composed of the old and the young, the learned and the unlearned, and I wish ever to write of such things, and in such a manner, as will interest all, and be beyond the comprehension of none.

And now to my task. The largest temple on the Acropolis is the Parthenon, and the approach to it is inexpressibly grand and beautiful. A broad flight of steps, or rather a carriage way in the centre, with steps on either side, of white marble, leads up to a portico, about seventy feet broad, having six fluted pillars, twenty-nine feet in height, and fifteen feet in circumference. From this portico, two wings projected, adorned with columns, which are now more or less in a ruinous state. The walls and ceilings of this portion of the temple, the "Propylæa," were once adorned with paintings, now, alas! "among the things that have been." Scattered along the pavement now, are fragments of pillars, broken statues, and choice bits of sculpture, found among the ruins; and here one sees the perfection to which the art was brought in the palmy days of Greece.

And now we have reached the Parthenon, which Wordsworth says is the "finest edifice on the finest site in the world, hallowed by the noblest recollections that can stimulate the human heart." The Parthenon was built under the administration of Pericles, and was finished four hundred and thirty-eight years before the Christian era. The matchless sculptor, Phidias, was entrusted with the general superintendence of it, and his name alone ought to be a sufficient voucher for the merit of the work. It was built of Pentelic marble, except the tiles of the roof, which were Parian, and the whole cost of the building is estimated at three millions and a half dollars. It is nearly two hundred and thirty feet long, and about one hundred wide, and has a portico at each end of eight columns, and a colonnade on each side of seventeen. All these columns are fluted, of the Doric order, and are nearly thirty feet high by six and a quarter in diameter. Of all these pillars, but thirty-two are standing, and of the frieze, which was once adorned with rich sculptures, but little now remains.

I have given you these few dry statistics, that you may be better able to form some idea of the far-famed Parthenon of Athens, but, like many other things, it must be seen to be appreciated. I should enjoy very much seeing it by moonlight, but at present that is impracticable, from the moon rising quite too late at night for me, or rather too early in the morning.

Near by the Parthenon is the small temple of "Victory without wings," built in honor of the victories gained by the Athenians, in the time of Miltiades and Cimon, over the Persians. It is only twenty-seven feet long by eighteen wide, but has some beautiful sculptures, representing battle scenes. For nearly two hundred years, this temple was lost to sight, but in 1835, on a Turkish battery being removed, some fragments of sculptured marbles were brought to light, and on further researches being made, the various parts of the temple were discovered, and under judicious and able superintendence, were collected and re-arranged, according to the original plan of the edifice.

Next we visited the Erectheum, the most revered of all the ancient sanctuaries of Athens, connected too with the earliest religious legends of Attica, for here was once the oldest statue of Athens, the guardian of the city, which was made of olive wood, and which was said to have fallen down from Heaven. Here, too, were the sacred olive tree, the well of salt, and the tomb of Cecrops, and of the god Erectheus. Of the various parts of the temple, none pleased me so much, as one of the porticoes, the roof of which is supported by six columns called Caryatides, in the form of young maidens, in flowing drapery, their hands resting on their hips. This term, Caryatid, meaning a female figure supporting an entablature, is said to have been derived from Carya, a city in Arcadia, which took part with the Persians against the Greeks, and was consequently destroyed by their enraged countrymen, the men slain, and the women carried away captives. Male figures representing

Persians, were sometimes used for columns, when historical scenes were to be portrayed, and consequently Grecian sculptors, used for a like purpose female figures, thereby commemorating the punishment of the women of Carya, or the Caryatides.

Some of these columns are mutilated; one has been furnished with a new head and bust, and one is of plaster, sent out from England to replace that carried off by Lord Elgin, as great a robber of Grecian marbles, as the barbaric Turks, but even in this mongrel form, they present a beautiful appearance, in their picturesque attitude, with their drapery floating gracefully around them.

In our walks among these ruins, we were constantly meeting exquisite bits of sculpture, fragments of statues and bas-reliefs, which told us how very, very beautiful these temples must have been in their days of glory.

Here too, are collected in a rude kind of Museum, vases and urns, and lamps found among the ruins, and marble heads, and hands and feet, and a thousand like objects of interest. Absorbed as I was in gazing upon the records of the past, collected on the Acropolis, I paused a great many times to look on the magnificent scene, stretched below and around me. One of the peculiar charms of the whole, is the soft haze like a thin blue mist that invests the mountains as with a halo, giving them ever a purple, amethystine hue, which is perfectly lovely, particularly when blended with the clear sky above. Then, too, the hills slope down so gracefully into the valleys, and the plains swell up so beautifully towards the mountains, and the blue mist enshrouds all, softening down every asperity, and concealing every rugged spot, that it seems to me the scenery of Greece thus far, must be totally unlike any thing found elsewhere.

If we turn to the sea, behold the islands clothed in the same ethereal garb, tinged with the same delicate hues, rising abruptly, yet with exquisite grace from the blue waters spread around, and when you add to these physical beauties, that every island and every mountain peak, and every hidden vale, have their legends of heroism and love, you can conceive the fascination Greece must ever have for the lovers of the beautiful.

Come stand with me on this elevated point, and look abroad over as fair a scene, as was ever presented to the eye of man. Far down the blue gulf, see that island folded in its garment of blue mist; that is Ægina, and yonder is "sea-born Salamis," and under that "rocky brow" Xerxes once sat, and "counted at break of day" the "ships by thousands" which "lay below" and the "men in nations," and still farther on, are the mountains of Eleusis, and range upon range of blue hills. And what an air of repose dwells upon all; what a delicious calm reigns over the whole scene! Not a bird darkens the clear air, not a sail ruffles the blue waters. Is it not lovely?

Look below. Do you see that rugged rock rising up at your feet? There St. Paul once stood, and preached his memorable sermon to the "men of Athens." Beyond, on that rocky platform Themistocles and Demosthenes once swayed the masses assembled around them, and in that cavern in yonder hill, was the prison of Socrates, that philosopher, whose life and death and doctrines, approached nearer, than any other heathen sage, those of the blessed Jesus.

Turn once more; see that green belt that engirdles the plain; it is the grove of Academus, where Plato and Aristotle and Zeno and Epicurus and Socrates (I do not arrange these names in chronological order, but write them down, just as they come into my mind,) and a host besides, discoursed of high and abstruse subjects with the Athenians gathered around them.

If you are not tired of whirling round on this airy height, take one more tour and look down. At your feet rests Athens, not the "august Athena" of old, but the modern town, its wilderness of houses broken here and there by a venerable church, true specimen of old Byzantine architecture. The garden that surrounds the Palace, is almost the only green spot for the eye to rest upon, and back of that, rises "flowery Hymettus," which still "yields his honied wealth," and through the plain beneath "Ilissus rolls his whispering stream" along, and the fair pillars of Jupiter Olympus rise up in their beauty. Where'er the eye turns, "'tis haunted, holy ground,"

> "Till the sense aches with gazing to behold
> The scenes our earliest dreams have dwelt upon;
> Each hill and glade, each deepening glen and world."

Perhaps you have had enough of sight-seeing by this time, so if you like, you can descend from your lofty perch, and come home with me to breakfast, for which my long walk had given me a famous appetite.

As we were warned not to be out too much during the heat of the day, we spent the remaining hours very quietly, reading, writing and sleeping, and after dinner, we drove out. What a luxury, after donkey, camel, and horse riding, to lean back in an open carriage, and enjoy the comforts of a quiet drive!

A short time after leaving the city, we came to a hill on our right, a part of the site of the ancient Academy of Athens. Here a column of white marble marks the spot where the distinguished antiquary and scholar, Miller, is buried. Farther on, we came to a lovely garden, said to be the spot where Plato once lived.

We left our carriage, and walked for some time amid clusters of ripening grapes, and under the shade of spreading sycamores and "silvery olives in all their poetic glory." But the beauties of the present, could not wean our minds from the associations of the past, and as we slowly wandered back and forth, it seemed we could almost hear the teachings of him, "on whose infant lips, the bees shed honey as he slept."

Once more in the carriage, we drove on through vineyards and groves of fig and olive trees, along the bank of the Cephissus, now almost dried away, but the murmur of the little rivulet as it rolled by was in gentle harmony with the soft rustle of the leaves.

We returned home by the old "sacred way" that led from Athens to Eleusis, and the sun went down,

"Not as in northern climes, obscurely bright,
But one unclouded blaze of living light,"

and the blue mountains looked more and more ethereal, till their "tenderest tints" owned "the hues of Heaven." Years ago, Milton described Athens in "words that burn," and one sentence in that description constantly recurred to me that evening. It was, "pure the air," and certainly purer air was never breathed by mortals, than the air of Greece. It really makes one in love with life. And then came "solemn night, and spread her pall wide o'er the slumbering shore and sea," and the lustrous stars shone out, and the soft breeze blew, and our hearts beat in unison with the time and place; till we were suddenly recalled to the notice of the present by finding ourselves in the streets of Athens, not left in their natural obscurity, as in other towns in the East, but actually lit by street lamps, a convenience we have not seen since leaving England, nine months ago.

There, I have certainly written enough for one letter, so now good night.

LETTER LVII.

English Church—King and Queen of Greece.—Tower of the Winds.—Agora.—Mars Hill.—Pnyx.—Prison of Socrates.—Sliding Stone.—Temple of Theseus.—Garden of the Palace.

ATHENS, July 17th.

MY DEAR P.:

I resume my record of sight-seeing in Athens. Yesterday we attended the English Chapel all day, where the Rev. Mr. Hill, though an American, is the Chaplain, and when I heard J's familiar voice in the pulpit, I closed my eyes on Athens, and was once more in my own loved church at home.

As we were coming from prayers in the evening, we saw a party on horseback dashing down the street, and although there was but little pomp and parade to mark their station, we immediately concluded it was the King and Queen of Greece. The King and Queen rode in advance, followed by the maids of honor, two or three aids and the servants in livery. The Queen had on a purple skirt, with a white jacket, a straw hat trimmed with white, and has a so-so face, with bright eyes and florid complexion. She is excessively fond of riding, and rides splendidly, managing her spirited horse with ease and grace. The King rode on her right, and wore the Greek costume, which consists of a "fustanella," a short full skirt, reaching to the knees. This skirt is of white linen or cotton, and is made all of gores, a full skirt often having two hundred of these gores, giving a peculiarly lofty, majestic gait to the wearer, as the folds sway back and forth as he walks. Red gaiters ornamented with gold embroidery, and reaching to the knee and fitting the leg with exquisite nicety, a cunning little red jacket with loose flowing sleeves, covered with embroidery, a red scarf tied around the waist, a cap of red velvet, adorned in front with magnificent diamonds, completed the costume of King Otho. From his face, I should never have thought him a German, but should have taken him for a Greek. He is not forty yet, but his face looks worn and haggard. His eyes are splendid, and his smile a blending of majesty and grace. I did not take all these observations at one glance, but this evening we stood at the gate of the Palace, and saw them mount and come leisurely towards us. About twenty or thirty persons were there assembled, and every head was uncovered, as their Majesties appeared, but there was no cheering, or sign of enthusiasm. The King and Queen looked around on the people, and acknowledged their silent greeting by a gentle bend of the head, and as we stood at a little distance from the group, and made our own salutations, we received a bow and a smile from each. Shakespeare once said, "uneasy lies the head that wears the crown," and I imagine few crowned heads lie more uneasily, than those of King Otho and Queen Amelia.

8

This morning, we were up a little after four, and out before five, and I really thought it required the courage of a martyr, to brave such early hours. The morning was lovely. A golden light was in the sky, and each mountain top stood out distinctly in its gauze-like haze. Through the streets of the city we wended our way, and unseasonably as the hour was, many of the inhabitants were astir, for in these Eastern climes, the generality of the people rise early, rest during the heat of the day, and come forth with renewed vigor towards evening.

Passing by two or three venerable churches built in true Byzantine style, a magnificent portico, half in ruins, one or two Mosques, now used for barracks, and walking through narrow streets, where in the time of the Turks were the bazaars, we came to the "Tower of the Winds," or the water-clock of Athens. It is octagonal in shape, each side facing one of the eight winds, into which the Athenian compass was divided, and having bas-reliefs representing the qualities and ideal form of that wind. Thus on the north side, is the figure of Boreas, wrapped in a thick mantle, and stout buskins, while the side next this, towards the east, presents an abundance of olives, that wind being favorable to their production and growth. The side facing the east, exhibits a rich profusion of flowers and fruits, and the very next compartment shows us Eurus with scowling face, threatening a hurricane. Then comes the south wind, ready to deluge the ground with showers, from a large urn which he holds in his naked arms, and next a ship is seen, apparently in rapid progress, that wind bringing success to the navigator. Floating gently on, appears Zephyrus, showering flowers beneath him, while his next neighbor carries a vessel of charcoal in his hands, to dispel the cold, he, himself, has produced. Each face has a sun-dial too, and when it was noon, the water which was brought from a fountain near the cave of Apollo and Pan, in the hill below the Parthenon, rose to the top of the tower, and ran down over the side.

And now having passed under an arch or gateway, we are in the Agora, where once assembled the people of Athens to discuss the news and politics of the day. Here patriots and demagogues sowed the seeds of glory and of sedition, and here arose the first whispers against "the just" Aristides and the immortal Socrates.

But a far more interesting spot to us than this even, was Mars' Hill, where once stood the intrepid "Apostle of the Gentiles." We ascended to the top, by a flight of steps cut in the solid rock, and after gazing around us a few minutes, sat down and read the account of St. Paul's memorable visit to Athens. How vividly came the whole scene before us! Here, where the great and solemn council of the Areopagus sat, here where the Athenian mind, if ever, could be awed by the solemn associations of the spot, famous as it was for the trials which had there taken place of causes connected with crime and religion, from the legendary trial of Mars, (hence the name of Mars' Hill,) down to those of later times; here eighteen hundred years ago stood St. Paul, and preached to the Athenians, who were ever ready to tell, or to hear some new thing, a "doctrine" which might emphatically be called "new." Hark to the voice of the Apostle! "Ye men of Athens," he cries to the multitude who came thronging up from the Agora to "know what these things" meant, "I perceive that in all things ye are too superstitious," or "peculiarly observant of unseen influences." All around him were splendid structures built by "art and man's device," but not to these, was worship to be paid. On the rocky ledges of the Acropolis, which towered above him, stood the elegant Parthenon of Minerva, and in the plain below, the magnificent temple of Theseus, while in the Agora, were sundry monuments, all objects of "devotion" to the gay and frivolous Athenian. And as though these were not proof enough of their seeking after the abstract and the invisible, an "altar" had been erected "to the Unknown God." And now hear him proclaim, "whom therefore ye ignorantly worship, Him declare I unto you. God that made the world, and all things therein, seeing that He is Lord of Heaven and earth, dwelleth not in temples made with hands," and here, perhaps, he pointed his finger to the temples rising in their beauty and grandeur above him, or to those studding the rich valley beneath him. Then he proceeds to tell them further of the "Unknown God," ending with that allusion to the resurrection of the dead, and the day of judgment, on hearing which "some mocked, and others said, we will hear thee again of this matter."

The sermon was finished, and he "departed from among them," but his preaching had some effect, for "certain men clave unto him and believed; among which was Dionysius the Areopagite," and at a little distance from Mars' Hill, are the ruins of a small church named in honor of that Athenian disciple.

Next, we ascended the hill, or artificial platform, called the Pnyx, which was the place of Parliament, or assembly of the Athenian people. The area of this platform was capable of containing from seven to eight thousand persons, and sloped gradually down towards the centre, where was the pulpit or "bema" of the orator. It was not provided with seats, hence the assembled citizens either stood, or sat on the bare rock. It had no awning to protect the masses from the heat of the sun, but the assembly was generally held at day break.

Here have stood the far-famed legislators and orators of Greece, Solon, Pericles, Themistocles, Aristides and Demosthenes, and along the shore of the bay beyond, Demosthenes walked, strengthening his voice by striving to speak above the murmur of the waves. Ah me! as I thought of all these things, I seemed to go back many, many years, and to be once more a school girl, studying the History of Greece.

Near the Pnyx are two hills, one called "the Hill of the Nymphs," which is surmounted by an observatory, and the other "the Museum Hill," on the summit of which, is the monument of Philopappus, who lived in Athens in the first century of the Christian era.

In the side of this hill, is a little cavern or grotto, consisting of three chambers, and this is called "the prison of Socrates." One of the chambers was used for a chapel, the middle one for the bath, and the third is said to be the room where the greatest of all heathen philosophers was imprisoned. For the sake of his health, I should hope these rooms had a better odor in former days than now, for they are any thing but fragrant at present.

Here he drank the bitter cup of poison, and then laid down to die, and when life had departed, he was borne to another grotto, farther on in the hill side, and deposited in a sarcophagus, hewn out of the solid rock.

Once more the school girl feeling came over me, as I dwelt upon these scenes.

As we came down the hill, we saw a smooth, shining rock on our left, which is known by the name of the "sliding stone," and I must preface my remarks concerning it, by exclaiming, "Ye that have blushes, prepare to bring them out," for I am going to touch upon a delicate subject, which may cause some of you to turn away with rosy cheeks, and perhaps with eyes flashing with contempt for one who thus dares to set delicacy, in the American sense of the word, at defiance. It is said that if she, who has been a wife long, without becoming a mother, will but slide down this stone, in less than a year, her fondest hopes will be realized, and she will give birth to a child! The Greek wives must believe this legend, for the stone is worn to brightness and smoothness by having been often used.

And now we approached near the temple of Theseus, which we had long been seeing at a distance. This temple is by many spoken of as "the most perfect architectural relic of all antiquity," but I think that antiquity should be specified as Grecian or European, because one finds as "perfect architectural relics" in Egypt, which date back hundreds of years before the "antiquity" of Grecian temples. But be that as it may, this temple is a most beautiful "relic" of "antiquity." It is one hundred and four feet long, and forty-five wide, and has a portico running quite around it, the pillars of which are nineteen feet high, and ten in circumference. The bas-reliefs represent the labors of Hercules and Theseus.

This temple, though more than two thousand three hundred years old, is so admirably preserved, as at a little distance to look quite perfect and like a modern edifice. In the interior, is the national museum of Athens, and here we found a good many ancient statues and sculptured tablets to interest us. And when I compared the faultlessly chiselled faces, and exquisitely proportioned figures to the square, clumsy forms, delineated by Egyptian artists, I could not but acknowledge how far superior were the sculptors of Greece to those of Egypt.

After four hours spent in rambling among these interesting localities, you may be quite sure I was ready to come home to my breakfast. Seeing kind American friends, journalizing, and sleeping, served to fill up the hours till dinner, and after that, we walked in the garden back of the Palace. Here, various kinds of trees, and flowers of every hue, and quiet, shaded walks, and arbors paved with rare old mosaics, and glimpses ot the lovely sky and the blue hills, and ruined temples at a distance, charmed us greatly, and when the sun went down, and the sky was suffused with a soft rose tint, and Hymettus assumed a rich violet hue, I thought no where on earth could there be a lovelier scene.

And now good bye, for if you are not tired, I am.

LETTER LVIII.

Prisoners.—Cholera at the Piræus.—Trip to Pentelicus.—Grand view from the Summit.—Marathon.—Eubœa.—Isles.—Mountains.—Sacred Way.—Daphne.—Bay of Eleusis.—Eleusis.—Remains of Temple of Ceres.—Megara.—Lovely Sunsets.—Queen Amelia.—King Otho.—State of Greece.—Rev. Mr. Hill.—Episcopal Mission.—Phalerum.—Sickness.

ATHENS, July 22d.

MY DEAR P.:

At length we are prisoners! Do not be alarmed, for no hostile powers have taken possession of us, but the cholera, or what is thought to be the cholera, having broken out at the Piræus, five miles distant, the steamers have refused to take any passengers from here. How long this state of things may last, we cannot tell, but we hope not long. You may readily imagine it is not pleasant for us to be thus hindered from prosecuting our journey, but we try to bear it as patiently and cheerfully as possible. Fretting is bad any where, but in hot climates it is especially to be avoided, and we therefore make up our minds to patiently and quietly wait till permission is given us to depart.

If the weather were not so hot, and the mountains were not infested with bands of lawless plunderers, we might spend the time in making some excursions in Greece, but it is so hot we could not travel with impunity, except in the very early morning, and towards evening, and the prospect of being robbed, to say nothing of being murdered, is by no means a pleasant one, so we must remain in Athens, and while away the time as best we may. Then there is another difficulty. Our letters, containing, as we hope, remittances, are awaiting us at Vienna, and it will take a fortnight to write there and receive an answer, and before that time is over, we hope to be once more on our way. Our funds are just sufficient to take us to Vienna, but if we have to stay here a fortnight, or perform quarantine at Trieste, we shall have nothing to supply the loud demand for cash; however, we are relieved from that unpleasant predicament, by our banker here kindly consenting to advance us the needed sum, to be repaid when we arrive at Vienna, Rev. Mr. A. being our surety.

But then our letters from home! We are anxious to have them, and yet we refrain from sending for them, hoping ere they could arrive, to be on our way towards Vienna. As for the cholera, it brings us no alarm; we have had it around us at home, and the same kind Providence who protected us there, can watch over us here, and we therefore have no fears whatever, and I earnestly hope you will all feel as free from anxiety for us we do for ourselves.

Summer is rapidly hastening on, and we have yet much to see, before we once more brave the terrors of the Atlantic, and as I said before, it is unpleasant to be delayed in our journey, but that can't be helped; and as, time and again, we go over the whole subject, dwelling at large upon its most aggravating points, we sum up the whole by saying, and trying to feel what we say, "'Tis all for the best."

And now let me go back a few days. Once more we were called early from our beds, on Tuesday morning, for a long excursion was before us. We had talked about going to Marathon, but much as I wanted to see that celebrated spot, I was forced to give it up, when I found, besides the distance we could go in a carriage, I should be obliged to ride six hours on horseback.

But even that was not so formidable as starting at four o'clock in the morning, which we should have been obliged to have done, to make so long an excursion in one day. So we decided to go to the top of Mount Pentelicus.

With my eyes half open, I went down to breakfast, for we could not think of starting on such an expedition, without first fortifying ourselves with something to eat, and by five o'clock, we were in the carriage, the saddle horses having previously been sent on. After leaving the city, we entered upon a wide plain, here and there dotted with a vineyard or grove of olive trees, but generally barren and brown, save where the purple thyme, or clusters of flowering oleanders, added variety to the scene. Perhaps, earlier in the season, this plain would look fresh and green, and have bright gay flowers, but now the country every where is parched and sere. On our right, Hymettus lifted its purple head, and on our left were the rock-crowned peak of Lycabettus, and the lofty range of Mount Parnes, Pentelicus bounding the prospect ahead.

After two hours' drive, we came to a thick grove of trees, where we left the carriage, and mounting our horses, we crossed a little rivulet, and began the ascent of the mountain. The first part of the way, the path was not very steep, but it was so covered with loose stones as to render the footing rather unsafe. But the stones in the path were not all the difficulties we met, for soon after leaving the carriage, it began to rain, at first slightly, then it increased to a heavy shower, till we were uncomfortably wet. There was no shelter near; we must either return to the carriage or press on to a grotto in the mountain, about half way up. We decided on the latter course, and hurried on as rapidly as possible, though in such a stony path, we could not go out of a walk. The thick bushes of oleander and the masses of brush-wood that lined the path, showered upon us, as we rubbed by them, and by the time we arrived at the grotto, we were about as wet as we could be. Water is as great a damper to enthusiasm as to many other things, and literally soaked when we arrived at the grotto, I cared not much for the sublimity of the scene around me.

Strattis made a fire of dried branches, and standing within the grotto, sheltered from the rain, I had ample leisure to look about me. Higher and higher rose the wreaths of smoke, encircling the ivy which grew in luxuriance over the rocky sides, and startling the owl from his perch, while the flames threw a lurid light over the roof and walls of the cavern. Around us were immense quarries, from which the Pentelican marble is taken, and below us were hills and plains, rolling on to the distant sea. Now, the valley was wrapped in mists, and now, the sun shone out, lighting up every nook, and shining upon every mountain peak. It was very, very grand, and being thoroughly dried, I quite forgot the previous wetting.

Out shone the sun at last, and with every leaf and shrub glittering with tiny drops, we mounted and pursued our upward way. Steeper and steeper grew the path, and wilder and wilder the scene, and the view below was becoming more and more magnificent, but I would not stop to look around me, determining to wait till I reached the top, that the whole might burst upon me at once.

And now the path became so rocky and steep that we

dismounted, and pursued the rest of the way on foot. Arriving at the top, which is 3500 feet above the sea, I sat down under the shelter of a high rock, and threw my eyes quickly around. What a scene! I drew my breath, and looked again. Strattis began to talk, and point out the different localities, and then what names I heard, so dear to every lover of Greece! First of all, at our very feet, lay Marathon, which

> "Preserves alike its bounds and boundless fame,
> The battlefield where Persia's victim horde
> First bowed beneath the brunt of Hellas' sword,
> As on the morn to distant glory dear,
> When Marathon became a magic word,
> Which uttered, to the hearer's eye appear
> The camp, the host, the fight, the conqueror's career."

Yes! the very name of Marathon brought the great, the memorable battle before us, which was fought there more than two thousand three hundred years ago, when a handful of Greeks put to flight "Persia's horde."

Between us and the plain of Marathon, a succession of rolling hills sloped gradually down, and beyond, the sea came up in a semicircular bay, protected by a long, low promontory. Still farther on, rose Eubœa from the sea, its shore beautifully indented with bold promontories and sheltered bays. On and on swept the sea, gemmed with beauteous isles, among which rose conspicuous Andros and Tinos, while away in the distance, Syra bounded the view. I turned around; the sea washed the peninsula on that side, and beyond queenly Egina and "sea-born Salamis," rose a range of mountains, at whose feet lay Eleusis and Megara.

Turning my eyes landward, I see "hills upon hills arise," Parnes and Cytheron swelling up in their majesty, while Helicon brings up the rear. And yonder towers Mount Geranea, and far away, amid those hidden recesses, lies Delphi, near which flows the Castalian fount, whose waters gave inspiration and power to the poet.

Over hill and plain, and wooded dell and rocky ravine, and a few villages gleaming here and there, my eye roamed, till it rested on Athens, almost engirdled by the groves of the Academy and by green vineyards. How plainly I saw the Acropolis, and so distinctly stood out the fair temples in their beauty, I could almost count the pillars.

Varied as this scene was, perhaps its predominant trait was the unbroken stillness that reigned over all. Not a moving thing was to be seen; not a sail broke the majestic repose of the dark blue waters. How many times I ejaculated, "Oh, glorious land of Greece!" And even while I ate my lunch, I broke out a dozen times with—

"The mountains look on Marathon,
And Marathon looks on the sea."

At length we must descend; we soon reached our horses, which were quietly browsing the scanty grass, and mounting, we descended the steep, stony path, which seemed to me almost as bad as some of the roads in Syria. We descended safely, however, and in due time arriving at the grove where we had left the carriage, we were soon on our homeward way, reaching the hotel about two o'clock.

The next day we were off on another excursion, to Eleusis and Megara, leaving here at five o'clock in the morning, and not getting home till nearly eight in the evening, but as we went the whole distance in a carriage, I was not at all fatigued.

We went out by "the sacred way," the road along which the religious processions of old were wont to pass, and occasionally saw remains of the ancient pavement and the marks of the chariot wheels, and niches in the sides of the hills, where the votaries of the gods deposited their offerings. Never was there a lovelier morning, and the mountains and the sea, and the

"Isles that crown the Egean deep,"

were clothed in the most delicate tints imaginable. Fair Greece, favored child of poesy and song, to me thou art charming!

Arriving at the little village of Daphne, we stopped to visit an old monastery, remarkable for nothing but the antique mosaics that line the dome of the little chapel. In a chamber beyond the chapel, we were shown the burial places of two of "the Dukes of Athens." From the roof, or as it is called here, "the terrace," of the monastery, we had a magnificent view. Before us stretched the famous "pass of Daphne," a narrow, rocky gorge, between two peaks of Ægaleos, at the end of which opened the Bay of Eleusis, its waters of the clearest blue, while the background was composed of hills clothed in amethystine hues.

Then on we went, along the Bay of Eleusis, the mountains on our right, and the blue sea on our left, studded with islands, among which Egina and "sea-born Salamis" shone the most conspicuously. This bay seems almost entirely land-locked, being encircled on three sides by rugged mountains, and almost shut in, in front, by Salamis. I have rarely seen a lovelier bay.

At Eleusis, there are some remains of the temple of Ceres, and we saw a large number of shattered columns and broken statues, and an immense medallion of

Pentelic marble, representing in bold relief the head and bust of a warrior in complete armor.

While we walked about, half the inhabitants, old and young, male and female, gathered about us, among whom, the most conspicuous objects were little girls and boys, apparently not more than four of five years old, having the care of babies, and of children two or three years younger than themselves. It seems to me this is one of the characteristic features of the East, and I think I have spoken of it more than once. Amid all these groups gathered around us, Mr. and Mrs. A, who were with us, could find but one who could understand Greek, as spoken in Athens, they being Albanians, and speaking a dialect peculiar to themselves.

After resting a while at Eleusis, not so much for our own sake, as for that of the horses, we went on to Megara, twelve or fifteen miles farther. Nearly all the way, our road lay along the bay, while the mountains almost encircled us. Once we crossed a plain, covered with the vine and the olive, but otherwise the country seemed barren and desolate, the ground looking parched and dry, though I am told in early Spring, every thing bears quite a different aspect.

At Megara we were told there was nothing interesting to be seen, and as it was excessively hot, we did not care about walking round to make any new discoveries, so we took possession of the upper story of a kind of Khan, ate our lunch, and then laid down on the floor to sleep.

On our way back, we took fresh horses at Eleusis, and then came on quite rapidly, arriving here before eight o'clock, the distance we travelled that day, being about fifty miles. As we came towards Athens, she looked lovely, dressed in her evening robe of beauty, the heavens being glorious with its many hues, the pillars of the Parthenon standing out clearly against the soft sky, while Hymettus, Lycabettus and Pentelicus were bathed in a flood of rosy light. The sunsets here are magnificent; they almost rival my cherished ones on the Nile. The thin haze that floats upon the mountains, the lovely hues of the sky, cloudless and clear as possible, the change that comes over the earth and the heavens as the twilight deepens; all these, and a thousand other charms, to which my feeble pen cannot do justice, serve to make a sunset at Athens exquisitely beautiful.

At a little distance from the city, Strattis suddenly announced the approach of the Queen. We drew up while her Majesty passed, it not being considered etiquette to be driving on, while a royal personage is passing, and I had a better view of Queen Amelia, than I had had before. She was in a carriage drawn by four horses, accompanied by her "mistress of robes" who sat beside her, and preceded and followed by three or four attendants on horseback. On mature observation, I should pronounce the Queen of Greece, not exactly handsome perhaps, but decidedly good looking, having clear, bright eyes, a full, florid face, and an exceedingly beautiful and winning smile. For the gratification of my lady readers, I will say she wore a silk dress, a cachemere shawl, and a bright pink bonnet, with flowers of the same color inside, which I am sorry to be obliged to add were exceedingly unbecoming to her high color.

Our good star again was in the ascendant, for a half hour afterwards, we met King Otho. I like his appearance much; his eyes are soft yet brilliant, though I should say wanting in soul, and in intellect. His smile and the look of his eyes, as he bends them on you, while he bows graciously, are exceedingly captivating, and to me, (I am frank enough to confess it,) the King of Greece, mounted on a spirited horse, dressed in the charming costume of the Albanians, the circumstances in which he is placed at present, investing him with a mournful interest, is peculiarly fascinating.

It is not my province, neither is this the time and place, to dilate upon the state of Greece, nor indeed of any country through which we may pass. You, with your constant access to books and newspapers, at present so full of these subjects, are probably more conversant with them, than I, in my wanderings about, am able just now to be, but one thing I must say for Greece, and that is, that at this moment she is probably at one of the most critical points of her life. How will she pass this crisis? Oppressed by enemies within, and foes without, will she be able to throw off the shackles that bind her, and appear once more before the world in her former brightness and glory, or will "she draw tighter the bonds that enslave her, and be lost in the shadow of mightier powers?" The future will decide. When I meditate upon the present state of Greece, and compare her with what she once was, I am ready to weep over her fallen greatness, and I sigh and mournfully exclaim, "Poor Greece!"

Yesterday we spent the day at Rev. Mr. Hill's, long known to the world at large, as one of the most successful Missionaries and Teachers in foreign lands. True, the work he has accomplished may not be counted by the numbers he has brought from the error of their ways, but in the seeds of good that have been sown, and of which a future generation will show the fruits better than this. I regret exceedingly that the holidays should have commenced before we arrived, as I should have liked much to have seen the schools in their full operation. As it was, I went yesterday all over the Mission premises, and had occasion to admire the neatness and order that reigned every where.

In the afternoon we drove down to the Phalerum, which before the time of the Persians, was the harbor of Athens. The road has lately been bordered with trees on either side, under the direction of the Queen, she frequenting this road very often, as she generally goes down to the Phalerum every morning to bathe.

We had a quiet ramble along the sea shore, but my pleasure during the whole day was greatly damped by sickness, which at last increased so much, that I was obliged to ask my kind friends to drive me home without delay. It is never very pleasant to be sick in a foreign land, but just now while the cholera is near, perhaps I shall be excused if I do feel a little degree of anxiety about myself. To-day I have not been out at all, but have tried to write a little to divert my mind from dwelling too much upon my own affairs. I have written this long letter at many intervals, and in much pain, which must be my apology for its defects.

LETTER LIX.

Prospects for Departure.—Queen's Farm.—Garden of the Palace.—Greek Costume.—Lycabettus.—View from top Acropolis.—Sunset.—Parthenon by Moonlight.—Farewell to Friends.—Cavia.—Maid of Athens.

ATHENS, Aug. 3d.

MY DEAREST P.:

We are still shut up here, as you will see by the date of this, and I am sorry to be forced to add, that we see no prospect whatever of getting away. Remonstrances and efforts amount to nothing; the steamers will not take passengers, and we cannot compel them to take us. Mr. King, in his capacity as consul, has made every exertion to procure us permission to depart, but thus far in vain. Two or three times our hopes of a speedy departure have been raised only to be dashed to the ground again with renewed violence. We try to be quiet and patient under the disappointment, and to trust that all will work out for good, and our friends here say, we bear it remarkably well, but it is a great hindrance to us, for summer is now hastening to a close, and we have not yet entered Germany. But there is no use in fretting. We talk over the affair every day, and amuse ourselves with wondering what comments you will all make on the subject, and with hoping every Tuesday, we may get away the next Friday, and every Friday, that we may be able to leave the next Tuesday.

Meanwhile we are as pleasantly situated as possible, under like circumstances. Our hotel is good, and what is of quite as much consequence just now, the charges are reasonable; we are surrounded by good friends, whose houses and hearts are ever open to us; twice a week we see the latest newspapers from the United States, and every Sunday we enjoy the great privilege of going twice to church.

And now I fancy I hear you ask, "what have you done to amuse yourselves all this time?" and this reasonable question I shall now proceed to answer.

For several days after my last letter, I was not well enough to do much of anything, except to read a little and write a little each day. That tardy journal of mine was halting a little behind, and I tugged at that every day to bring it up. Then it was such a luxury to sit quietly down and read, and we had so many books lent us by our good friends here, that the hours glided by almost insensibly in the company of an interesting author.

I had enough of early rising when circumstances compelled me to practice that virtue, so that I have indulged at will in morning naps. Every morning, between eight and nine o'clock, the band plays in front of the Palace, while the guard is changed, and the strains of music, oft of some well remembered air, mingle most deliciously with my late dreams, and my early reveries. During the heat of the day I have seldom been out, but after dinner we take a walk, ending each day with a quiet evening spent with some of our friends here.

To-day we are told we may leave next week; go as far as the island of Syra, where we must perform quarantine eight days, after which we may take the next Austrian steamer to Trieste. Think of that! What a prospect! Eight days' quarantine in that lazaretto, under a burning sun, without a tree to shade that glaring edifice!

The very thought of it makes me shudder. But we shall do that, rather than run the risk of being kept here till next September.

But allow me to enter a little more into particulars of our evening amusements. One day last week immediately after dinner we drove out to "the Queen's Farm," about five miles from town. This is a favorite ride of the Queen's, and she goes there nearly every evening to drink milk and eat ices, with which we should have been delighted to have been regaled, but unfortunately those good things are only served up for royal personages. We found everything there in the nicest order; a beautiful garden, well stocked with fruits and flowers; a fertile vineyard, with immense clusters of ripening fruit; a large barn yard, full of poultry, and fat cows, and frolicsome calves, and a small castle-like house, from the terrace of which we obtained a splendid view of Athens and its environs.

Another evening we went to the palace to see the King and Queen ride out. Looking into the garden, we saw the Queen in a little carriage driving two of the most charming ponies imaginable. After that, she mounted her horse and dashed by us, the King hurrying on to catch up with her. They are very particular in bowing to every one who salutes them, the King gracefully touching his cap to all ladies.

I enjoyed exceedingly a quiet walk in that lovely garden. The flowers, and the trees, and the clear sky, and the glimpses of ruined temples, and the people in gay attire, formed a beautiful and ever-varying picture. I am perfectly in love with the costume worn by the men; the full kirtle, the richly embroidered gaiters and jackets, the large open sleeve flowing behind and displaying the full sleeve of the shirt, dazzlingly clean and white, the red cap, hanging gracefully down one side, with its long blue tassel, combined with the graceful walk of these men, make them look like heroes on a stage. Unfortunately the women, except on great festivals, have dropped the peculiar costume of their country, and dress too much like other Europeans, except many of them wear a red cap, with a braid of hair twisted around it, or a handkerchief folded with peculiar grace around the head.

One day this week we climbed to the summit of Lycabettus, and a hard climb I found it, particularly after the weakness incidental to sickness, and to leading so inactive a life as I have lately done, but the magnificent view from the top more than paid for the labor of reaching it. Let me copy here a few words from my note book, written on the spot. "At our feet lies Athens, girdled by brown plains and rugged hills, except where the vineyards and 'olive groves of Academe, Plato's retirement,' present the appearance of a broad green belt. The hills are clothed in their robes of amethystic hue, while the blue sea glitters beyond, dotted with islands, queenly Egina, and 'sea born Salamis,' showing the most conspicuously. Yonder rises the Acropolis, and over its turreted walls, stands out every pillar of the Parthenon in bold relief against the glowing sky. And there too I see Mars' Hill, where the intrepid Paul proclaimed a new religion to the 'men of Athens.' How lonely stand the pillars of Jupiter Olympus, and yet how majestic, for the very heavens seem to rest upon them!

"And I can trace the bed of the Ilissus, from the margin of green that follows its windings, though the water itself has quite disappeared. Beyond, stretches up Hymettus, a few green patches shining out here and there, and further still, rises Pentelicus, with its rich quarries of marbles, while between us and that lay vineyards and olive groves. Out from the green trees peep forth white houses, forming many a picture of rural beauty. But the greatest charm of all is the exquisite coloring of the earth and the sky; the purple hills and the glowing hues that envelope all as with a rich veil."

The rocky summit of Lycabettus is crowned with a little church, and as I looked within, the air came wafted with rich incense, and the murmur of a soft sweet voice reached my ear. A young candidate for holy orders, (so I judged from his dress) was standing with rapt face, chanting a hymn, his clear olive complexion, and dark eyes, lighted up with enthusiasm, and his whole appearance showing that his heart and his soul were engaged in the worship he was offering up. His long black hair hung in wavy curls on his shoulders, and as he came out on the rock, and cast his eyes over the scene, the bright red spot glowing on his brown cheek, and the fire yet in his dark eyes, I thought I had never seen a more interesting face.

Yesterday evening we went again to the Acropolis. Did I before tell you that in ascending the hill we passed the ruins of the theatre of Herodius Atticus and of the temple of Bacchus? The arched openings in the massive walls of the theatre served as a frame to the picture beyond, a picture formed of undulating meadows, set off in the background by mountain peaks and a glimmering of blue water. I noticed last evening, what escaped my observation before, that there is a double row of pillars at each end of the Parthenon, and that all the pillars taper towards the top.

With difficulty we climed up a ruined staircase, and stood upon the top of the Parthenon, and saw the sun sink slowly behind the hills. What an exquisite scene it was! How matchless was the coloring that wrapped all as in a halo! The calm water, the sea-girt isles, the beautiful form of the mountains, "the flowery hill, Hymettus," the rock crowned Lycabettus, the distant Pentelicus, with its summit tinged with soft roseate hues, the varied tints of the sky, here like molten gold, there fading away to a delicate straw color; here a glowing crimson, there a pale pink or lovely lilac, the sober brown of the plains, and the rich green of "the olive groves of Academe," the temple and its age-stained pillars, each had its own peculiar shades and tints. Seen under that lovely sky, and through that pure air, even the scenes of earth took a heavenly hue.

And then we descended the stairs, and going to the upper end of the Parthenon, we seated ourselves in the marble chairs occupied by the King and Queen of Greece when they attend the meetings of the antiquarian society. Right through the massive portal, between the gigantic pillars, I saw a little glimmering sea, backed by purple hills, upon which rested a sky perfectly glorious in its tints of amber and gold. I sat rapt in admiration at the scene. No words could do justice to the delicious blending of colors in sea and sky, in hill and dale; and this exquisite blending is one of the peculiar charms of Greece.

Slowly, as though loath to depart, these glowing tints began to fade, and as they paled away, brighter and brighter shone the moon, and more and more lustrous glowed the stars. The beauty of the ancient Parthenon was said to be the roof of Parian marble, adorned with sculpture and paintings and gilding, but to me, there could be no fitter covering than the clear sky, studded with its countless stars. I don't know why it is, but a column standing alone, touches me more than to see a cluster of them together. It seems to speak of one who is left alone to battle with life's storms, without a friend to love him or to smile upon him.

How softly fell the moonbeams on the pale marble! How beautifully were brought out the pillars and the statues! You may laugh at me, and call it all enthusiasm, but I can assure you I would gladly have sat in that chair of marble, and gazed on that exquisite scene till midnight. Our two weeks' imprisonment here seemed not all in vain, since it gave us an opportunity to see the Parthenon by moonlight.

In all my roamings in and about Athens, I seem like one who treads upon consecrated soil, for is it not true, what Byron said,

> "Where'er we tread, 'tis haunted, holy ground?"

And oft and again I murmur some of the glowing lines penned by him, when he visited

> "Fair Greece, sad relic of departed worth,
> Immortal, though no more; though fallen, great."

And as I stood last evening on the top of the Parthenon, on

> "the giant height
> Which looks o'er waves so blue, skies so serene,"

I felt indeed,

> "That he who there at such an hour hath been,
> Will wistful linger on that hallowed spot,
> And slowly tear him from the witching scene."

Changed as Athens is from her former days of glory, to me she is still lovely, and as I view her varied beauties from one point or other, I say,

> "Yet are thy skies as blue, thy crags as wild;
> Sweet are thy groves and verdant are thy fields,
> Thine olive ripe as when Minerva smiled,
> And still his honeyed wealth Hymettus yields;
> There the blithe bee his fragrant fortress builds,
> The free-born wanderer of thy mountain air;
> Apollo still thy long, long summer gilds,
> Still in his beams Mendeli's marbles glare;
> Art, Glory, Freedom fail, but Nature still is fair."

Some of the time that we have been here, the heat has been intense, the air blowing as from an oven; at others, a north wind has prevailed, bringing comfortable days and cool, delicious nights. One comfort can be enjoyed at Athens, and that is, ices every evening. How often we have sat in the open air, under the clear canopy of heaven, and sipped an ice, front of some café, in company with the dear friends here. The remembrance of these scenes of earthly comforts will not soon be effaced.

Aug. 6th. Good news for you! We are off to-morrow! After "every thing said and done," we are assured we may go to-morrow evening in the French steamer to Syra, and after waiting there three days, take the Austrian steamer, and proceed at once to Trieste, without being obliged to perform quarantine at Syra. Is not this cheering intelligence?

We have made our last calls on our kind friends here, and I can assure you, though glad once more to be on the way, we are very sorry to part from them. Their kind attentions to us have been rendered to the last, and among my pleasant recollections of Athens, the hours I spent in friendly intercourse with them, will stand out in full relief. Long, too, shall I remember our quiet Sundays here, and the beautiful little church where we offered up our prayers and our thanksgivings.

I bid farewell here to one long-tried friend, my saddle, which has done me such good service in Egypt, Palestine and Syria, but which I shall no longer need, as I shall soon be in the region of railroads and diligences.

Oh! but I must not forget to tell you of a drive we took yesterday, part way up Hymettus, to the village of Caraa, where we had the pleasure of being introduced to the far-famed "Maid of Athens," at present known to the Athenian world as Mrs. Black. She has recently lost her oldest son, under trying circumstances, and her face is very grave and sad, true heart-sorrow being shadowed forth in her eyes, which are very, very mournful. I cannot fancy her ever being beautiful, though doubtless in her youth and bloom, she had a speaking, interesting face.

And now I must say adieu, for night is waning, and I have much to do to-morrow.

LETTER LX.

Departure from Athens.—Hindrances.—Arrival at Syra.—Trouble about Lodgings.—Syra.—Evening Promenades.—Tinos.—Miraculous Shrine.—Exquisite Views.—Old Town.—Convent.—Church of St. George.—Delicious Evenings.

SYRA, Aug. 10th.

MY DEAR F:

Thus far we are on our destined way towards Trieste, and here we have been waiting, this is now the third day, in an uncomfortable hotel, and in weather, the heat of which would prove trying to a more amiable person than myself.

Up to the last moment of our leaving Athens, it seemed uncertain about our getting away, the agent of the Austrian company saying he was by no means sure the steamer would take us from Syra, and confidently telling us we might have to be shut up in this little island for a month. Not a pleasant prospect, to be sure! On the reception of this intelligence, a "palaver" was held, at which some said one thing and some another, but the general conclusion was, that if we were to be shut up in any place, that place would better be Athens than Syra. I will not burden you, nor this sheet, with the pros and cons; suffice it to say, we were willing to try our chance of being shut up here, or of going on to Trieste. Dr. Beretti, an eminent lawyer from Pera, who came with us from Constantinople, and who had been fellow-prisoner with us in Athens, was determined to make a bold push to get home, having been kept from his business three weeks, and we decided to share his fate, feeling confident if he could go to Constantinople, we could to Trieste.

The boat was to start from the Phalerum, instead of the Piræus, which is still in quarantine, and the hour of her departure was given at six. It seemed to me we should never get away from Athens, for every thing went wrong. At first, the horses would not move, and the coachman was obliged to send to the stable for other horses. At last, after innumerable delays, we were off, but the very first hill we came to, the new horses stopped. I was sure we should be left, and my blood rose to fever heat, and I grew nervous and irritable. I could not attempt to count the times we started and stopped, but at last, the coachman meeting a return carriage, made a bargain for us to be taken down in that, so out we bundled, with all our luggage, and in a few minutes were dashing furiously towards the harbor. Will you believe it, when we arrived there, we found the steamer would not leave till eight o'clock, the French ambassador having sent down a message for them to wait till that hour for dispatches! I made an inward vow then never to be impatient, nor to fret again, which I am very much afraid I shall break at the first temptation.

I witnessed one more sunset, equal in beauty and gorgeousness of coloring to any I have ever seen, and then I bade farewell to Athens, not the last adieu, however, as we must go back there to-morrow.

I never saw a lovelier night than that on which we ran from Athens here. The sea was calm, the sky cloudless, the moon and the stars lustrous, the views matchless, as we passed amid a succession of islands, rising up like fortresses from the sea, and presenting new and varying scenes of beauty. I was in ecstacies with all I beheld, and went from side to side, murmuring snatches of poetry and song about fair Greece, till my enthusiasm was raised to the highest pitch, and I recited to my Greek companion Fitz Halleck's beautiful poem of Marco Bozzaris, with which he was delighted. I was sorry when the time came to exchange the lovely prospect from the deck for the close cabin, but there was no alternative; my companions were tired, and I could not stay on deck without them. There was a port-hole in my berth, and more than twenty times I awoke in the night and looked out, and always I saw the glittering sea and a mountainous shore.

When morning came, we were in the harbor of Syra, and as the wind was blowing freshly, there was what the English call such a "nasty motion," we were all glad to get up, dress in a hurry and come on shore. When I complained so bitterly of the heat, as we lay in this harbor four weeks ago, I little knew that the heat was saving us from what would have been far more unpleasant, namely, short, quick, "bobbing" waves, trying to the strongest head and stomach.

I need not dwell upon our search for lodgings; the three little hotels of Syra were full, and not a room was to be had. What "money," however, could not procure, "love" obtained, for a friend of Dr. B.'s, Judge Cassimati, kindly offered us his room, which was the largest and best in this hotel. I need not say we were delicate about accepting such an offer, even though made in the most polite and friendly manner; but what was I to do? The gentlemen might "rough it," and sleep on beds made up in the hall, but I must have a room some where, so I gladly and thankfully accepted the offer, made in so kind a spirit. An extra bed is put up at night for J., Dr. B. sleeps in a closet, while Judge C. occupies a narrow passage leading to our room. In this room we all congregate during the day, when the heat is too intense to permit us to go out, and reading, conversation and eating fill up the time. We sit with our doors and windows open, to catch what little air is stirring, and we have been much amused by the conduct of two of the waiters and the landlord, who, at little intervals, come to the door of the room, stand still a moment, casting their eyes all around, then deliberately turn about and walk away. At first I supposed they were looking for something, and I invariably asked them in Italian, Greek being a "dead language" to me, what they wanted, but they never vouchsafed a reply. At last, Dr. B. could bear it no longer, and at the next visitation on the part of the waiter, which happened while Judge C. was reading aloud, he jumped up and ran out into the passage, showering a torrent of Greek upon the astonished waiter, and ending by asking him what he meant by coming into the room and looking about in that manner. The cool reply was, "Because God has given me two eyes to see all that is going on!"

But now let me tell you a little about Syra. As I said before, it is a small island, being only ten miles long and five wide. The old town is built on a conical hill, rising abruptly, while at its foot, and on either side, is spread the new town, which has well paved streets, and some very handsome houses. In the hills back of the town, abound mica, slate, and an inferior kind of marble, and garnets are occasionally found, and iron ore in considerable profusion. Some travellers have praised the wines of Syra, but they must like a mixture of acidity and rosin better than I do. Homer once described the island as

> "Fertile in flocks, in herds, in wine, in corn,"

but I believe that description can hardly apply to the state of the island at present. The importance of Syra depends now upon its being one of the principal ports of the Levant, vessels from all parts of the world stopping here.

When the heat of the day is beginning to subside, all the inhabitants betake themselves to different promenades and places of resort, and, of course, we followed the multitude. We first went to a high cliff, on the right of the town, and here we had, not only a refreshing sea breeze, but one of the most delightful prospects imaginable, the blue sea, stretching for miles and miles away, dotted with islands clothed in as lovely tints as the sea itself. Tinos and Mycone and Paros were all clustered within a little distance of us, and the white houses and the pretty churches of Tinos seemed almost beneath our feet, though more than twelve miles off. In one of the churches at Tinos is a miraculous shrine, and the believers in this shrine dwelling at Syra, come to this cliff every evening, and as the sun goes down, kneel upon the hard rock, with their faces towards the favored isle, and offer up their vesper song and prayer.

I wish I could convey to you the irresistible charm there is about these sea-girt isles, with their exquisite tints, and the delicious sky above, perfectly glowing and radiant with beautiful hues, but my powers of description are quite too feeble for the theme, and I must content myself with feeling their power, without being able to impart their fascinations to others.

In a pretty square, in the centre of the town, newly laid out and planted with trees, we sat down, to refresh ourselves according to our respective tastes, one taking coffee, another a pipe, while others contented themselves with the less excitable beverage of cool lemonade. Around dozens of little tables, similar groups were seated, engaged in similar occupations, while the waiters, from an adjoining coffee-house, were flying hither and thither, administering to the various wants of the company. Night came on, soft and beautiful, and still we sat, and talked of Greece and her prospects, a subject of which I never tire.

Then we walked to another cliff, o'erhanging the sea, and there we found hundred of persons walking about, or sitting round little tables, eating and drinking, and listening to fine music from a band stationed in front of a café. The night was perfectly lovely, the sea calm and noiseless, the moon and the stars lustrous, while the different islands reared themselves proudly and beautifully from the blue waters. Gay groups were constantly passing, the soft and musical language of the Greek mingled occasionally with the flowing Italian tongue, and the harsh Turkish. The "tall Albanian, kirtled to the knee," walked majestically by, and as I looked on their noble forms and handsome faces, and eyes on which a shadow of mournfulness rested, I could but think perhaps they, too, were meditating upon the past glories of their country, and daring to hope and to pray that "Greece might yet be free."

Yesterday afternoon we walked to the summit of the old town, and a curious place it is too, with its steep, narrow streets, many of them consisting of flights of steps leading from one height to another, the roof of one house being on a level with the ground floor of the one above it; and singular little houses they were too, each one having its tenants of men, women, children and pigs.

On our way up we stopped at a convent, where is an English girl, whose mother I often met in Athens, and as I thought of the lone mother in her widowhood, deprived of her children, (for another daughter is in a different convent) I could but mourn over those mistaken notions of duty and religion, that could thus shut the hearts of children to the claims of home and affection.

The church of St. George crowns the height upon which the old town is built, and from the terrace in front we had an extensive view of hill and vale, sea and isle. Many of the hills were covered with vineyards, dotted here and there by white houses peeping out from among the vines, but the fairest view of all was "the sea, the deep blue sea," and the purple islands, mingling far away with the very clouds.

The evening was ended on the cliffs, and I, for one, can never forget the two delicious evenings spent at Syra. As far as hotel comforts are concerned, we have had nothing to boast of in that line during our three days' sojourn in this island, but we have had, what hotels rarely furnish, the charms of delightful intercourse with heart and intellect, and that has cheered and softened all, making even the heat endurable, for we could sit still and talk, and badly cooked food, and swarms of vermin at night, only heightened this delight. But all these things, pleasant and unpleasant, must now be left behind, for the Austrian steamer has arrived, and there is no impediment thrown in the way of our leaving; so in a few hours we are off, and with saddened hearts we must bid farewell to friends whom we may never see again.

LETTER LXI.

Departure from Syra.—Incident.—Pleasant voyage.—Piræus.—Cerigo.—Modon.—Navarino.—Zante.—Ionian Islands.—Cephalonia.—Ithaca.—St. Maura.—Paxos.—Corfu.—Ruins of Pola.—Trieste.

TRIESTE, Aug. 16th.

MY DEAR P.:

At length our long voyage of more than a thousand miles is ended, and we are landed safely on the shore of Austria. And a pleasant voyage it has been too; lovely days and quiet nights, the sea almost without a ripple, and the sky without a cloud. Being the only lady passenger, I have had the ladies' cabin quite to myself, and every night I have lain with the window in my berth open, and many times I have wakened and looked out upon the calm sea, and the distant shore. Nothing can exceed the beauty of these summer nights, excepting always those of Egypt and the Desert. The sunsets have been resplendent, the moon and the stars bright yet soft, while ever and anon, across the heavens, has darted some brilliant meteor. Every evening while we were in Athens, we saw such meteors repeatedly, and bright and beautiful things they were too, leaving often a train of light behind them which would last several minutes.

We came on board the steamer Thursday evening the 10th, but though we were told to be there by seven, the anchor was not weighed till long after I was in my berth. At the hotel where we were staying in Syra, there was an Italian lady, a widow, who with her two children was coming to Trieste, her home, which several years ago she had left, to go with her husband to Crete. Unfortunately her little boy had been ill, and when they came to the steamer, some objection was made to taking them on board, but their objections were finally overruled, and she took possession of her allotted place. But in a few hours, the child changed rapidly, and when the captain and the agent came on board, they refused to allow them to go on, so late in the evening they were put in a small boat and sent to the lazaretto, for the steamer being in quarantine, they could not immediately go back into the town. My heart ached for the poor afflicted woman, but all remonstrances were in vain, the agent assuring us that if we came to Trieste with that sick child on board, or that if he died on the passage, we should inevitably be put into quarantine for at least fifteen days. I said all I could to comfort the sorrowing mother, for she looked as though her heart was breaking, and as though she felt she was without friends in the world. I suppose, too, her means were straitened, and I don't know how well she could bear this further hindrance in a pecuniary point of view. I did not like to offer her money, but I gave her my hearty sympathy, and she thanked me gratefully for it, and the last I saw of her, was after she was seated in the small boat, pressing her sick child to her breast with one hand, and her handkerchief to her streaming eyes with the other. Silently the oars were dipped into the water, and then the boat glided away in the distance and darkness—fit emblem of the sadness that was brooding over the group in the stern.

When I came on deck the next morning, we were at Piroeus, the harbor of Athens, the Acropolis towering up in the distance, backed by Lycabettus and Hymettus, while at their feet slumbered the city of Athens.

And there we lay that long summer day, without any communication with the shore, except sending off and receiving the mails. Small boats, with their dazzling white sails darted by us, but none dared to stop even within hail. It seemed as though we were already doomed to death, and that the shadow of pestilence was really brooding over us.

The rocky peninsula of Piroeus is supposed to have been originally an island, but gradually changed into a peninsula by the accumulation of sand between the island and the main land. The fortifications of the harbor, of which there are at present but few remains, were erected by Themistocles, whose name stands forth proudly in the annals of Greece.

As the sun went down, more and more distinctly stood out the pillars of the Parthenon, Lycabettus and Hymettus assumed deeper purple hues, and the sky grew perfectly radiant with its tints of gold and crimson, and sapphire.

At length we were off, and the city faded away in the distance, and the hills mingled indistinctly with the clouds, and the fair and goodly pillars of the Parthenon were no longer visible, and then I felt I was bidding a long and perhaps lasting adieu to Athens.

Among "isles that crown the Egean deep," our course lay, till it was time for me to go below. Early the next morning I was awakened by the stopping of the steamer; I looked out my window, and found we were before the island of Cerigo, having as far as my eye could reach, a rugged mountainous coast. In classic days this island was called Cythera, and was said to have received Venus after she arose from the wave; and to have been afterwards her favorite place of abode. The island is about twenty miles in length and twelve in breadth.

We had now sailed down the whole length of the eastern coast of Greece, and after rounding the capes, leaving the land at a goodly distance, we began our progress up the western shore. We passed between two or three large islands and the main land, and occasionally caught a glimpse of an ancient looking town, or a fertile spot, but generally the coast of Greece is of a stern and severe aspect, befitting well the character of the old Spartan, and the present wild and warlike Mainote.

We passed the town of Modon with its Venetian looking fortresses and almost hidden by a rocky island, saw the bay and town of Navarino, where was fought in 1827, I think, the battle that for a time decided the fate of Greece.

Towards evening we came in sight of Zante, celebrated the world over for its currants, but all we could see of the island, that for a long time was called "the flower of the Levant," was the dim outline of a mountainous ridge. During the night, to my great regret, we passed the islands of Cephalonia, Ithaca, St. Maura and Paxos, all more or less celebrated in classic lore.

Cephalonia is the largest of the Ionian islands, being about one hundred and twenty miles in circumference. Ithaca was the scene of many of Homer's narratives, and has always been called Ulysses' own isle. Santa Maura too is mentioned in Homer, but the spot in the whole island which is most particularly interesting to lovers and poets is the high cliff called Sappho's leap, which rises precipitously from the sea, to the height of two hundred feet. This is "Leucadia's far projecting rock of woe." Here it is said the gifted daughter of song, when enamored of Phaon, leaped from the rock into the sea, and in later days victims of unrequited love have followed her example. Moore calls it,

> "The very spot where Sappho sung
> Her swan-like music ere she sprung,
> (Still holding, in that fearful leap,
> By her loved lyre,) into the deep,
> And dying, quenched the fatal fire
> At once of both her heart and lyre."

Paxos is a very small island, not more than five miles long and two wide, but there is such a beautiful legend connected with it, I cannot forbear from repeating it. "At the time of our Lord's most bitter passion and death, a cry was heard announcing the death of the great god Pan, and this cry was accompanied by such piteous outcries and dreadful shrieks, as the like of hath never been heard." It is to this legend Milton so beautifully alludes, in his ode on the Nativity.

> "The lonely mountains o'er,
> And the resounding shore,
> A voice of weeping heard and loud lament."

When I came on deck Sunday morning, a delightful prospect greeted my eyes. On the right rose a precipitous mountain coast, yet showing here and there a fertile spot, or a cheerful looking little village peeping out from among the rocks and hills, and on the left was a shore sloping more gradually up, dotted over with vineyards and clumps of trees, and these verdant slopes and green trees were exceedingly refreshing to the eye, after the bare hills and arid plains of Attica. Villages and villas were scattered here and there, and white sails glided over the clear waters, and mists rolled over the distant mountain tops, now enshrouding all, now revealing hill and dale and wild ravine. I turned eagerly to the captain to ask him where we were, and found we were between the island of Corfu and the coast of Albania.

About nine we entered the harbor of the town, and saw before us the two rugged peaks on which the citadel is built, while the other parts of the town stretch along the shore, and extend far up the hill. All around were vineyards and groves and pleasant meadows, and I longed to exchange the deck of the steamer for a ramble on the hills, and the privilege of attending Divine service in the chapel connected with the garrison. But we were in quarantine, and were allowed to have no communication with the shore. Occasionally small boats would come off, and their occupants hold a screaming conversation with the officers or passengers of the steamer, and towards evening large baskets of fruit were handed up the side of the steamer, the persons having them in charge being very careful not to come in contact with any one on board. And what delicious fruit it was too. All the time we were on board "L'Egitto," we had the nicest grapes, melons, peaches, pears, plums and oranges at breakfast and dinner, and notwithstanding the prevalence of cholera, I revelled in fruit, for you know I always go on the principle that ripe fruit will never hurt any one.

Nearly all that day we played round in the harbor, now lying directly before the town, and now going to the lazaretto to land freight, and in so doing, we got different views of the town and the adjoining country.

The island of Corfu is about forty miles long, and at its greatest width twenty miles across. It was mentioned by Herodotus, though under the name of Corcyra then I think, and its existence is known to have dated as far back as seven hundred and thirty-four years before the Christian era. After being subjected to many different governments, the Ionian islands are now erected into what is called "a free and independent State," under the immediate protection, however, of the English government, which maintains a garrison in every important island.

After dinner we left, and then we glided along a narrow channel, the rugged coast of Albania on the one hand, and the diversified shore of the island on the other. On the mainland we occasionally saw an old town and a bright green patch, but on the island the whole country seemed fertile and well cultivated. The sun went down just as we were off the north end of the island, and then the ocean once more swept before us, though the coast of Albania was still on our right, and as the twilight deepened, the mountains in their robes of purple hue, could scarcely be distinguished from the clouds that hovered over them.

Nearly all day Monday, we were in the broad Adriatic, entirely out of sight of land, till towards evening, when we caught a glimpse of a low range of hills. The sea was of the loveliest blue, and the air was delightfully refreshing and invigorating. The hot breath of the East and the South seemed to be left far behind, and we began to realize we were approaching the cooler regions of the North.

Yesterday we skirted the shore of Dalmatia and Istria, and had enchanting views of pretty islands, and fertile fields, and smiling villages, backed by a range of dark mountains. Some of the scenes were exquisite. While we were at dinner, we came in sight of the ruins of Pola, and we all made a rush for the deck, and saw before us an immense amphitheatre of reddish stone, and scattered here and there over the shore, large pillars and broken columns.

One of the prettiest features of the scene yesterday, was the boats we were constantly meeting, having sails of a dark yellow color, each sail with a large cross painted on it.

From the time we came on board "L'Egitto," the most exciting topic of conversation was the question whether we should be obliged to perform quarantine or not at Trieste, and what would be the length of our imprisonment in the lazaretto? and although it was nearly eleven when we arrived here last night, I could not think of going to bed till the important question was settled. To our great joy, before the anchor was dropped in the harbor of Trieste, a small boat came alongside, and we heard the delightful response of "no," to the captain's question "is there quarantine?" Late as it was, the greater part of the passengers came on shore, but we preferred to stay on board, and came off about seven this morning. I told J. if you had been here you would have been off by sunrise, but I take everything as easily as possible.

Trieste is situated, as you know, at the head of the gulf of Trieste, and its capacious harbor holds vessels from all parts of the world. The town lies in a semicircular form around the gulf, while it is backed by a lofty range of green mountains, along whose slopes appear many a pretty village and charming country-seat. We are at the Hotel Eliseo, and while we were waiting for breakfast, I commenced this letter. After breakfast we took a carriage and drove through several streets, which we found wide, well paved and adorned with handsome houses of white stone. Indeed so large and fine looking are the houses, that we were constantly wondering where the poor people lived.

In the principal streets the shops were fine, and I had to stop many times to admire the tempting goods. A crowd of people was in the streets in all sorts of costumes, the Greek in his becoming fustinella, the Italian lady in her gay attire, and the bare-headed and barefooted German and Swiss women, many of them carrying immense loads on their heads and backs.

We rode to the top of one of the mountains that environ the city, and had a splendid view of the far-reaching Adriatic in front, and hills and mountains rising up in the back-ground, spotted with vineyards and pleasant fields. I cast many a longing look across the gulf, where I supposed fair Venice to lie, and longed once more to see that "city of a hundred isles," but we have not the time, as we must press on towards the North. Our seats are already taken in the diligence for Adelsberg, and at six we must be off. Our luggage must now go to the custom house to be examined and sealed up, to escape undergoing a rigid examination at Vienna, and I have time to add no more.

LETTER LXII.

Diligence.—Grotto of Adelsberg.—Laibach.—Railroad.—Beautiful Country.—Arrival at Vienna.

VIENNA, Aug. 19th.

MY DEAR F.:

It is raining fast, and I cannot go out, and having just refreshed ourselves with looking over a package of fifteen letters from our dear home, I turn my thoughts towards you, and commence at this early period after our arrival here, to give you an account of our journey hither. It seemed strange, after an interval of thirteen years, to find ourselves once more in a diligence, though much smaller this one was than those we were formerly accustomed to in France. We soon left Trieste behind us, and began to ascend the mountain, and for more than two hours we were constantly on the rise, each turn giving us a more extensive view of the city below, and the sea beyond.

Our diligence was small, carrying two persons in the coupé, four in the *intérieur*, and four in the rotund. We were in the *intérieur*, two Germans, a man and a woman, being our companions. Night came on, and I settled myself in my corner to sleep, and, with occasional wakings, slept quite nicely till little past two, Thursday morning, when we arrived at Adelsberg. There we found the inn full, and we were shown into the coffee-room, to wait till a man could go out and procure us lodgings. Late as it was, we found three men sitting round a table, playing cards, a pile of money before them, showing to what extent they had been gambling. They were a hard looking set, I can tell you.

At three o'clock, we were in good soft German beds, and at nine we went back to the hotel, had our breakfast in a room where at least a dozen men were smoking, and then we prepared for our visit to the celebrated grotto of Adelsberg. A walk of nearly a mile brought us to a mountain, in the side of which is the opening into the grotto. At the entrance we waited a while for the guides to go in before and light up some of the chambers. All due preparation being made, we at last commenced our subterranean tour. I had heard so much of this wonderful grotto, from some of our fellow-travellers in the East, that I had fully made up my mind to be disappointed, but in this expectation I was disappointed myself, for it certainly proved to be a most magnificent affair. For more than two hours we wandered about in the bowels of the earth, and when we ended our walk, we were told we had not half explored the cave. In fact, no one seems to know how far it extends under the mountains, but it is supposed ten miles at least. Parties have started to explore it, taking provisions with them, and after being there for more than two days, have returned without finding the extremity. The guides had arranged the lights to show the different chambers to the best possible effect, and the number and variety of these chambers exceed all belief. At one time we seemed to be among the aisles of an immense Gothic church; at another, in a dimly lighted sculpture gallery, surrounded by figures of every form and size; now we stood in front of a huge pulpit, with a heavy, old-fashioned sounding-board hanging over it; and now we walked in a garden, every crystal seeming to be shaped like some fruit or vegetable. Here we almost groped along a dark passage, a foaming torrent dashing along far beneath our feet, the darkness, and the roar of the rushing water rendering the scene fearfully grand. This stream is supposed to be the same as the Unz, which bursts forth from the mountain several miles beyond, pieces of wood thrown into the stream, at its entrance into the grotto, being seen ten or twelve hours afterwards in the Unz.

Some of the stalactites that adorn these chambers are immense, being as large as many of the pillars in many churches, and it is really wonderful into how many shapes these stalactites have wreathed themselves. Now you see a figure called the Virgin Mary, and it requires no stretch of the imagination to behold a figure with a crown on her head, and holding an infant in her arms; and here you see the chair of St. Peter at Rome, with its pillared canopy. There you see a butcher's shop, with a round of beef on one side, and a flitch of bacon overhead, and here a pillar, which, on being struck, emits the sound of a bell. From the ceiling of this chamber hangs a curtain of stone, and yet so transparent that the light shows plainly through it, and along the border depends something that looks precisely like lace, so thin and fragile it seems, and yet it would require quite a blow to break it. In that room, you see stalactites arranged in regular form, like the pipes of an organ, and but a little distance off, there is quite a different formation still, resembling perfectly a waterfall.

One large cavern is called the ball-room, and in Whitsun week a ball is given here. A natural gallery at one end, adorned with a balustrade of stalactites, is for the music, while around the hall, are niches and recesses, all formed by nature, remember, which are used for supper and dressing rooms. This room was brilliantly lighted up for our examination, and it was like a scene in fairy land, those pillars and arches glittering like diamonds, and I tried to fancy how much more brilliant it would look, illuminated for the ball, lights shining from every part, and bringing into view each hidden nook and recess. And how splendidly must the music sound, echoing and re-echoing among the arches and pillars, and stealing far away into dim, obscure chambers!

Not the least striking feature of this grotto, is the variety of colors seen, one pillar being of a delicate rose tint, while another would resemble yellow alabaster. And then the crystals sparkling in the pillars, and gleaming forth in the roof of the caverns, shining here and there like stars, rendered it all perfectly radiant and dazzling. To all this beauty there was one drawback, and that was the excessive dampness that reigned every where, water constantly dropping on our heads, while the ground beneath our feet was wet and cold. The walk back to the inn, in the bright sunlight, was very pleasant, along a lane bordered with trees and gemmed with wild flowers. Adelsberg is pleasantly situated in a sheltered valley, high hills rising all around it. The houses are of stone, and look clean and comfortable.

We did one stupid thing at Trieste, for in having our luggage sealed up there for Vienna, we never thought of the two days which must elapse before we should reach this city, and of the things we might want in that time. We dared not open any of the packages, for fear of exciting suspicion on our arrival at Vienna, and so we got along as well as we could. The worst of it was, my writing desk was sealed up too, and I could not write at all, except in my note-book, which I always carry about me. Fortunately, too, we had a few books out, so the remainder of the day did not pass so very heavily. Besides, as we were to take the diligence at half past two on Friday morning, a "nap" in the afternoon did not come amiss.

The fear of not being ready when the diligence should come along, the uncertainty about our finding vacant places in it, the question constantly coming up whether we could arrive here in season to-day to receive our long expected letters, all this served to render our sleep rather broken, so that by one o'clock, we were up and dressed, in readiness to depart.

But oh! the tediousness of that long hour and a half that intervened. At last, the cracking of the whip was heard, and we hurried to the door. But the waiter would never wake up, and the key was not in the lock, and the conductor was thundering on the door! The sleepy servant at length appeared; the key was found in the wrong place; two seats were vacant in the *intérieur*, but the conductor grumbled at our luggage, and declared he could not and would not take it. At last, even this difficulty was settled; each box and bag were stowed away, and off we rattled through the streets. In a few minutes I was fast asleep, and I did not waken till the sun, vigorous body that he is, had been up a long time. Bradshaw's Guide gave but two trains leaving Laibach, one in the morning, the other in the evening, and as it was long past the hour for the morning train, we began to feel pretty sure we could not see Vienna to-day, in season to get our letters.

Fortunately, Bradshaw was wrong, for on reaching Laibach, at ten o'clock, we found a train would start at noon, going through in eighteen hours. Not having eaten any thing since four o'clock the day before, we plunged into a breakfast with a hearty appetite, having first washed and "prinked" in a room given up for our special use, in the depot. And I could not but think what a capital thing it would be, if in our immense depot at home some rooms could be fitted up, where weary travellers could thus refresh themselves, and get a little nap, while waiting to go on by another train.

Punctual to the moment, we were off at twelve, a man sounding a horn, the whistle answering the signal, and then away we went. What a novelty to be on a railroad! Just ten months to a day since we went down from London to Southampton, and that was the last time we were on a railroad. The country was lovely, so green and so fresh, so fertile and so well cultivated. The road lay through a valley, along a rapid river, high mountains hemming us in on both sides. Green and wooded, these mountains were to their very summits, often crowned by a picturesque looking church, or fortress-like castle. Such pretty houses, too, we passed, belonging to the railroad, and occupied by men employed on the road, every house having its little plat of flowers, and often a rustic little arbor. And the people looked clean and healthy, and seemed industrious and happy. Soon after leaving Laibach, we met with an accident, I don't know what, for it was raining fast, and no one cared to get out to see, but I think the breaking of a wheel, and there we had to wait three long hours, till the broken carriage was taken off the track, and we were once more ready to move on.

The carriage we were in was very comfortable, having high-backed seats to rest the head against, and I slept very soundly till morning. How magnificent was the scene when I awoke! Higher and higher rose the mountains, some of them craggy and bare, and the road wound through ravines, passing over gorges and precipitous descents, now darting through a long tunnel, and now spanning a fearful height, by a bridge of immense length and strength.

I cannot tell you how much we enjoyed this ride. The contrast between this country, so green, so fertile, and those through which we long travelled in the East, was startling in the extreme. Never in Erin's Emerald Isle were there fields clothed in a lovelier green than those we saw between Laibach and Vienna.

For an hour or two, before reaching this city, the mountains receded, and the plain grew broader and broader, every inch of the ground cultivated and rich as a garden. In fact, for miles it seemed like one vast vegetable garden, not a fence or a hedge to be seen, dividing one field from another.

Never was there a quieter entrance into a large city than our entrance into Vienna. In fact, so little did I see around me that looked like a city, I doubted for a long time whether we had arrived, and I did not stir from my seat till every passenger had left the carriage we were in. A porter took our luggage to the door of the depot; there we found carriages, and jumping into one, were soon on our way to the Golden Lamb, recommended to us by our good friend Mr. R.

At the barrier we were stopped for our pass, the passport having been taken from us two or three hours before, and a pass given us instead, and then the seals of our luggage were examined, and we were allowed to pass on. And this was the formidable entrance I had so long dreaded, into the Austrian dominions! The examination of luggage was not an hundredth part so strict as I thought it would be, not beginning to compare with that we underwent on our arrival in England.

It was raining fast, and I could see but little of the streets through which we passed, but after an interminable ride, as it seemed to me in my hungry state, we arrived at our hotel, which is situated in the suburb called Leopoldstadt. A capital breakfast, and good news from home, refreshed us, and as soon as the weather will admit, we shall be ready for sight-seeing, upon which I enter with new zest after my long rest at Buyukdere and Athens.

I can't tell you how strange it seems to see chambermaids about, for with the exception of the two weeks we were at Jerusalem, the care of our rooms has always devolved upon men ever since we left London. How near home seems to me, when in three weeks from the time a letter was written, I am reading it. But the weather seems to be clearing up, and so I am off for a walk.

LETTER LXIII.

Situation of Vienna.—Walls.—Glacis.—Suburbs.—St. Stephen's Church.—Companions in Sight-seeing.—Belvedere Palace.—Lower Belvedere.—Ambras Collection.—Church of the Capuchins.—Hotel.—Imperial Palace.—State Carriages.—Schonbrunn.—Dinner in the open air.—The Prater.—Gardens.

VIENNA, Aug. 22d.

MY DEAR FRIENDS:

According to my usual custom, before entering upon any account of this city, I shall give you a little idea of its situation. Though Vienna is said to lie on the Danube, the river is about two miles from the city, but a branch of it runs directly in front of our windows, and a dirtier looking little stream I would not wish to see. Vienna derives its name from the Wien, an insignificant river which runs through a part of the city, or rather through the suburbs.

If you had a good plan of this city to refer to, you would give your assent to some writer's remarks, that the situation of Vienna, and the arrangement of the streets, might be compared to a spider's web, the centre of the web being the "place" around St. Stephen's Church, from which all the streets radiate, to the walls of the city, and thence, across what is called the "Glacis," to the suburbs.

The city itself, not large in circumference, is surrounded by a high wall, so thick that the top of it is arranged as a walk, and forms one of the numerous promenades of the inhabitants. Within so small a compass is the city collected, that one can walk with ease completely around it in less than an hour. But the suburbs are large, and extend over far more ground than the city itself, from which they are separated by a wide, open space, planted with trees and carpeted with the richest grass. This is what is called the Glacis, and was originally a part of the fortifications. Like the parks of London, this spot may be termed "the lungs" of this city, for here the inhabitants come to breathe the pure fresh air. The number of inhabitants within the city and the suburbs is estimated at four hundred and eighty thousand. And now let me proceed to other themes. I have written to you so fully from the East, that I shall merely glance at what I see in this part of Eur̀ope, or my "Budget" would swell to an interminable length. And so for sight-seeing in Vienna.

After it had ceased raining on Saturday, we went out to take a little stroll. Crossing the bridge built over the arm of the Danube, and passing through a massive gate, we entered at once the busy streets of the city, paved with large flat stones, but without any sidewalks, so that in my eagerness to look into the shop windows, I was in constant danger of being run over. Compared with the cities of the East, the streets of Vienna are wide; compared with those of more modern towns in the Western world, they are narrow. The houses are of stone, from four to six stories high, and some of the shops are very elegant, and I may add, exceedingly tempting.

Suddenly emerging into an open space, we stood before a magnificent cathedral, in the richest Gothic style, ornamented with towers and a spire and a wilderness of delicate fretwork, its high peaked roof being covered with colored tiles, arranged in fanciful mosaics, so as to form the Austrian eagle. I needed not to enquire its name, for I was sure it could be no other than St. Stephen's.

Its appearance is grand and imposing in the highest degree, and, rich in historical associations, and a perfect gem of architecture, we were exceedingly interested in it. We entered the church; it was the hour of evening prayer, and a number of people were kneeling here and there, each one repeating the prayers in a loud tone. We silently paced up and down the nave, and at every turn stopped to gaze with new zest on the "long drawn aisle," with its massive pillars and ornamented arches, and delicate tracery. Through the windows of richly stained glass, the softened light fell, gilding altars, and tombs, and chapels and statues with a matchless radiance. How lovely, how exquisite it was! But even with all this effulgence of beauty before me, my mind often wandered to a far humbler church, having the same name, in my own distant home, and I sighed to think how far the two St. Stephen's were from each other.

The first foundations of this church were laid more than seven hundred years ago, though it was not finished till the fifteenth century. Its length is three hundred and forty-five feet, and the width, from one arm of the cross to the other, two hundred and thirty. The spire, or south tower, is four hundred and forty-four feet high, and is a conspicuous object from every part of Vienna. It is a perfect specimen of a Gothic spire, tapering off beautifully, and adorned with a profusion of arches and buttresses.

We have since been to the top of the spire, and I may as well tell you about it now, as to wait for it to come in in its proper place. We went up by five hundred and thirty steps, and I thought I should have dropped down with fatigue before we reached the top. Round and round, and up and up we went, till my head ached as badly as my feet. We stopped, however, several times, to see different objects of interest, the great bell, weighing three hundred and eighty tons, made from nearly two hundred pieces of cannon, taken from the Turks in their last siege of the city, and the room for the fire watch, stationed there day and night, to watch for fires, and to inform by signals in which part of the city one has broken out.

The view from the top of the spire was magnificent. The city, the green band that encircles it, the surrounding suburbs, lay at our feet, and beyond, stretched the beautiful country, green fields and high hills, while the waters of the Danube glistened here and there, as the river meandered through the rich valley. The eye, too, can take in Napoleon's battlefields of Loba and Wagram, Aspern and Essling. It was a toil to reach the summit of the spire, but I thought not of the stairs, when I was gazing at the vast prospect spread out before me.

On Sunday, it rained pouring all day, and I did not leave the hotel, to my great regret, as there is an English church here, and I should have liked so much to have attended it.

One of our letters from home announced to us that our fellow townsman, Mr. P., had sailed for Europe. J. thought he saw him the morning we arrived here, and on sending to the Police office, we found not only that he was in this city, but the name of the hotel where he was staying. And now he and a young friend of his from Boston are our companions in sight-seeing.

It was so long since we had seen any fine paintings, that our steps were turned first, on Monday morning, towards the Belvedere Palace, which was built by Prince Eugene, and where he resided during the latter part of his life. It is situated in the midst of a park-like garden, and it was with difficulty I could leave the lovely picture without, to gaze on other beauties within. We went through room after room, lined with paintings from the Italian, Venitian, Flemish, Dutch, German and other schools, and though the collection is inferior to many galleries I saw in Italy, I found a good many gems of beauty. But I will not dwell upon them more at length, for fear of wearying you, and of filling up this sheet too much.

Passing down a part of the garden, along a sheltered walk, shaded by lofty trees, through which we caught glimpses of shorn lawns, dotted o'er with beds of flowers, we came to what is called the Lower Belvedere, where is the Ambras collection of antiquities, so named from the castle of Ambras, in Tyrol, where it was originally placed. Let me see what I put down in my note-book, that particularly interested me.

Some sarcophagi, covered with hieroglyphics, brought from Egypt, statues and urns, found in different places; and a large collection of ancient armor, among which those that pleased me the most were the suits of Francis I. of France, a full suit of armor for man and horse, bearing the imperial arms, and belonging to the Emperor Maximilian; a steel skirt, fluted, and looking like the fustinella of the Greeks, belonging to Albert the Bear, Elector of Brandenburg, and a magnificent suit ornamented with gilded bas-reliefs, which was once worn by Alexander Farnese, Duke of Parma. The saddle and bridle were adorned with splendid turquoises. Besides these, we saw, the tomahawk of Montezuma, the horse-tail standard of the Grand Vizier, Kara Mustapha, the banner and weapons of Stephen Fadinger, the leader of the insurgent peasantry in 1626; guns inlaid with ivory and adorned with rare old carvings; a crossbow, with etchings in ivory on the stock, done by Albert Durer, and bearing his monogram beneath; a collection of curious old portraits and pictures; a stag's horns, enclosed in the trunk of a tree; specimens of rich carvings in wood and ivory; tables of inlaid woods, highly polished; miniature cabinets, adorned with pearls and precious stones; ancient musical instruments, many of them now quite out of date, in fact, unknown in modern times; a set of the most charming little toys, made for the children of Francis I. of France; the "dearest little" cradle of wood, inlaid with ivory, used by the children of Prince Ferdinand; and dozens of other curiosities, of which I could not stop now even to give the names.

Next we turned our steps to the Church of the Capuchins, in the vaults of which are seventy coffins, containing different members of the imperial family. Some of these coffins are of bronze, and the rest are of lead, except that of Joseph I., which is of silver. A few are elaborately carved, while the remainder bear simply a cross and the name of the deceased. Three particularly interested me; those of Maria Theresa and her husband, an immense sarcophagus of lead, adorned with statues as large as life, and bas-reliefs representing different cities in their dominions; and the plain coffin of Maria Louisa and the Duke of Reichstadt, wife and son of Napoleon Bonaparte. All unused as I am to weeping over the woes of those unknown to me except by fame, I could not help my eyes filling with tears, as I stood by the coffin of the unfortunate Duke, and thought over the melancholy events of his short life. Born to a throne, he died a prisoner in deed, though not in name, and now he sleeps in this cold, damp vault, beside his mother and his mother's kindred, far away from the ashes of him whose proud heart once doted upon him with such o'erpowering love.

To this cold, dark tomb came Maria Theresa, every Friday, for thirteen years, to weep and pray beside the coffin of her husband, and here, at last, she was borne, and laid by his side, one coffin sheltering both. Do you remember the childish enthusiasm with which, years ago, I used to read every thing I could find about this celebrated Empress? Imagine, then, how this enthusiasm has been renewed, when all around me I see portraits and relics of her, and, at last, have stood beside her very coffin.

Once more the heavens opened, and the rain poured down, and we were glad to give up sight-seeing, and to come home for our dinner. This hotel here is conducted on quite a different plan from those we have known in the East, and I am told all the hotels throughout Germany are on the same plan. There is no "table d'hote," but every body orders from a "carte" what he wishes to eat, and is charged accordingly. Thus, if a person's wishes are moderate, he may live very cheaply in this country. We have a double bedded room, for which we pay two florins a day; our breakfasts cost about two florins, and our dinners three. A florin is about forty-four cents our money, and thus it costs little more than three dollars a day for two persons, which is not dear for a first class hotel in a large city like Vienna. Candles are extra; they cost us at the rate of seven or eight cents an evening; but even with this addition, all our hotel expenses may be brought within three dollars and a quarter a day.

I dwell upon these little particulars, because one hears so much about the cheapness of living in Austria, Germany, &c., though at the same time I ought to say, by having plainer and less expensive dishes than we do, one could live at a much cheaper rate.

This morning, to our great joy, the sun shone out brightly, and we once more set off to view the lions of Vienna, and as it was necessary to have a clear sky for the purpose, we went up into the spire of St. Stephen's, an account of which I have already given you. We next went to the Imperial Palace, but we could not gain admission; we tried the Treasury, where the crown jewels are kept, and met with equal success, so we turned our steps to the imperial carriage house, where we saw carriages of almost every shape and size, from the small buggy in which the Emperor himself sometimes drives, to the magnificent state coach, resplendent with gilding and carving and crimson velvet. There are about a dozen of these state coaches, and the gilding alone on them cost more than a half million dollars. What do you think of that? Some of the sleighs were very beautiful; one of them, shaped like a Roman car, and covered with gilding, Maria Theresa herself used to drive out in. The imperial establishment, in all, consists of six hundred carriages, quite sufficient, one would think, to satisfy the desires of one family.

In Vienna, it is useless to attempt to see any thing between twelve and two; every thing is shut up, for every body goes home to dinner. At first it seemed very strange to me to see so many of the shops closed, and for us, who do not dine till five or six, it is a very inconvenient arrangement, but we are obliged to submit to it. Finding we could see nothing more for two hours, and the weather being so very pleasant, we took a carriage and went out to Schonbrunn, one of the summer palaces of the Emperor, two or three miles distant from the city.

The palace stands within an immense park, diversified with winding walks, beautiful lawns, clumps of trees, and plats of flowers. We were conducted over the palace by a veteran, who seemed to have the whole history of Austria at "his fingers' ends," and we could understand him quite easily, for it seemed to me his German was like broken English, when spoken by one having a hot potato in his mouth. As usual, I shall only tell you about the rooms that particularly interested me. In this palace, Napoleon took up his abode in 1805 and 1809, and in a large hall, he was standing talking with his Marshals, when a German student fired at him from without, and we saw the hole over the window, made by the ball. Here were many things which spoke to us of Maria Theresa; the room where she used to dine, waited upon by her ministers, the dishes being handed up through openings in the floor; a screen and a stool worked by her own hands, and the furniture of one entire room, consisting of two sofas, two divans, (the four having ten pillows,) and four stools covered with silk, all from one dress of hers. When this was told me, I marvelled greatly at it, but when I saw in another room a portrait of the Empress, in a dress rising, from the stiffness of her hoops, almost to her ears, and swelling out to a prodigious rotundity, lengthened out, moreever, by an immense train, I no longer wondered that the silk of one dress could cover so many pieces of furniture.

The walls of another room were covered with paintings representing the marriage of Joseph II. to the Duchess of Parma. All the figures portrayed there being portraits, dressed in the costumes of the day, we found them exceedingly interesting. One of the pictures represented the entrance of the bridal party into Vienna, in which there were eighty coaches, each drawn by six horses. What a display that must have been! Another picture represented the family of Maria Theresa, among whom were grouped thirteen Kings and Queens, all descended from her. A royal family, truly!

Nor was the unfortunate Maria Antoinette forgotten, for here we saw a series of beautiful paintings done by her, bearing her initials in one corner. Nor were these all that interested us. Here we saw the chamber occupied by Napoleon, and the bed on which he slept, where afterwards in 1832, (I think,) his son died. A writing desk stood in one corner of the room, and there Napoleon often sat and wrote, and there the Duke of Reichstadt wrote his last letter to his mother. How vividly these things brought before us the departed great! I really don't know when I have been more interested than in visiting this palace. The mighty years that have rolled on since these royal personages passed away were as nothing, for I seemed to stand in their immediate presence, and to see them face to face.

We spent an hour or two rambling through the garden, now pausing to see the myriads of gold fish in a pretty pond, and now stopping to notice a beautiful avenue of stately trees, or to admire the velvet smoothness of the lawn. At the upper end of the garden is a little temple called the "Gloriette;" and from the roof of it is one of the most lovely views the eye ever beheld. Around us lay the beautiful park, trees and flowers and green lawns, all blended so perfectly, and away stretched the rich country, till it was bounded by the distant hills on the one hand, and Vienna, with its countless roofs and beautiful spires, on the other.

In another part of the garden are the wild animals, monkeys, birds, &c., and although we have seen larger collections in Paris and London, we stopped a while to look at these.

We dined at Schonbrunn, in a large garden attached to a café there, and while we sat under the trees, and ate an excellent dinner, a band was discoursing most eloquent music. How much I enjoyed this life in the open air, and for the thousandth time I said "why cannot our people at home have pleasures like these?".

After we came back to Vienna, we drove along the Prater, one of the fashionable places of resort for the Viennese. A broad road, bordered with trees, extends for miles beyond the city, and on either hand are green meadows, dotted beautifully with clumps of trees, where on Sundays and holidays, the people come in crowds to amuse themselves. Farther on is a deer park, and here we saw a number of those beautiful animals, browsing and gambolling about.

We ended the day by a visit to one of the gardens near the Palace, where we saw hundreds of well dressed people sitting on benches and around little tables, the ladies having their work, and sewing and chatting, eating and drinking, they seemed the very picture of sensible enjoyment, while groups of children were playing games under the trees. In different parts of the garden bands of music were stationed, and sitting down before a little table, I ate an ice while J. drank a cup of tea, the strains of music falling delightfully on our ears.

But this is quite enough for one letter, so I will say "good night" to you.

LETTER LXIV.

Copy of Last Supper.—Monument of Archduchess Christina.—Imperial Library.—Cabinet of Minerals.—Arsenal.—Dance.—Imperial Printing Office.—Polytechnic Institution.—Public Garden.

VIENNA, Aug. 25th.

MY DEAREST P.:

All day out seeing " sights and wonders," and every evening and early every morning, jotting down what I see, I have not a particle of leisure. And yet, busy as I am, I enjoy every moment. But much as I delight in the pleasures of sight seeing, I assure you I shall not be sorry when, our journey over, I find myself on the way to my own loved land again. Strange as it may seem to you, I did not think half so much of my home, when far away in the East, as I do now, when I am comparatively so near it. Should I live to see all I love on earth once more, I defy the whole world to produce a happier person than I shall be. But I must not run on in this way, or I shall quite forget where I am, so I will tell you what we have been seeing the last three days.

In one of the churches in this city, is a beautiful picture in mosaic, done by the order of Napoleon, a copy of the celebrated "Last Supper" of Leonardo da Vinci. It is a master piece of art, worthy of the great original.

In another church is the monument of the Archduchess Christina of Saxe Teschen, by Canova, perfect in design and in execution. It consists of a pyramid of gray marble, about thirty feet high, placed against the wall of the church. An opening like a door, in the centre of the pyramid, represents the entrance into the vault, and before it stand two groups, in attitudes most striking and impressive. The first in advance, bears the urn containing the ashes of the deceased, and by her side walk two young girls, with torches in their hands. Ascending the steps of the pyramid appears the figure of Benevolence, supporting on her arm a man bent almost double with age and infirmities, his tattered garments hanging in disorder about his withered limbs. Beside him stands a little child in touching attitude, his hands clasped before him, his head drooping, and his long robe flowing loosely around his feet. Never was there a lovelier contrast than that between this tottering old man and the fair gentle child. It is old age and innocent childhood in perfection. On the other side of the entrance into the vault reposes a lion, and near him sits a figure representing desponding Genius, the wings drooping, the face full of sadness and grief. All these figures are as large as life, and admirably well done; in short the monument may be considered as one of Canova's master pieces, and again and again I returned to look at it.

In a chapel in the rear of this church, are the hearts, contained in silver urns, of the different members of the Imperial family of Austria, while their bodies repose in the vaults of the Capuchin church.

Of course we made another effort to visit the Palace, and to see the crown jewels, but still without success, so we turned our steps towards the Imperial library, which contains four hundred thousand volumes and sixteen thousand manuscripts. Among these last, we found many interesting relics of olden times, extending from the fourth to the sixteenth century, among which were the prayer book in gold letters, of Charlemagne; a Greek testament of the thirteenth century, collated by Erasmus, Tasso's "Jerusalem delivered," in his own hand-writing; a roll of Mexican hieroglyphics, presented to Charles V. by Cortez, and a number of other things interesting to look at, but perhaps a great deal of the interest would be lost in narration, so I will not trouble you any further on this subject.

Let me see, where did we go next? Oh, to the cabinet of minerals, and here I can assure you I was deeply interested, though my own little collection at home suffered in comparison with this extensive one. Here marbles, crystals, quartz, precious stones, petrifactions, &c., shone in all their wealth of beauty and of richness, and I sighed more than once to think my limited means could not procure some similar specimens. Here too, we saw a large collection of meteoric stones, which have fallen from the heavens in different parts of the globe. One immense piece, weighing seventy-one pounds fell in 1751 near Agram. This is no hoax, for it was actually seen to fall by some peasants. A bouquet of flowers, composed of precious stones, belonging to Maria Theresa, attracted a good deal of attention, both from its richness, and because it belonged to her.

A long walk brought us to the Imperial arsenal, and here we saw a large collection of ancient armor, and guns and pistols to the amount of three hundred and fifty thousand, arranged in fantastic forms; sometimes representing the arms of Austria, at others, different parts of fortifications, &c. The objects of interest to us were an iron chain of eight thousand links, thrown across the Danube near Buda, by the Turks in 1529, to hinder the navigation of the river; a coat of elk skin, worn by Gustavus Adolphus at the battle of Lutzen, having a small hole in the back, made by the bullet which caused his death; the balloon used by Marshal Jourdan to reconnoitre the Austrian army; a large number of standards taken from the French, the Italians and the Turks, among which was the green banner of the Prophet, taken by John Sobieski in 1683, and a variety of orders worn by emperors and generals and other military heroes.

All these things being duly seen and registered in my note book, I was quite ready for one, to give up sight seeing for the remainder of that day. In the evening, we went to a café in the suburbs, much frequented by the mechanics and trades-people, milliners and dress-makers of Vienna, and here in a large hall, plentifully adorned with supper tables, dozens of couples "tripped the light fantastic toe," an orchestra at the other end of the hall giving excellent music. Most of the dresses were in good taste, and some of the dancers acquitted themselves very well. All fortified themselves first by a supper, more or less light, and between the intervals of the dances, beer, good, wholesome German beer, was drunk in abundance, and cigars plentifully indulged in by the male portion of the dancers. I was much pleased with a group that sat around a table near us, consisting of the father and mother and three young daughters. I at first looked on with astonishment at the supper they were eating, and I doubted whether much agility could be displayed in the dancing line, after such feats in eating. But soon, first one and then another were whirling round in the giddy waltz, and I did not see but their feet moved as nimbly as though their stomachs had not been well supplied with substantial food. When a partner came to solicit the honor of the hand of one of the young ladies, he first bowed to the father and mother, and then to the maiden, and when he led her back to her seat he kissed her hand.

During the pauses in the dances, the waiters darted back and forth, with mugs of foaming beer, and plates of cold ham and chicken, and other good things, and after a few moments devoted to eating and drinking, the music again struck up, and away flew the flounces, as round and round went the gay couples. Altogether it was a pleasant scene of good homely enjoyment, and as long as they liked it, why should we find fault with them?

Yesterday and to-day it rained again; in fact it has rained every day but one since our arrival at Vienna. I regret this the more because the beauty of Vienna is its environs, which abound in pretty gardens and parks, not seen to good advantage in a heavy rain, to say nothing of their being quite deserted by the crowds who throng them in pleasant weather.

We visited with much pleasure the Imperial printing office, an immense establishment, having in constant employ eight hundred men, and keeping fourteen steam engines in operation. Here are types for two hundred and six different languages, and besides the vast amount of printing done here, photography and lithography are carried on in all their branches. Dr. Auer, the director of this establishment, has lately invented a "natural self-printing process," by which flowers, leaves, mosses, patterns for embroideries, &c., can be engraved very easily and very beautifully. Unfortunately we were there at the hour the workmen were dismissed for their dinner, and therefore could not see the method of taking these impressions, but it was explained to us in a very able and scientific manner.

We went to the polytechnic institution, another large establishment under royal patronage. Here, besides a vast number of models of different machines, bridges, engines, steamboats, &c., we saw specimens of all the different manufactures of the country, for the last three hundred years. This was exceedingly interesting to us, as not only giving us an insight into all the manufactures, but also enabling us to see collected together, some of the most beautiful productions of art, such as magnificent specimens of porcelain and glass, rich carvings in wood and ivory, and a thousand other things that I have not time to enumerate. Among the articles, curious for their minute size, I cannot forbear mentioning a chess-board, about one inch square, of pearl and ebony, the set of men for which was contained in a cherry stone; and yet each piece, minute as it was, was perfectly carved.

The clouds having dispersed toward the close of the day, we took a walk yesterday after dinner, around the ramparts, ending our walk in the public garden, in which is the temple of Theseus, built after the model of that in Athens. Here I sat down on a seat between two ladies, diligently engaged in knitting, and as I looked on with interest to watch the manner in which they throw the thread over with the fore finger of the left hand, instead of the right as with us, one of them accosted me very politely, though in broken English. From talking of the difference between English and German knitting, our conversation glided into other subjects, till at last I mentioned how much pleased I was with the beautiful gardens and parks about Vienna, and to find too they were so much appreciated by the inhabitants as to be frequented by them in such numbers. She told me in fine weather she came to the gardens every afternoon at three o'clock, and staid till seven at least, always taking knitting or sewing with her. When I told her my countrywomen did not indulge in out of doors life, she shrugged her shoulders and said she would not like to live in such a country. I told her I hoped some time they would have more correct ideas on such subjects, and that I might live to see the day when they would, in respect to exercise and being in the open air, imitate the customs of the old country.

The streets of Vienna are brilliantly lit with gas, though a great many of the shops are closed in the evenings, the merchants and trades-men being in the gardens. Towards evening they are filled with people in all sorts of costumes, the white fustinella of the Greek, mingling with the short gowns and tight jackets of the peasant women. One particular feature of Vienna is that the signs of the shops in addition to the names of the occupants, are painted to give you an idea of the contents within. And the paintings are well done too, not daubs, as sometimes seen in our streets, but remarkably well executed.

To-morrow we go into Hungary for a little excursion, and after that we shall be ready to proceed Westward and Northward.

LETTER LXV.

Excursion into Hungary.—The Danube.—Marchfield.—Presburg.—California of Hungary.—Islands.—Komorn.—Magyars.—Gran.—Vissagrad.—Pesth.—Buda.

VIENNA, Aug. 28th.

MY DEAR F.:

This is our last day in Vienna, for although we have by no means exhausted its sights, we have no more time to devote to them. As I said before, the greater part of the environs, that I should have taken so much pleasure in visiting, have been shut out from us by the weather, and although in the city there is a large number of picture galleries and museums, we have not cared to tire ourselves out in racing from one to the other. Selecting the best, we have devoted our time and attention to those, content to leave the others unvisited.

And now I will give you a brief account of our excursion into Hungary. We left here Saturday morning, at six o'clock, taking a small steamboat on the branch of the Danube which runs in front of our hotel, and going in that two or three miles, till we came into the Danube itself, where we took a large steamer. The river ran with a strong current, so that we were enabled to go down very rapidly. At first the banks were low and flat, and covered with trees, but after a while the country had more variety; along the river were well cultivated fields and thriving towns and villages, while lofty hills reared themselves in the background.

On the left bank, between Vienna and the mouth of

the river March, there is an immense plain called Marchfield, and here Rudolph of Hapsburg gained that victory over the king of Bohemia which laid the foundation of the present Imperial house of Austria. Here too, in later days, were fought other battles between the Austrians and the French, known to us as those of Aspern, Esling and Wagram. Among the multitudes of wooded islands through which we threaded our way, we could not make out which was Lobau, the scene of another of Napoleon's victories.

From the river, we saw at a little distance the birthplace of Hayden, a town called Haintz, I think, though I can't be sure, and at present I have no book of reference near me to decide the question.

The March, running into the Danube, forms the dividing line between Austria and Hungary, and on a precipitous rock, washed by the two rivers, stand the ruins of a lonely tower. Here, it is said, came, years gone by, a nun accompanied by her lover, who had snatched her away from the arms of the church. But even to this stronghold they were followed, and finding escape from their vindictive pursuers impossible, they twined their arms around each other, and threw themselves into the roaring Danube beneath, thus preferring certain death to separation.

Three hours after leaving Vienna we arrived at Presburg, formerly the capital of Hungary. It has about forty thousand inhabitants, but it presents rather an ordinary appearance from the river. Still, notwithstanding its old and dilapidated looks, it is rich in historical associations, for here occurred that interesting episode in the life of Maria Theresa, which in my earliest girlhood, had for me the charm of romance.

In 1741, when she was menaced by enemies on every side, and deserted by all her allies, Great Britain alone excepted, she came to Presburg, and calling together her Hungarian nobles, threw herself upon .them for aid. Wearing on her noble head the crown of St. Stephen, and carrying his sword, both sacred objects in the eyes of the Hungarians, and clothed in the deepest mourning, she told them the sad story of her present situation, ending her tale by boldly demanding their assistance. Who could resist an appeal like that, from a young and beautiful woman, when that woman too was their sovereign? The blood of the Magyars was fired to noble deeds; with one accord every sword was drawn, and every voice was heard as the cry of one man "Let us die for our king, Maria Theresa," for woman though she was, they called her king rather than queen.

In the old cathedral in Presburg, the kings of Hungary were formerly crowned, and every king, immediately after his coronation, went to a mound at a little distance from the town, and from the summit of it, made in the air the sign of the cross with the sword of St. Stephen, (not St. Stephen the martyr, but the first king of Hungary) waving it towards each point of the compass, as a proof of his determination to protect his dominions on every side.

For some time after leaving Presburg, the river was very wide, and the banks low, and covered with trees, and in many places walled up to prevent the ill effects from the inundations, which occur every Spring after the ice has broken up. We repeatedly saw men and women digging along the banks, and on inquiry were told they were digging for gold, this part of the country being called the California of Hungary, though gold is by no means so abundant here as there, a laborer here finding, one day with another, only about two dollars a day. The number of islands dotting the Danube, give great variety to its scenery, and render the navigation of it very difficult, the current sweeping so rapidly round some of these islands as to form a perfect whirlpool, through which at times it was exceedingly difficult to pass. We met but few boats, and occasionally saw large rafts going down the river, on which was often quite a family, a " little cubby house" being fitted up for their accommodation.

Once more the scene changed ; the trees disappeared, and rich meadow lands usurped their place, diversified here and there by a neat looking village. Then we came to Komorn, one of the strongest fortified towns in Europe, and having seventeen thousand inhabitants, almost exclusively Magyars. One Hungarian gentleman told us that these Magyars were of Asiatic origin, and formed a class of people quite distinct, living by themselves, and never intermarrying with other nations, and being moreover of rather roving and warlike propensities. Shortly after, in conversation with an Austrian who has resided for several years in Hungary, in speaking of the Hungarians he used the word Magyar. I asked him in what sense he understood the term, and he said Magyar was the word used in the Hungarian language for a Hungarian, and that at present it was used to designate any person born in Hungary, no matter of what parentage he was, just as a citizen born in America would be called an American, even if his parents were German and he could not speak a word of English. He said originally the term " Magyar" designated a tribe that probably came from Asia centuries ago, and settled in Hungary. I dwell thus long upon this subject, because lately quite a question has arisen in the United States upon the Magyars.

Again there came a change; the banks swelled up into hills, and the hills increased into mountains, some, vine-clad, and others well wooded. Among the hills lies Gran, a town of eleven thousand inhabitants, the residence of the Primate of Hungary, and said to be the richest see in the world, the revenue being two hundred thousand dollars a year.

Beyond this town the mountains swell out bold and grand, now being ragged and jagged, and now covered with vegetation to the very summit; now a half-ruined fort or a castle perched on some giddy height, gave a picturesque feature to the scene; while the river, narrow and deep, was often so hemmed in by the mountains, as to present the appearance of a beautiful lake. I very much doubt whether the vaunted Rhine can present finer scenery than this part of the Danube, and yet how seldom has it been mentioned by tourists.

Vissagrad was once a favorite resort of the sovereigns of Hungary, and here on a steep hill, are the ruins of a fine old castle, where the valiant Sigismund was once held in captivity by his powerful subjects. At the foot of this hill there is a little church, and all along the roadside leading up to it are small chapels or oratories, where the pilgrims to the church stop to offer up a prayer. I counted fourteen of these oratories. Almost hidden in a clump of trees by the water side, is another pretty little church.

This bold mountain scenery continued for some distance, and then the scene became less wild, and more lovely, verdant meadows, and vine clad hills, and wooded islands, and cultivated fields, forming a beautiful picture, such as the eye loves to rest upon. Soon we began to see Pesth, the capital of Hungary, and on the opposite side of the river, Buda, the capital at one period, and in eleven hours from the time of coming on board, we stepped once more on shore. I enjoyed the sail down the Danube very much, for every thing was new. The boat was crowded with passengers, ladies and gentlemen in their rich furs, and peasants in their homely garb, the men wearing large white trowsers, immense jackets, and broad brimmed black hats. The only drawback to my enjoyment was the weather, for it was rather too cool for comfort. While in the burning East, I languished for the cool breezes of the North, but when the cool breezes came, I sighed for the warm air and bright sun of the South and the East. Such inconsistent creatures are we, ever seeking for what we cannot have.

We found great trouble in getting lodgings that night, for the town was full of strangers, an annual fair being now held in Pesth. At last we took possession of one room, in a large hotel, but while we went to another part of the house to see what accommodations were to be had for the Messrs. P., our room was taken possession of by a party of Germans, who refused to give it up, the landlord siding with them. So once more we were cast adrift, but at length we found quarters, in what proved to be a second class inn. However, they provided us with a good supper, and we had a nice, clean room, but our friends were obliged to sleep over the stable, which did not furnish them with the best odors imaginable.

We found the streets well lighted and well paved, and lined with handsome houses of stone, but although the town was said to be so full, we met very few people. The booths along the quay were all closed, and the greater part of the shops, though it was not nine o'clock. The next day being Sunday, there seemed to be but little going on. We went to a church in the morning, where a sermon was preached in an unknown tongue to us, but the preacher seemed fervent and eloquent, and the congregation attentive and devout. The peasant women wore little jackets with large sleeves, and a short petticoat and full apron, and immense boots, thick and strong. We walked out twice, and found the streets clean and wide, and the houses of quite a superior order.

We crossed over to Buda by a handsome suspension bridge, which was opened for the first time on the fifth of January, 1849, to allow the army commanded by Kossuth to retreat, when pursued by superior Austrian forces. We walked through a part of the town, and found many of the streets grass grown, and the generality of the houses of one story, built of stone and stuccoed. The Palace, however, is a large handsome building, and in it are kept the crown jewels of Hungary, which are guarded with jealous care.

We went up the hill on which stands the old fortress, seven hundred and sixty-five feet above the level of the sea, and from this height we had a magnificent view of the two cities at our feet, of the river winding between, and of the country stretching around, a vast plain encompassing them about, except just in the rear of Buda, where are hills covered with vineyards.

We went to the "Hotel of the Queen of England,"

situated on the quay at Pesth, and had an excellent dinner at a very reasonable price. Late last night we took the railroad for Vienna, and arrived here about six o'clock this morning, greatly pleased with our Hungarian trip. Letters from home awaited our arrival, and when we read letters, written only three weeks since, it seemed as though we were almost at home.

We have devoted a greater part of the day to our arrangements for leaving Vienna, doing a little shopping, taking our last walks, and attending to that pest of all traveling business, packing trunks and carpet bags. To-morrow morning we are off at an early hour, so adieu for the present.

LETTER LXVI.

Up the Danube.—Linz.—Fine View.—Politeness.—Fertile Country.—Gmunden.—Traun-see.—Ischl.—The Emperor, Francis Joseph.—Costumes.—Beautiful Scenes.—Salt Bath.

ISCHL, Aug. 31st.

MY DEAR M:

We left Vienna at six o'clock on Tuesday morning, and after riding an interminable distance, reached the river, where we went on board a steamboat, bound up the Danube. We found the scenery on this part of the river even more varied and charming than that between Austria and Hungary. In fact, I can imagine nothing more romantic and beautiful than the banks of the Danube, and I can only repeat my expressions of wonder, that it is not oftener visited by travellers. At times, only a narrow plain intervened between the river and the mountains, which were sometimes rock-ribbed, but generally covered with woods, or terraced off into vineyards, or divided into green patches and smiling fields.

Often, on the very summit of a precipitous rock, and scarcely discernible from the rock itself, stood a strong old castle, each one having some interesting legend or historical anecdote connected with it, but which it would require more space to relate than I have at my present disposal. Two or three of them are of peculiar interest, as having been the prison abode of Richard the Lion Hearted. We found going up the river against a rapid current quite a different affair from going down, with the current in our favor, and we were not able at any time to make more than six miles an hour. And yet I did not find it at all tedious, for at every bend some new feature was presented, either a bold mountain peak or a wild ravine, a pretty town, with its church crowning the hill, or a sheltered vale, where all bore the marks of beauty and fertility. Convents and churches always occupied the most conspicuous spots, and many of these are of great renown through all the country round, the people flocking to them in crowds at certain seasons of the year.

Occasionally a steamboat would dart by us, or we would pass a raft, or a rude boat crowded with peasants, each boat bearing aloft a cross. At almost every town we stopped, so that the passengers were constantly changing. In short, what with gazing on the country, and looking at the people, reading a little and sewing a little, I had enough to occupy my attention till evening, when, so difficult is the navigation of the river, the boat "lay to" to wait for daylight, to proceed on her course. There were no berths in the cabins, and therefore no sleeping accommodations, except such as the chairs furnished. However, by spreading the thinnest possible mattress over two or three stools, a bed was provided for such as chose to pay a florin and a half for it, and among this number I was glad to be included, as I have quite enough fatigue to encounter by day, without being deprived of sleep at night.

By daylight the next morning, the boat was once more on the move, and I went on deck quite early, that I might lose nought of the lovely scenery. The mountains had receded far into the background, and the banks of the river were very low and flat, walled up in many places, to prevent damage from the rapid rise of the river in the Spring. Soon, however, the mountains once more encircled us, and the banks became varied and beautiful. Almost every town we passed on the river had its interesting historical associations, connected with the warlike deeds of some Prince or Emperor, and every church, pointing with its taper spire toward heaven, seemed to have its own tale of miracle and healing virtue.

We arrived at Linz about nine o'clock, and there we left the boat to go on its way up the river, while we pursued a different direction. The scenery about Linz is enchanting, and I only regretted we could see so little of it. Finding the train did not leave till one o'clock, we started off for a walk to the top of one of the mountains back of the town, whence, we were told, we should have a charming view.

After going through a part of the town, seeing the peasant women with their fruits and nice, sweet looking butter, and passing many handsome houses, we came to a public promenade, shaded with fine trees. On stopping to make some inquiries concerning the way, of a tall, noble looking old man, he politely offered to be our escort to the top of the mountain. He spoke French very fluently, and told us he was a Belgian by birth, but that he had lived in Linz more than fifty years.

Our road wound along up the mountain side, by vineyards and orchards and gardens, and every house we passed had plats of flowers in front, and geraniums, roses, pinks, &c., in pots in the windows. Every where here the people seem fond of flowers, and always they are arranged in an artistic manner.

Near the summit of the mountain, there is a large college belonging to the Jesuits, and an imposing church, and all along the mountain sides, villas and gardens dotted every slope. The view from the top was enchanting. The lofty mountain peaks, so dark with thick woods, the sunny slopes with their bright fields and rich vineyards, the smiling valleys stretching for miles away, the Danube glistening among green fields, and suddenly breaking through a mountain gorge beyond, the city sleeping at our feet, the white houses peeping out here and there from thick groves of trees, distant mountain ranges blending their lofty summits with the o'erhanging clouds, what a combination of beauty and grandeur did these all present! What lovely scenes there are in this world of ours! Yet how often do we shut the eyes and the heart to them!

On coming back into the town, we urged our kind conductor to go with us to a café for some refreshment, but he politely declined, and left us, though not without many thanks from all the party for his courtesy towards us. After leaving him, we lost our way in going to the railroad, and on Mr. P. (who speaks German a little) asking the direction from a gentleman, he turned to go with us, and would not leave us till we were in sight of the railroad. I record these little instances, to show the natural politeness of the people of this country.

From Linz to Gmunden, on the Traunsee, a distance of forty miles, there is a railroad, but as yet no locomotive has been put on the line, and the carriages are drawn by horses. We were seven hours going these forty miles, but the country was so lovely I did not find our progress at all too slow. Almost the entire distance, our way lay through a rich plain, well watered and well cultivated, immense fields of clover and buckwheat and potatoes stretching as far as the eye could reach. And there was not a fence to be seen, so that it seemed as though we were passing through one immense meadow. Women were at work in the fields, some of them protected from the sun by large straw hats, but the greater part of them with no covering on the head, except a silk handkerchief or a muslin cap. In many places the grass had just been cut, and the smell of the new hay was delightful. How like home it seemed, the merry hay-makers, and the mounds of green hay, and the loaded wagons!

At times we passed through large forests of dark firs, and at the end of the long vista, Traun mountain reared its head of granite, and seemed quite to shut in our path. And then other mountains appeared, but they looked green and bright, compared with the rocky mass of Traun-stein. It was almost dark when we caught a glimpse of the waters of Traun-see, glistening among the distant trees, a circle of lofty mountains hemming it completely in. When we arrived at Gmunden, lake and mountains were shrouded in darkness, and it was left entirely to our imaginations to picture the scene that might be presented by daylight.

Our supper, or dinner, rather, consisted of fish from the lake, but I have eaten as nice elsewhere, though a good appetite gave them the proper relish. We washed them down with a glass of capital German beer, which I drink every day, for two reasons; the first, because I like it; the second, because I am in hopes it will help fill out my thin cheeks, made so thin by my fatiguing Eastern journey. By five o'clock this morning, I was out of my bed, and standing at the window, gazing on the little lake spread out before me. All there lay in deep shadow, but the mountain peaks were lit up with the early beams of the sun.

From Gmunden we crossed the lake, in a small steamer, to Eben-see, a distance of nine miles. The morning was clear and cold, like our mornings in October, but the sail along the whole length of the lake was one exquisite picture. The vivid contrast between the bold granite peaks and the verdant slopes of the forest-covered mountains, the wild ravines and precipitous gorges, the little villages, nestling at the foot of the hills, the placid waters of the lake reflecting every crag and tree and shrub, the sunlight playing here and there, now gilding a mountain top, now lighting up a sheltered vale, and here and there a little stream, like a silver thread, leaping down the mountain side, formed a beautiful picture, perfect in all its parts.

Arriving at Eben-see, we chose a nice, open carriage, in preference to a close, lumbering diligence, and came on here very comfortably, a distance of twelve miles, the road running alongside of the Traun river, a wide, rapid stream, which sweeps down from the mountains beyond, and empties into the Traun-see. Here and there along the road, were little oratories, containing a small altar and pictures and wreaths of flowers, or rude crucifixes and images of Christ and the Virgin Mary. Beggars of every age and condition beset the carriage, and children ran after us for miles, clasping their little hands and beseeching us for alms. Many of the women had large goitres on their necks, like those we used to see in Switzerland, and in some of the fields we saw women wielding the scythe as skillfully as any man.

When we arrived here, we were quite ready for our breakfast, having been up more than five hours. We are at the hotel Kaiserin Elizabeth, or in plain English, Empress Elizabeth, and a capital hotel it is too, nice, clean rooms, and an excellent table and a civil and obliging landlord. As we knew the Emperor was at Ischl, we began at once to make inquiries about him, for we wished to have an opportunity to see him, if it was a possible thing. But we were told he had just left for Vienna! This was rather provoking intelligence, but fortunately it proved to be untrue, for while we were still at breakfast, we heard a great clattering in the street, and we had just time to run to the windows and see the royal carriages go by. The young Empress, whom I wished most of all to see, had passed before I reached the window; the next carriage contained the Ex-Empress and the Queen of Prussia, all in mourning for the late King of Saxony, and in the last carriage was the Emperor Francis Joseph, in a plain military undress. He is quite as youthful looking as his portraits represent him, and has a light complexion, and hair and mustache inclining to sandy. I understand he is very popular among his people, and is disposed to rule them with a just and firm, yet a gentle hand. Ischl is one of his favorite places of resort in the summer, and while here, I am told he walks and drives about in a simple, unpretending manner, coming almost daily to this hotel, where he makes himself quite at home.

The remainder of the day we have spent out of doors, returning only at five o'clock to dinner. The various walks about Ischl are delightful, and I would gladly spend a week or two here, if we had the time to spare. It is famous for its salt baths, and is a fashionable place of resort during the summer, not only for the imperial family, but for the Austrian nobility, as well as for English tourists.

Ischl lies in a lovely valley, watered by the Ischl and the Traun rivers, and is completely girded around with mountains, a few of them craggy and bare, but the greater part wooded, or divided off into green and sunny patches. Stretching up along every mountain side are beautiful country seats, and the clumps of dark trees contrast charmingly with the bright green of the meadows. Here and there, in a gorge far up some mountain peak, the snow glistens, looking cold and pure, while the valley below is bathed in warm sunshine.

We went up a mountain side, and had a delicious view of the valley, with its sparkling rivers and pretty white houses, and lovely meadows dotted over with trees, and of mountain after mountain, rising majestically around us. Through the murmur of the trees came the soft gush of a distant waterfall, and the velvet sward beneath our feet was enamelled with sweet flowers. It was very, very lovely, though I utterly despair of giving you any adequate idea of it. Wherever we turned, some new beauties unfolded, and a wild, romantic glen or a dark ravine, a towering peak or a smiling vale, had its own peculiar charm.

All the men about here wear tall, conical black hats, with a bunch of flowers on one side, or a tuft of feathers, while the women wear tight-fitting jackets, with sleeves large at the top, a skirt of different color and materials, and a full apron, reaching quite round the waist. The men are fine looking, but justice requires me to add that the women are the homeliest set I ever came across. I think there must have been some fête, for we met multitudes of peasants in holiday attire.

After dinner, we walked to the top of a hill called "Calvary Hill," near the summit of which is a church decorated with an unusual number of pictures and images, and surrounded by a multitude of shrines and oratories, before which many people were kneeling and praying. I followed a path leading far back of the church, where the trees were thick and dark around me, but through openings in them, I caught enchanting glimpses of the rich vale below. All along this path were tall crosses, or large crucifixes, each having, in addition to the image of the Saviour nailed to it, a full sized figure below, of the Virgin Mary.

Night came on solemnly and grandly amid these exquisite scenes, and as I gazed on the vale beneath me, wrapped in dark shadows, and then looked on the peaks far, far above me, shining out beautifully and clearly, in the last beams of the sinking sun, I thought of those stricken ones, who are often called to walk mournfully and sadly through the vale of life, darkened by the shadows of sin and suffering and sorrow, but while all is dark around them, the eye of faith looks up, and sees bright and sunny hills, illuminated by the blessed rays of the Sun of Righteousness. Happy, happy ones, who can look thus from earth below to Heaven above!

After we came down from the mountain, we walked to the entrance of the imperial grounds, and then came back through the streets of the town, to a promenade thickly shaded with trees, running along side of the river. I walked there till I was tired, and then both fatigue and dampness drove me to my room, where I have charmed away my fatigue by gossipping with you.

I shall long remember this day among the mountains, and hope to have a few more as pleasant in our further journey through the Tyrol. Oh! I had forgotten before to tell you I tried a salt bath this afternoon, and liked it much, better than I did a glass of the water I forced myself to drink.

And now good-bye for a while.

LETTER LXVII.

Departure from Ischl.—Open carriage.—Mountainous Country.—Wolfgang-see.—Churches.—Cemeteries.—Beggars.—Students.—Travelling Journeymen.—Salzburg.—Queen of Prussia.—Ex-Empress of Austria.—The Square.—Birthplace of Mozart.

SALZBURG, Sept. 2d.

MY DEAR P.:

We left Ischl yesterday morning in an open carriage, preferring that mode of conveyance to a close diligence, where we might be shut up with a party of smoking Germans, who smoke and spit rather more than the Americans. As there are four of us, it is quite as cheap to hire a carriage by ourselves, as to go in the diligence, and far more pleasant, for we can stop when we like, and pause on the way as long as we choose, if there are interesting objects to attract our attention.

Our road was all among the mountains, yet what more can I say of them, than of those around Ischl? I never enjoyed a day's ride more in my life, than yesterday, for we were among some of the grandest scenes of nature, high mountains and beautiful valleys, and gushing streams and fountains, and thick forests and sunny glades, and though the snow rested on many a lofty peak, we were in bright and genial sunshine, and the air was deliciously warm and invigorating.

We left Ischl about seven, though we ordered the carriage at six, and having to wait more than an hour for slow German movements, was by no means an agreeable commencement of our journey. However, when we found we could not leave here yesterday, and accomplish what we wished to, we grew more reconciled to the delay.

It was a pretty sight for the first hour or two after we started, to watch the mists as they rolled away from the mountain tops, now disclosing a patch of meadow land, now revealing a dark forest, and now enshrouding all in obscurity. Later, when the mists had disappeared, we had magnificent views of the mountains, and far away saw the glimmer of a lovely lake, called "Wolfgang-see." Clearer and clearer shone out the beauteous lake, as we approached nearer to it, and the water lay so perfectly placid that every tree and leaf were reflected distinctly as in a mirror. Our landlord at Ischl advised us to leave the carriage at that part of the lake, and row across to the other end, where the carriage would await us, but I did not fancy going so far in a small boat, so we swept around the margin of the lake, and had quite as good views of it as though we had been in a boat.

By not stopping there, however, we lost our breakfast, as there was no other good inn for several miles farther on, so that we got nothing to eat till after eleven, and by that time we were ravenous, having been up since five o'clock, without eating a mouthful.

When we stopped to breakfast, it was near a church, where some interesting service seemed to be going on, for it was crowded with the peasantry, in their very best attire, the women in large straw hats and nice jackets, and nearly every one of them having on a necklace, composed of small silver strands, fastened around the throat with an immense clasp. Every man had either a nosegay or a feather in his hat, and all, both men and women, looked the picture of health and happiness.

All along, we saw women working in the fields, or driving carts, or carrying immense burdens in baskets or tubs slung over their shoulders. In these countries, where a large standing army is kept, a great many of the men must be soldiers, while the burden of field labor rests upon the women.

Oratories and images lined the road, and beggars beset the carriage in such numbers it was impossible to give to all, without draining the purse rather too much, so I selected the old and the infirm as objects of my bounty.

Passing an ordinary looking inn, we saw under the portico a number of laborers sitting round a table, drinking beer, eating coarse bread, and smoking. One of them held a little girl in his arms, apparently between three and four years old, who had a pipe between her lips, occasionally taking quite a whiff! This is beginning life early.

The churches we passed had little cemeteries around them, filled with crosses and images, each grave having one or more, and many of them decked out with flowers beside. The churches were always open, and many a passing traveller stepped in to offer up a short prayer before a hallowed shrine. Every body we met was polite and civil to us, the men taking off their hats, the women bowing and smiling, and the children kissing their hands.

Every hour we meet numbers of men journeying on foot, knapsacks on their backs, boots and boot brushes in plain sight. Some are students, spending their vacations in going about in this cheap manner, to see the world, and as they generally stop at second class inns, where the fare is plain and unexpensive, their journey, though it is often a long one, costs them but little. The greater part, however, of these travellers are journeymen, who, before they can obtain their freedom, are obliged, according to a regulation prevailing in Germany, to travel a certain number of years, stopping at such places where they may profitably work at their trade. On their way from place to place, they are often obliged to beg from their countrymen, or from passing travellers, and they consider this no act of degradation whatever. Whenever their prescribed term of wandering has expired, they return home, when they are obliged to exhibit some specimens of their handicraft, and if this is approved by the corporation or trade to which they belong, they receive their freedom, and are allowed to do business for themselves. I have dwelt thus minutely on this national custom, because it is often alluded to by Goethe and other German writers, and because otherwise a traveller cannot account for so often being accosted by stout, healthy young men, who modestly, yet unhesitatingly ask for alms.

Through an opening in the hills, about three o'clock, we descried Salzburg, seated in a lovely plain watered by the Salz river, and surrounded by lofty mountains, from the summits of which castles, monasteries and churches, looked down upon the plain beneath. The effect of the contrast between the bright green vale, and the dark forests on the mountains, was delightful, and as we rode on, new scenes of beauty were revealed to our admiring gaze. Upon a lofty mountain, rising precipitously from the town, stands the citadel, a castle-like looking edifice, seeming of strength sufficient to defy time and change and hostile attack. A thick wall runs around the town, and the moat beyond is covered with grass of the richest green imaginable.

When we arrived at our hotel, (Golden Ship,) we found every body on the look-out, and we were told the Queen of Prussia was about to leave the town, so we rushed to a window, where we saw horses and carriages, and liveried servants and soldiers, and had ample time to look at these, as it was quite a half hour before the royal personage made her appearance, and then we had more of royalty than we had expected, for she was accompanied by the wife of the Emperor Ferdinand, who renounced the throne in 1848. Both ladies are in the decline of life, and both were dressed in mourning, in honor of the late King of Saxony. After escorting the Prussian Queen a short distance on her journey, the Ex-Empress returned to her palace, which is on one side of the square on which our hotel stands.

Opposite the hotel, is the cathedral, an imposing edifice, and on the other side of the square is the guard-house, the clock of which, at morning and evening, sends forth the most dulcet chimes imaginable. In the centre of the square is a magnificent fountain, where, from the mouths of four bronze horses, pour incessantly little streams of water, which fill the air with their soft, rippling sound.

We ordered dinner, and while it was being prepared, took a stroll to see the town, which, though only containing thirteen thousand inhabitants, covers a good deal of space. The streets are wide and well-paved, and lined with nice houses and handsome churches. One street is so entirely under a mountain, that its summit seems to hang over the roofs of the houses, producing a most singular effect.

In this town, the great Mozart was born, and the house is still shown that was honored by that event, and in a square near our hotel, a noble statue of him, in bronze, has been erected.

Some of the shops are filled with beautiful specimens of carving in wood, ivory and bone, done by the Tyrolese, into the purchase of which I should have enjoyed entering at a large expense, if I had not been hindered by prudence.

I must reserve the remainder of my remarks about Salzburg till to-morrow, so good-bye for now.

LETTER LXVIII.

Quiet Sunday.—Visit to salt mines.—Costume for the mines.—Amusing appearance.—Mode of getting the salt.—Chambers.—Inclined planes. —Wooden Horse.—Miners.—Holbrunn.—Promenades.

SALZBURG, Sept. 3d.

MY DEAREST FRIENDS:

We have spent a very quiet day to-day, going out this morning to one or two churches, where, as we could not understand the services or the preaching, we hoped we might hear some good music, but in this we were disappointed, there being no music at all in either of the churches. After dinner we walked to the top of the hill on which the citadel is built, and had an extensive view of the whole country around, Alps rising on Alps, and the beautiful vale slumbering at our feet. We saw the sun set from this elevated spot, and then came home by a winding walk through dark forests and across bright green glades. And very quiet too it was, "that Sabbath eve in summer tide." We met occasionally a group of neatly dressed people, but the usual resort on Sundays is the park of Holbrunn, or some adjoining garden.

And now I will tell you about our adventures yesterday, when we had quite an exciting day, for we visited the celebrated salt mines, a few miles distant from here, when once more I was tempted to go far into the bowels of the earth. We took a carriage to Hallein, a small town where the salt works are carried on, and then we had rather a fatiguing walk of nearly an hour up the mountain side. But nothing could exceed the charming views we enjoyed in this walk. The mountains above us, in their robes of dark green, the smiling valley below, with its sparkling river, the lovely meadows surrounding the town, gave us delicious pictures, and more than a hundred times I said, " this is the country where I would like to spend weeks, and even months."

And here I will digress a little to say that perhaps you may think it strange for us when we are pressed for time, to travel about in these mountainous regions in this slow way, when we could see so much more by going from city to city on the railroads. But as I fully believe the maxim uttered by Pope or somebody else, that " God made the country but man made the towns," I prefer the handiwork of God to that of man, and have wished to spend some of the time we have for Germany, in seeing the glorious views of nature, rather than in visiting museums filled with curiosities, and galleries of paintings, even though many of them may be the works of the great masters themselves. Man may exceed man, but nothing can ever surpass the works of God.

Arriving at the entrance of the mines we were told we must divest ourselves of our usual habiliments, and be attired in a costume adapted to the mines. To this I had no great objection, as I had done it once before in England, but when a loose jacket and trowsers were brought for me to put on, I stoutly demurred at thus disguising myself, and declared " up and down," I would not go dressed as a man. The loose sack I was willing to put on, but the trowsers I respectfully declined. I exhausted my broken German in trying to convince my female attendant they were not necessary, but all in vain. She talked fast, and perhaps convincingly on the subject, though I did not understand one word in ten that she said. At last, finding me incorrigible, she called up our French "valet de place," who politely informed me that the trowsers were indispensable, as I should be obliged to slide down several inclined planes, where petticoats, (to speak right out in plain English,) would be very much in the way. "Silenced but not convinced," I consented to put on the "unmentionables," but here a new difficulty arose. They were of white linen, which would have been rather thin for those subterranean regions, and so I was obliged to put them on over all my clothes, which was no easy job, as I was dressed for a cool day. However, by dint of rolling up in some places, and pulling down in others, I made out to get on the pantaloons, over which I wore the loose white linen jacket or sack, fastened around the waist by a leather belt, the end of the jacket making quite a respectable frill below the waist, so that altogether I flatter myself, I looked quite like a fashionable Bloomer. The effect of this unique costume was somewhat heightened by the pantaloons being tied tight around the ancle, and by my wearing on my head a coarse cap of blue cloth.

When I joined the gentlemen, I found them dressed precisely like me, with the exception that they each had on a leather apron, (not before, where aprons are generally worn,) but behind, to protect themselves while sliding down the inclined planes, and a stout glove on the right hand, with which they were to hold on to the rope while sliding. As soon as I saw the glove, I asked why I did not have one also, and was told that I was not to hold by the rope, but by the shoulder of the guide who would always precede me.

The first few minutes were spent in laughing at each other's appearance, and then we entered the mines; first a guide carrying a lantern, then one of our companions bearing a large candle, followed by my transformed self, and the two other gentlemen, the rear being brought up by another guide with a lantern. Tramp, tramp, we went through a long passage cut into the mountain and walled up, or pierced through the solid rock, our procession of white figures, looking in the dim light like a company of ghosts. Occasionally we came to places where strata of salt glistened in the rock, sometimes of a dazzling white, sometimes of a deep yellow or delicate lilac. On either hand of us was a large pipe, one for conveying fresh water into the mines, the other for carrying the salt water out. And here I will say, that the salt in these mines does not lie like pure rock salt, or in large masses, which can be quarried like stone, but is scattered along in veins and threads, mingled with clay, marl and gypsum, which are soft, and easily dissolved in water. To obtain this salt, pits and galleries are cut through the limestone rock, till the beds are reached which contain the salt, and then a small chamber is excavated, and pipes laid down to it from above, and leading out of it, but those leading out below are stopped up with valves, which can be opened and shut at pleasure. A stream of fresh water is then introduced from above into the chamber, until it is full up to the very ceiling. The water immediately attacks the sides and roof, dissolving the salt it imbibes, the clay and other matter falling to the bottom of the pool. As fast as a void is made in the chamber, more fresh water is let in, and more salt is imbibed, and this process is continued till the water is perfectly saturated with salt, and has become a strong brine. In these mines three weeks are sufficient for this process ; in some others a longer time is required, sometimes even a whole year being necessary.

Then, the pipe leading out of the chamber is opened, the mountain being tapped as it were, and the salt water is drawn off and carried in pipes to the boiling houses. When the water is thoroughly drained off, the chamber is found to have extended upwards and to have become wider by one or two feet, while the floor is considerably raised by the refuse particles deposited at the bottom. After taking out the rubbish and beating down firmly the mud and the earth, fresh water is again let in, salt is imbibed as before, and the brine made, and the process is repeated till the chamber becomes so large there is danger of its giving way, and then it is no longer used. There is a large number of these chambers in this mine, and we passed through one of them in a flat boat drawn along by a rope pulled by invisible hands. This chamber was three hundred feet long, and two hundred wide, and was lighted up by a multitude of little tapers fixed in the wall, and these were reflected in the black looking water, but failed to penetrate the darkness above our heads. This immense chamber was entirely devoid of any pillars to support the roof, and when I thought of the mountain over our heads, and the water, to the depth of seven or eight feet beneath us, I shuddered at the idea of any accident befalling us in so dreadful a place.

But I have gone a little too far ; let me return again to the gallery we first entered. Judging by the time it took us to walk through it, we thought it must have been nearly a mile in length, and although we were so far under ground, the air was remarkably pure. At last we reached one of the inclined planes down which we were to slide, far, far beyond what the eye could see. It seemed, indeed, like making "a leap in the dark." It was so dark I could not see exactly how these planes were made: all I know is, I had to put my feet over a smooth log, rest my hands on the shoulder of the guide, who was seated in like manner astride the log, holding by a firm gripe to the large rope on the right, which served to steady his course. His lantern he fastened to his waist, and after seeing that I was firm in, or rather on my seat, he darted ahead, and I followed. I scarcely dared breathe, and I only remember of thinking that I no longer wondered that trousers and a leather apron were indispensable in such a slide as that. This first descent was three hundred and fifty feet long, at an angle of between forty and forty eight degrees, and we accomplished it in a minute and a half; Was it not fearful progress?

As soon as I was on "terra firma" I paused to see my companions come down, and I can assure you it was a strange sight, first to catch a glimpse of their lanterns and white clothes peering out from the darkness, and then, before you could say "Jack Robinson," see them darting down the steep descent.

Then came other galleries and deserted chambers, and four more inclined planes, some shorter, some longer, and then we seated ourselves on what was called a "wooden horse," on which truth compels me to add we were all obliged to ride astride, and with one miner pulling before and another pushing behind, we traversed a passage cut out of the solid rock, extending more than a mile in length, and here we found the air both damp and cold. When we had gone about half the distance, the guide pointed to a glimmering star far ahead; it was the light of day peeping in at the end of the passage. Brighter and brighter grew this star, and more and more quickly our "wooden horse" darted on, till at length after more than a quarter of an hour in this last passage, we found ourselves in the open air on the mountain side, where our "valet de place" awaited us with the articles we had left in his care.

We were more than two hours in this mine, and at one time had a large church over our heads, and at another were more than two thousand feet below the surface of the earth. In different parts of the mines there are monuments of the emperor of Austria, and some other distinguished personages whose names have quite escaped my recollection. In one of the chambers we saw some beautiful crystals and petrifactions, some of them of very large size, which have been found at times in the mines. These mines are so very extensive that the guide told us it would require more than a week to go over them. They extend quite beyond the Bavarian frontier, but Austria alone has the right of working them.

The miners go to their work at six o'clock in the morning, and work till noon, when they are relieved by another set of hands, who work till six in the afternoon, so that the labor of the miners is by no means hard. These mines yield a great revenue to the government, producing annually on an average six hundred thousand quintals of salt.

They are of very ancient origin; in fact the date of their origin is lost in obscurity, though it is proved to a certainty that they were in existence more than twelve hundred years ago, being known not only to the Romans, but to the nations that preceded them.

On our way back to the village we went into one of the boiling houses, where we saw the process of converting the brine into salt. Then we had a lunch of bread and butter, honey and beer, after which, refreshed in body and mind, we started on our homeward way. About three miles before reaching here, we stopped to visit the park and chateau of Hollbrunn, once belonging to one of the powerful archbishops of Salzburg, but now the property of the Emperor of Austria, who rarely visits it however, (in fact the chateau is entirely unfurnished) preferring to stay at the Palace in Salzburg, whenever he visits this part of the country.

The grounds are very extensive, and abound in lovely scenes, and the view from the upper story of the chateau is magnificent, taking in at one glance the valley of the Salza, and its surrounding mountains. The fountains are more extensive and varied at Hollbrunn, than any I have ever seen, and I could not give you a full account of them without going into a most elaborate description, and so I will just mention a few of them. In a grotto there is a figure surmounted by a crown; the man who has charge of the water works turns a crank, a stream of water gushes from the figure, raising thereby the crown into the air to the distance of fifteen or twenty feet. In another grotto, water gushes from the floor, the roof, the sides; in fact we scarcely had time to step from one place, before a stream of water started up from below our very feet. In still another place there was a table with seats ranged round it. The visitor is invited to take a seat, but woe be to him if he accepts the invitation, for water darts up through apertures in the seats, and this might not be agreeable on a cold day. But most of all was I interested and amused with a series of figures representing the different trades and occupations of men. Before a large temple stood soldiers on duty, and around the temple were shoemakers, masons, carpenters, &c., each at work at their respective trades, while a number of peasants were dancing. By the action of water each of these figures is put in motion; the soldiers walk back and forth on their post, and each one works as busily at his trade, as though he was impelled by animal life, instead of machinery. I was particularly amused with a scene in a field, where a man is whetting his scythe, while a woman turns the grind stone. I did not count them, but I should think there must have been more than two hundred figures in that small space. We could not help saying to each other, "how much amused the——children would have been here."

Leaving the grounds of Hollbrunn, we came along a wide road, shaded by large trees, and bordered by meadows enamelled with flowers, which filled the air with their delicious odors. The last part of the road runs along by the Salza, and this forms one of the favorite promenades and rides of the citizens of Salzburg. And I must confess no one feature of German cities and towns pleases me more than this, the pains that are every where taken to have public gardens and promenades, where the people can enjoy the fresh air, and see the beauties of nature besides, and I can't help sighing when I think how long it will probably be before my countrymen will be ready to follow this European custom. And yet, has not every city in the United States some favored spot, which, by a little expense, might be converted into a park, that would serve as a public promenade. In answer to this I may be told "there are already squares, and parks, and commons in almost every city, but they are rarely used except by poor people, or nurses and children." And why are they not used by the higher classes of our citizens? Simply because it is not fashionable, and because our fine ladies do not care enough for the rules of life and health, to seek the open air oftener than is necessary. But if I once launch out on this theme, I shall not know where to stop.

In this part of the world we have met with the first specimen of bed clothes, peculiar, I believe, to Germany. This consists of a light, puffy sort of feather bed, which is laid outside the sheet or counterpane, and is, I must say, a most uncomfortable piece of bed furniture, for if I have it over me, or rather on me, I am half suffocated, and if I throw it off, I am almost frozen, the nights being quite cold.

There, I am too tired to add another word, except to say "good night."

LETTER LXIX.

Leaving Salzburg.—Grand Scenery.—Cheap Traveling.—Innsbruck.—Sight-seeing.—Cathedral.—Monument to Hofer.—Tomb of Maximilian I.—Ambras Chateau.

INNSBRUCK, Sept. 6th.

MY DEAR FRIENDS:

On Monday morning we left Salzburg in a different carriage from the one we had from Ischl, for which we agreed to pay thirty-five florins, the driver to furnish us with three horses for the whole distance, to provide for himself and his horses, and to pay tolls, &c., on the way. In addition to this, if he performed his part well, we were to pay him on arriving here, four florins "drink money," the German "buksheesh."

Just as we were leaving the town, the "valet de place" we had on Saturday, came up to the carriage to wish us "a good journey," and to bring me a beautiful boquet, an offering delicately made, so evidently done without an expectation of any thing in return.

We rode that day, from quarter to seven in the morning, till eight in the evening, the distance from Salzburg here, being one hundred and ten miles, to be performed in two days with the same horses. We stopped to breakfast and dine, each time the horses being well cared for, so that we jogged on quite comfortably.

The scenery was grand; mountains, and vales, and running streams, and well cultivated fields, and romantic passes, and dark precipitous gorges, and here and there a gleam of snow, made the ride one of ever varying charm and interest. How like Switzerland it seemed! Houses, with projecting eaves and galleries around the upper story, and immense piles of wood near by, ready cut for the long winter's use, all reminded me of my former journey in that beautiful country. Almost every house had a bell on top, and heavy stones along the roof, for what purpose it puzzled us not a little to account, though we "guessed" they were to keep the roof from blowing off when the high winds prevail.

Sometimes the mountains were masses of rock, looking desolate and grand, at others they were thickly covered with trees, through which the sun seemed to penetrate with difficulty. At times the valley was but a narrow strip of meadow land, and then it would gradually enlarge, till it swelled out into quite an extensive plain. Rustic fences or hedges separated the fields, which were cultivated to their utmost extent. We saw but few fruit trees, and those did not seem to be overburdened with fruit.

Quite as pretty a sight as any, was to see the houses peeping ever and anon from up the mountain side, and the village church, with its graceful spire, and surrounding circle of cross-crowned hillocks. The sunset was magnificent, and the night came on with its bright stars and fair moon, and the mountains looked like majestic sentinels, keeping watch over the sleeping vale below.

That night we stayed at a very nice inn, where our sleeping accommodations were remarkably good. After we arrived, we had a supper of fried fish, and bread and butter, with the addition of tea for J., coffee for the other gentlemen, and a glass of beer for myself, and Tuesday morning, our two friends had coffee, and we all had bread and butter, and for all this, supper, rooms, good beds, candles, and a light breakfast, we paid but ninety cents, for four persons! Travelling would be cheap, if all expenses could be as moderate as these.

Yesterday we rode from before seven in the morning till after nine in the evening, through a lovely country, rich and grand. But I can say nothing more about it, for I have utterly exhausted my vocabulary of words, expressive of admiration of these mountain scenes. A great part of the day our road lay along side of a river, which ran by with a rapid current, at times dashing over rocks, so as to form quite a waterfall. Once we caught sight of distant glaciers, three distinct peaks being covered with "seas of ice."

We are in excellent quarters here, at Hotel Maulick, and find Innsbruck a charming spot, so embosomed among the mountains, that every time I go out, I think a dark cloud is coming up, whereas it is a mountain towering above us. The river Inn runs through the town, and the name Innsbruck means, I believe, "bridge over the Inn."

This day we have devoted to sight-seeing, walking about the streets, some of which are exceedingly handsome, darting into churches, rushing into shops to look at specimens of wood carvings, sauntering through lovely gardens, and visiting the museum, rich in Tyrolese articles. The charm of the country about Innsbruck, to me, is its association with the deeds of the noble Hofer, leader of the Tyrolese peasantry in the war of 1809. One of the most fascinating chapters in Alison's History of the French Revolution, treats of the daring of Hofer and his followers, and as you can read it much easier than I can give you an account of my hero, I must refer you to that for the present. In the cathedral here, there is a monument to Hofer, on which he is represented in his Tyrolese dress, and in the museum there is a splendid specimen of wood carving, showing him and a few of his chosen followers taking the oath to live and die for the liberty of their fatherland. Here, too, we saw other memorials of the peasant hero, his sword and rifle, and coat, and the last letter he wrote.

Beside these interesting relics, we saw a fine collection of Tyrolese manufactures, among which, in my eyes, wood carvings shone conspicuously. There is also an excellent collection of minerals found in the Tyrol, and a good cabinet of stuffed birds.

In the church where Hofer's monument is, there is a superb tomb of Maximilian I., having, on the outside of it, twenty-four compartments, each one representing, in bas-relief of white marble, some scene in his life. The sculpture is admirably done, each face being carved with as minute and perfect accuracy as if it had been designed for a cameo. I never saw any thing more beautifully done, even among the exquisite gems of Italy. The artist was Alexander Colin of Mechlin.

After a capital dinner, we drove out to the Ambras chateau, where is a fine collection of ancient armor and warlike implements, rare old cabinets, and relics of Philippina Welser, Archduchess of Austria, but the most interesting sight of all, was the splendid view from the roof of the chateau. The mountains around, down one of which a waterfall was dashing, the beautiful meadows, darkened here and there by clumps of trees, the handsome town with its sparkling river, the lights and shades thrown over the whole landscape, all formed as exquisite a picture as I ever saw. Again I said, "I should like to spend weeks here."

We drove home another way, to see the scene of one of Hofer's hard-fought battles, and as we stopped, in the deepening twilight, and looked up the mountain gorge he so bravely defended, my heart swelled with enthusiasm at the recollection of the strong-souled hero, whose life was given to his country and his God.

As we came farther down into the valley, the bell of a village church rang merrily out, and its sound was borne on the air, kindling a dozen mimic echoes in the hills around. Dark and mysterious the mountains looked, girding us about, like a huge wall, and far up in a deep gorge, the pale snow gleamed out like a ghost, from the dark scene. I leaned back in the carriage and gave myself up to thoughts in consonance with the hour and the place. It is no wonder a country like this should have inspired such enthusiastic love in the hearts of her children, and that they should have braved all dangers, and been willing to shed the last drop of their blood, to save their cherished fatherland from the hands of their enemies.

I have written this letter at intervals during the day, and that must be my apology for the rambling and disconnected manner of it. While the gentlemen of the party have been making arrangements, and settling bargains with our coachman to take us to Munich, I have been able to scribble away, only stopping to give my advice when asked, or occasionally to proffer it, woman-like, when it was not needed.

You must not think Innsbruck presents no more objects of interest and beauty than those I have mentioned, for as I told you before, I have neither time nor space, without swelling out this Budget to an unreadable and unbuyable rate, to dwell as minutely on the scenes I visit now, as I did on those of the East, not only because that country inspired me with more heartfelt interest, but also because it is less known to the generality of readers at home, and I might also add, because it has seldom been so thoroughly visited by an American woman. I therefore am compelled to pass lightly over many things which have interested me, and I doubt not would interest some others also, as every country has its own particular admirers.

And now I will release you for the present, and you and I both can pause to take breath.

LETTER LXX.

Mountainous Scenes. — Achensee. — Kreuth. — Tegernsee. — Munich.— House of Lola Montes.—St. Michael's Church.—Pinacotheque.—Crystal Palace.—Royal Palace.

MUNICH, Sept. 9th.

MY DEAREST S.:

Our mountain journey is over, to my great regret, for I should have liked it to last much longer. We devoted as much time to the Tyrol as we thought we could spare, considering the short period that is allowed us for the rest of Germany, to say nothing of wishing to take a peep at Holland and Belgium, for we have now decided to sail from Liverpool for Boston nine weeks from to-day, and in eleven we may hope, if prospered in our journey on land, and our voyage on the sea, to behold your dear faces once more. I scarcely dare think of it, for fear something might occur to mar our happiness. Much as I have enjoyed this journey, delighted as I have been with all I have seen, I can assure you that I shall be glad when the hour comes for us to embark on the sea, for then I shall feel our faces are really turned homeward. But I can dwell on this no longer, so must hasten to other themes.

We left Innsbruck Thursday morning, before six o'clock, and rode till after eight in the evening. For two or three hours we retraced the journey of Tuesday, going along the river Inn, which we crossed by a magnificent suspension bridge. The morning was charming, the mists rolling in fantastic forms from the summits of the mountains, disclosing glens and valleys of surpassing beauty. The road was full of peasant women, going into town with the productions of the fields and gardens, some dragging along little wagons filled with vegetables, others having strapped on their backs large baskets or tubs, loaded with fruits and garden produce. Most of them wore no other covering on the head than a black silk handkerchief, twisted around the head, and tied behind in a neat bow, the ends hanging down on the back.

We stopped to breakfast at Schwatz, at an inn kept by one of the Rainer family, who, perhaps you may remember, were in the United States several years ago, giving concerts. After leaving Schwatz the valley narrowed till it became a mere strip of meadow land, and a little while after we came into scenery of the wildest kind, mountains towering above us, no longer green, but bare and rocky, while the villages were very few and far between, and the houses scattering. And then we began an ascent, which lasted for more than an hour, the gentlemen walking ahead, and leaving me in undisputed possession of the whole carriage. The scene was almost fearfully grand and majestic, and when shortly after, mountains covered with dark forests, were mingled with those of granite, the striking contrast added new interest to the scene. On our left was a brawling mountain torrent, which leaped and rushed over the rocks, mingling the noise of its waters with "the soft and soul like sound" of the forests of pine. Up and still up we went, the horses puffing and blowing, and the driver cheering them on, walking by their side, and allowing them to stop every few minutes to get a little rest.

At last the ascent was gained, and then the country became less wild and more cultivated. Soon we came in sight of the small lake called Achensee, along the whole length of which, a distance of six miles, the road ran, being cut out of the solid rock, the mountain towering far over our heads. Across the lake, other mountains reared themselves, the whole scene forming a picture of sublimity and grandeur.

After we left this lake, we came again into wild scenes, dark forests of fir, being occasionally varied by a field of corn, or a meadow covered with long green grass, ready for the mower. Although we crossed the Bavarian frontier, no one came to examine our luggage, and we went on in the coming darkness, till all at once we were aware the scene was changed, for we seemed to be in a lovely valley, surrounded by gentle hills instead of lofty mountains. At a sudden turn we found ourselves in front of a large hotel, and our driver informed us we had arrived at Kreuth. It was too late to walk out, or rather too early, as the moon was not up, and as I was very tired, I was glad to go immediately to bed.

Yesterday morning opened dark and stormy, and we were obliged to have the carriage well shut up, so I saw but little of Kreuth. It lies in a beautiful valley, surrounded by high green mountains, and is one of the principal watering places in Bavaria, having celebrated mineral springs, which make it a great place of resort every summer, the royal family setting the example. The walks through the beautiful valley, and along the mountain paths, are said to be exceedingly fine, but I was obliged to take this upon trust, it being too wet for me to walk far. The situation of our hotel, and of the bath rooms is very good, opening upon a lawn covered with velvet like grass, and commanding fine views of the surrounding mountains. We went into the "pump room" where visitors assembled in the morning to drink the water, which I was not tempted to taste.

Soon after leaving Kreuth, the valley opened wider and wider, till at last the mountains were almost entirely behind us, and in front extended one immense plain. Before we quite left the mountains we came in sight of the Tegernsee, a lake about ten miles long, on the borders of which the king of Bavaria has a palace, and many of the nobility, country seats. We drove by pleasant grounds, adorned with flowers, and fine trees, and handsome houses, the lake, with its shining waters, and the distant mountains, adding beauty to the scene.

The remainder of our way lay across a plain, sometimes covered with forests, sometimes fertile in grain and vegetables. In the midst of this vast plain, watered by the "Iser rolling rapidly," lies Munich, one of the finest cities of Europe, containing about one hundred and ten thousand inhabitants. We are at the Hotel Manlick, where we have every thing nice and clean. At present Munich is quite deserted by strangers, the cholera having been severe in its ravages here, more than two thousand dying of the fell disease.

Last evening we took a long walk through the streets of the city, but very few people seemed stirring, and almost all the shops were closed. Some of the streets were lined with imposing edifices, but the great difficulty with this city is that its public buildings are scattered over so large a space, half their effect is lost.

Munich has the title of being the greatest city of modern art in Europe, having been greatly embellished under the reign of king Louis, who abdicated in 1848 in favor of his son Maximilian. Under his patronage the arts flourished, public buildings were erected, and galleries of painting and sculpture opened. Such an impetus was given to the fine arts, that at one time nearly eight hundred artists were residing here. Louis had but limited resources at his command, but these he used with the utmost ability, and in addition defrayed the entire expenses of several of the public buildings from his own privy purse. True, it is sometimes said, he impoverished somewhat the rest of his dominions to build up the capital, and make it, what it is universally admitted to be, one of the handsomest cities in Europe.

It was at the court of this Louis that the famous, or rather infamous Lola Montez flourished for a while, and in walking through one of the streets to-day, we were shown the house where she once lived.

This morning, under the direction of a good "domestique de place," we commenced the arduous duties of sight-seeing. There are so many objects of interest here, that a fortnight would scarce suffice to see them thoroughly, if one wished to see every thing. We want to see only the very best, so we select such things as would please us most, and devote what time we have to those. We have seen so many picture galleries, and museums, and cabinets of antiquities, and magnificent churches, that really we do not care to see many more, except as far as they illustrate the character of some particular country, or have special reference to historical events and personages.

Our first pause was to look at St. Michael's church,

which is remarkable for its great length, unbroken by any pillars to support the roof, being nearly three hundred feet long. But it was not this that attracted us there, but the monument to Eugene Beauharnais, duke of Leuchtenberg, by Thorwaldsen, consisting of a statue of Beauharnais, (said to be a capital likeness) by whose side sits the historic muse penning his deeds and his virtues. The figures are capitally done, and worthy of the great Danish sculptor.

Next we went to the new Pinacotheque, a long distance off, for as I said before, the public buildings of Munich extend over much ground. At first we went through fine streets, every house worthy to be called a palace, and then the houses became "few and far between," while the unpaved streets lined with trees, seemed more like some country town, than a part of a great city. We passed on the way fountains and monuments and statues, all perfect specimens of art.

The Pinacotheque contains a collection of modern paintings of the German, Bavarian and Dutch schools, in which we were much interested; and for one, I must confess, I did not know the modern school of painting had been brought to such perfection, for really we saw some magnificent pictures in the gallery. Among many excellent ones, I must be allowed to particularize three, as eminent for expression and beauty of coloring, and these were a vivid picture of the Deluge, a peasant girl of Albano, and the destruction of Jerusalem.

To get a good idea of the present manufactures of this country, we went into the Crystal Palace, lately opened for an exhibition of the productions and manufactures of Germany alone. The price of admission was exceedingly low, being only about eight cents of our money, but even at this low price the visitors were exceedingly few, for the cholera has not only kept off foreigners and strangers, but also frightened away many of the citizens of Munich. More than four hundred policemen are on constant duty there, and I should think the receipts could not begin to equal the expenditure, so that altogether it must prove a losing concern to those who got it up.

We found a great many things there to interest us, the gentlemen particularly admiring the machinery, fire-engines, carriages, &c., while I looked, with eyes of wonder, on the beautiful porcelain and glass ware, the rich furniture, silks, embroideries, shawls, linens, gloves, muslins, and a thousand et ceteras, all the productions of German manufactures alone. We spent more than four hours in wandering about the different parts, and then we went to the Royal Palace, where we walked through a score of rooms, attended by a guide who could not speak a word of English, and only two or three of French, so I came out but little wiser than I went in. I noted down a few things that specially interested me, and here they are for your benefit.

The ball room, adorned with paintings in fresco, copied from Pompeiian pictures, an immense room with chandeliers and candelabras capable of containing one thousand wax candles; the "halls of beauty," so called because they are filled with portraits of beautiful women, all Bavarian, among which are some of the loveliest faces I ever saw, and I was not a little anxious to find out who they were, for I felt somewhat suspicious when I found Lola Montez was among them, but all I could extract from our guide was, that they were portraits of persons living, at the time they were taken, in Munich, and put there for their beauty. Next came a large room, with fourteen immense pictures of battle scenes, and beyond this were other rooms, with paintings illustrative of events in the lives of Charlemagne, Frederick Barbarossa, and Rudolph of Hapsburg. The throne room was very fine, having chairs of state for the king and queen of red velvet embroidered with gold, under a canopy of the same. On either side of the room are statues in bronze gilt of the Wittelsbach family, the line of Bavarian sovereigns. The floors of these rooms were of polished woods, arranged in mosaics of different forms.

By the time we had made the rounds of the palace it was half past five, and we were quite ready for our dinner, I can assure you. As I was rather tired this evening, and as there was nothing particular to see, I declined accompanying the gentlemen on their evening promenade, and have spent the time as pleasantly, and I hope, as profitably, in writing to you.

The remainder of my observations on Munich you shall have in another letter.

LETTER LXXI.

Expense of Travel.—Romish Churches.—Public Garden.—Parks.—Museum.—Royal Library.—Ancient Pinacothek.—Glyptothek.—Church of St. Boniface.—Bavarian Hall of Fame.—Ludwig Schwanthaler.—Statue of Bavaria.—English Garden.

MUNICH, Sept. 12th.

MY DEAR FRIENDS:

Notwithstanding my uneasiness at Beyrout, when I thought our luggage was lost, and my firm determination not to part with it again, I have been tempted to break my resolution, and to consent to send to Paris every thing for which we have no immediate need. The expense of traveling with much luggage in Germany is very great indeed, for on many of the railroads only a few pounds are allowed each traveler, and on others none at all, so that all must be paid for by weight, which often makes the luggage cost more than the ticket for the traveler. There is a government agent here, who takes charge of packages to Paris, and who promises to keep them safely till they are called for, and to him we have entrusted our large trunk, a box of minerals we bought in the Tyrol, and the bundle of canes cut from holy mountains and from memorable spots. Now we have one small trunk, two carpet bags, (one of which contains my important journal,) my writing desk, two cloaks and a great coat, an umbrella and a parasol, and a bag I always carry on my arm, containing guide-books, note-book, toilet apparatus, &c.; few articles compared with those some travelers are burdened with, and many compared with what others carry.

Amid all the confusion of selecting and laying aside articles for use and those that may be dispensed with for several weeks to come, and the noise caused by a man hammering away while he adds a strap here and a few nails there, to repair the ravages made by careless porters and reckless coachmen, I have taken out my pen and paper to continue my account of Munich, at such intervals of leisure as will fall to my lot, when at times for a moment or so, there will be nothing I can do towards bringing the labors of packing to an end.

And with this long exordium, I will take up now the thread of my narrative, broken off last Saturday evening. Not having had the privilege of attending church since we left Athens, we had looked forward with great pleasure to our Sunday here, knowing there was a chaplain attached to the English embassy, who regularly performed divine service every Sunday. Judge then of our disappointment, when we found the English ambassador was out of the city, and that his chaplain had accompanied him. So there was no church for us last Sunday. To compensate in a measure for this disappointment, we were told there would be fine music in two of the Romish churches, in one at ten o'clock, and in the other at eleven. So at the appointed time we went, first to one, and then to the other, but were disappointed at both places, for at the first church we heard mass, and in the second a sermon a half hour long, interesting no doubt for those who understood it, but for those who knew not a word of what the preacher was saying, it was what I call "tough." At the last church, there were present several thousand soldiers, who stood during the whole sermon. The congregation seemed devout and attentive. Many of the women had on curious head-dresses, little caps of satin or gold thread, set very jauntily on the back of the head, while others wore an odd shaped cap of black silk, with immense "streamers" of ribbon of the same color behind.

At this hotel there is a "table d'hôte" at one o'clock, but that is rather an inconvenient hour for us, coming thus in the middle of the day, so since Saturday, we have dined at four. After dinner on Sunday, we went out for a walk in the gardens beyond the city. One small garden has an arcade, or colonnade, running around three sides of it, and the walls are painted in frescoes illustrative of events in Bavarian history. Interspersed with these are views of some of the celebrated cities of Italy and Greece. Is not this a capital method of teaching the Bavarian children the noble deeds of their ancestors, and of giving them a glimpse, at the same time, of other parts of the world? Beyond this garden lies a park, several miles in length, beautifully laid out with winding paths, and avenues, and clumps of trees, mingled with green lawns and beautiful meadows, watered by the river Iser. Here and there are statues, and on a gentle knoll, a pretty circular temple, from which we had a fine view of the park around, and the spires and roofs of the city. Groups of people in their holiday attire were in the gardens and the streets, and there was nothing to show that a grievous pestilence was brooding over the city.

Yesterday we were out all day, running here and there, till I was thoroughly wearied out with sights and sounds. First, we went to the Royal Palace, where we were on Saturday, an immense building, surrounding two or three courts, but we went only to see the chapel, which after all we did not see to good advantage, as staging was up for repairing the ceiling. There is another chapel called "the rich chapel," from the rare marble that adorns its walls, but from some cause or other, we could not procure access to it.

Through an interminable maze of courts, passages and stairways, we arrived at a museum or "royal collection of antiquities," where, amid a vast number of things, more or less interesting according to the places they came from, or their historical associations, I shall merely mention some beautiful specimens of carvings in ivory, the pen with which king Louis signed his abdication of the throne, March 21st, 1848, a plain deal table once belonging to Schiller, two of his pens, and a lock of his hair.

Once more we were in the street, and passing palace after palace, and noble statues and fine monuments, we reached the Royal Library, a princely building, in a street of palaces. Truly may Munich be called "one of the finest cities of Europe." The entrance to the library is by a magnificent staircase, lined with marbles and adorned with statues of its founder and its munificent patron, and busts of eminent writers, not of Germany alone, but of foreign lands also. The library contains seven hundred thousand volumes, arranged according to their subjects, in seventy-six rooms, and the collection of manuscripts and rare works is exceedingly rich, extending from the sixth to the fourteenth century. Let me see, there was a copy of the orations of Demosthenes, of a very early date; a book containing the laws of Alaric, king of the Goths; a tournament book, filled with rare old pictures illustrating games and sports of the day, and the first writing paper made in the fourteenth century. There was a missal, in a cover of gold, inlaid with ivory and precious stones, for which one of the former kings gave a city in return; and there was the first book ever printed with movable types, besides some that were printed with block types. Then there was the handwriting of Luther to look at, and of Goethe, of Charles I. of England, of my favorite Maria Theresa, and of Louis XIV., so that altogether our visit to this library was full of interest and information. How eagerly we looked at every thing, and how industriously we took notes. The man who showed us round looked frightened when he saw three of us take out note-books and pencils.

Again we darted off, through new and unpaved streets to the ancient Pinacothek, where is the gallery of paintings by the old masters. And here I was disappointed, for amid a large collection, I saw but few that merited more than a passing glance. I am beginning to like the German school of painting more and more. It may be wanting in the ideality that characterizes the Italian school, but it has more of the reality I think. The matchless glories of the Madonna and the Holy Child, the awe-inspiring sufferings of the Man of Sorrows, the convulsive agonies of imaginary saints, form the subjects of the greater part of the Italian pictures, and certainly some of them are the finest the world ever could produce, but the German artist does not so often touch on these, what some might call, forbidden subjects, but to him, real life and every day deeds has its charms, and a living face, a scene in a cottage, a group of children or peasants in their holiday garb and sports, call out his energies and his enthusiasm, and he produces on the canvass a picture of life, of life as it is, and matchless coloring and varying expression give to it an irresistible charm. You may think it strange that one so ignorant of art as I am, should set myself up for a critic, but I am not criticising for others, but for myself. Do not understand me to say I do not like Italian pictures. On the contrary, I value them highly, and have spent delightful hours in gazing on the greatest masterpieces the world ever has produced, but I mean to say, that now as I see more and more of the German school I am learning to appreciate it better.

The Glyptothek next attracted our attention, but if you expect me to give you a definition of all the hard words I use you are mistaken, for although I do not generally use a word I do not know something about, I am obliged to swerve somewhat from this rule, when I copy words descriptive of particular things. The word Glyptothek, with so many consonants, is, the catalogue tells us, of Greek origin, and then it learnedly gives us the Greek words from which it is derived, but as I am ignorant of that language, I am obliged to turn to my companions, more erudite than myself, and they go off into a disquisition from which I derive the information that the plain English of this word, difficult to pronounce, as well as to write, is "Sculpture Gallery."

The building itself is worthy of all admiration. Each hall is beautifully decorated with marble columns and vaulted ceiling, panelled with gold and rich frescoes, and filled moreover with gems of art from the Greek, the Roman and the Etruscan, as well as the modern schools, and we often had occasion to pause to admire a noble or a queenly figure, sculptured with matchless grace. But the prettiest thing of all in my eyes, was a "young girl fastening on her sandal," by Schadow. The childlike purity and innocence of the face, the dimpled arm and slender fingers, the graceful attitude, so easy, so very natural, are all inimitable. Each statue, and bust, and urn, stand on a pedestal of rich marble, in most cases, the natural productions of the country.

There were still other gems of art, and collections of antiquities which our guide praised up as being well worthy of admiration, and we did not doubt it; but we had seen quite enough in that way for one day, and our eyes as well as our minds were weary, so after dinner we drove out to get a general view of the city and its environs, which on account of the plain on which Munich is situated, cannot boast of as much beauty and variety as some of the other cities we have visited.

Oh! I forgot to say that while we were waiting for the Glyptothek to be opened, we visited the church of St. Boniface, an imposing edifice, with four rows of handsome marble pillars, and beautiful frescoes, built after the design of "St. Paul, without the walls," at Rome. The objectors to King Louis say that the fault of Munich is, there is nothing original about its public buildings, for that every palace, and church, and gallery, are copies from those of other cities. But better to have a good copy, than a crude, rough original, I say, though I have no doubt the German architects could have designed as good models as those they have so well copied.

Not far from the walls of the city, on a gentle slope

which rises from the midst of the vast plain that sweeps around Munich, stands the "Bavarian Hall of Fame," consisting of a Doric portico, running around three sides of a quadrangle, adorned with busts of those Bavarians who have distinguished themselves either in war or in peace, and this is not only to include the men of the past, but those of the future also, so that hereafter, a place shall be given to every son of Bavaria who has performed noble deeds for his country.

In the open space in the centre of the quadrangle, rises the bronze statue of Bavaria, represented by a female figure, having in her right hand a wreath, and in her left a sword. Beside her couches a lion. It is sixty-four feet in height, and stands upon a pedestal thirty feet high. It is magnificent! The artist's name is Ludwig Schwanthaler, and he may justly be called the Thorwaldsen of Bavaria. This morning we visited his studio, where we saw some very beautiful statues he is executing for noblemen of England. We bought a miniature copy, in plaster, of this statue of Bavaria, which I hope will cross the Atlantic in safety.

But I have wandered from the statue in bronze to the one in plaster; so now, with your good permission, we will return to it. A winding staircase within the pedestal and statue, leads up to the very top, and so up we went, not only to get a view of the surrounding country, but for the novelty of standing within the head of a statue. And there we stood, four full grown persons, and had a plenty of "elbow room" besides. Through little openings we gazed out upon the immense plain around us, and the distant mountains, standing out clearly and boldly against the golden sky. You can have no idea how hot it was up there; the inner surface of the statue was so heated by the sun's rays, I could scarcely bear my hand upon it.

Then we came back to town, and drove through some of its finest streets, every building in which is worthy the name of palace. We passed the University, which stands on a little "square" or "place," having in front a handsome fountain, and went again out of the city, under a noble triumphal arch, built after the model of the Arch of Constantine, at Rome, and surmounted by a figure of Victory, in a car drawn by four lions—a spirited piece of work.

Evening came on while we were driving along the winding roads of the "English garden," and the soft light fell through the thick branches over our heads, or slanted across a green meadow, or faintly lit up the rustling stream, forming a beautiful scene, quiet and peaceful, wonderfully refreshing to me after the day's excitement and fatigue.

This morning we took advantage of an hour's leisure, to visit an exhibition of modern paintings, where we found many beautiful pictures. On our way home, we stopped at the studio of Schwanthaler, but this I have already mentioned. And now, my record of Munich is finished, for in less than two hours we leave it behind. I am well aware that a hurried description, like mine, cannot do it justice, for it is a city that, to the lover of art, would well pay for a much longer sojourn than we have been able to give it.

LETTER LXXII.

Augsburg.—The Three Moors.—Augsburg Confession.—Fuggerville.—Nuremberg.—The Red Steed.—Objects of Interest.—Caspar Hauser.—Manufactures and Inventions. Passport Arrangements.—Crown Princess of Saxony.—Leipsic.—University.—The Battle Ground.—Monument of Poniatowski.—Rosenthal.

LEIPSIC, Sept. 15th.

MY DEAREST F.:

While we are waiting for breakfast, I sit down to commence a letter to you, without having the slightest idea when I shall be able to finish it. We left Munich Tuesday afternoon, for Augsburg, and although it was only forty miles, we were nearly four hours in accomplishing that distance, as we were in what is called "the slow train," which stops at every station, and takes freight as well as passengers. The country between Munich and Augsburg was level and fertile, but not beautiful or interesting, and so I pass it by without further comment.

At Augsburg, we stopped at the hotel of "The Three Moors," which is said to be one of the oldest inns in the world, there being records of it as far back, as the year 1364. Here, at one time, lived Anthony Fugger, surnamed "the Rich," and here were entertained Maximilian I. and Charles V., and we saw the rooms they occupied.

Full of interest in the old town, we went out for a walk, almost the very moment after our arrival, but although the street on which our hotel stands is wide, and lined with noble houses, and adorned with beautiful fountains in bronze, scarcely a light was visible in any of the houses, and not an individual, except a few soldiers, was to be seen.

The next morning our companions left us, to pursue their way into Switzerland, while we, under the guidance of a *valet de place*, advanced in years and infirmities, strolled around the town. And a quaint old place we found it, many of its houses having high, peaked roofs, often with three, four and even five stories above the eaves. Many of the streets are grass-grown, and look deserted, perhaps because Augsburg, like Munich, has been greviously visited with the cholera.

It has some flourishing manufactures, and noble old churches, and the palace yet stands where, on June 25th, 1530, the famous declaration of Protestantism, known as the "Augsburg Confession," was read before the Emperor Charles V. Here, also, in 1532, took place the conference between Luther and the Cardinal of Gaeta.

Within the centre of the city, (I forgot before to say Augsburg has about thirty-five thousand inhabitants,) is a collection of houses called "Fuggerville," in which are tenements of two or three rooms, let to poor people for a small sum, not more than a dollar or two a year. This little community lives quite by itself, having a school and church of its own.

At 12 o'clock, we left Augsburg for Nuremberg, and this time we were so fortunate as to get into the "fast train," so we got on quite comfortably and rapidly, the distance being little over one hundred miles. The country was mostly level and fertile, and we saw immense quantities of flax, tobacco and hops growing.

Arriving at Nuremberg about five, we went to the "Red Steed," and as soon as we had seen our luggage deposited in our room, we strolled out, and, yesterday morning, with a guide whose mixture of French, German and English was exceedingly difficult to understand, we went through the town with a rush. And what a quaint town it is! Even many of the new houses are built after the fashion of the ancient ones, and their high roofs, pierced with small windows, and their little turrets and balconies, present a most picturesque appearance. We walked through the market place, full of people buying and selling; stopped to look at fountains of diverse designs and forms; visited the church of St. Sebald, once a Catholic, but now a Protestant church; paused to look at a fine painting by Vandyck, in the church of St. Egidien; saw the old Town Hall, a good specimen of ancient architecture; went into a beautiful Catholic church, where mass was being celebrated, and where the peasant women, with immense baskets beside them, were kneeling to offer up their morning prayers; picked our way among the crowds of people that thronged the Goose market, in the centre of which is a fountain, the water running out of the mouths of two geese held under the arms of a peasant; saw the house of Hans Sachs, the Nuremberg cobbler and poet; went up to the old castle, where we had a magnificent view of the city and country around, and saw two or three chambers filled with old furniture, books, china, pictures, &c., &c.; went by the house where Albert Durer, the painter, poet and sculptor lived; saw his statue in the Milk market; and finally ended the morning with visiting the antiquities collected by mine host of the Red Steed. There, if you are not tired after reading that long sentence, I am, and so I will pause for breath.

Nuremberg was once one of the most important places in Germany, being the centre of the trade between the north and south, particularly when the Dutch had possession of the East Indies. After they lost that, the trade and prosperity of Nuremberg declined, but within a few years, I am told, they are once more on the rise. Judging from the immense number of bags of hops I saw in the streets, I should think they formed a staple commodity. Do you remember the story of Caspar Hauser? Well, he was found in Nuremberg, and, of course, for a time, gave celebrity to the place. This city, too, is famous for its manufactures and inventions. The first watches were made here in 1500, and from their oval shape, they received the name of "Nuremberg eggs." We saw two or three of them, and huge, ungainly things they were, too. Whist players may be interested in knowing that cards, if not invented here, were made here as early as 1380. The first paper-mill was built in Nuremberg in 1390, and the first cannon was cast here in 1356. Here, also, was made, in 1517, the first gunpowder, and in 1360 a machine was invented for drawing wire, and in 1550 that alloy of metals, called brass, was discovered. There's a string of dates for you!

At 12 o'clock, we were once more on the move, and late last evening arrived here, the distance between the two places being about two hundred and twenty miles. The country was beautiful, varied with hill, and dale, and rushing stream. At one place the railroad crosses a deep valley, by a bridge one-third of a mile long, and two hundred and seventy feet above the deepest part of the valley. The bridge is composed of four rows of arches, one above the other, having in the whole eighty arches, the grandest structure of its kind in all Germany.

We are in good quarters here, at the "Hotel de Baviere," and this morning had the pleasure of seeing the Crown Princess of Saxony, the wife of the heir apparent to the throne of Saxony, in whose dominions we are at present. Although we passed, yesterday, from the kingdom of Bavaria into that of Saxony, there was no examination of luggage at all, and no flurry about the passport. Indeed, we are every day agreeably surprised with the contrast, in these two respects, between our former European tour and the present one. And here perhaps I may as well say, as to wait till another time, that we have thus far had no trouble whatever about our passport, and very little expense. On arriving at some of the cities, it has been taken from us at the barriers, and when it has not, it has been asked for immediately on our entrance into the hotel, and the question added, how long we should stay, and where we were going next. Whenever we were ready to depart, the passport was brought to us duly signed and sealed for our next stopping place, and a fee to the man who has had the charge of it, of ten or twelve cents, has covered all expenses. How much better is this than being obliged to rush through a town, as we used to in France and Italy, hunting up authorities to *visé* the passports, each of which demanded a fee, three or four times more than was necessary.

And now what shall I tell you of Leipsic? for since I began this letter, we have spent several hours in looking about the town. It is a much handsomer city than I expected to see, and has about sixty-five thousand inhabitants. Here are held, three times a year, fairs which last two or three weeks, and which are visited by hundreds and thousands of merchants and traders from all parts of the world. At one time the sales amounted to eighty millions of dollars annually, that of books alone amounting to more than two millions.

Here, too, is a University, the oldest but one in Germany, having been founded in the year 1400. At present, there are about eight hundred students, and one hundred and thirty professors and teachers.

Of the Library, the Museum, the Gallery of Paintings here, I can tell you nothing, for I did not go to see them, having neither time nor strength to spare for the undertaking. We ascended, by I forget how many stairs, to the top of the Observatory, to get a good view of the battle ground where, in October, 1813, was fought one of the largest battles ever recorded in history, there having been engaged one hundred and seventy-six thousand troops on the side of Napoleon, and three hundred thousand on that of the Allies. No wonder, with such an overwhelming majority against him, the star of Napoleon sank for the time. This battle, it is said, decided the fate of Europe.

Afterwards we went to the bank of the Elster, where Prince Poniatowski lost his life, by attempting to swim across the stream, and a little farther on saw the monument which has been erected to the brave Pole.

Like Vienna, Leipsic is surrounded by gardens, which form delightful promenades. We walked through a part of Rosenthal, a beautiful park, but I was too tired to go far, even though told that a half hour's walk would lead to a lovely little cottage once inhabited by Schiller. As I have said many times before, sight-seeing is fatiguing business; it not only tells upon the physical strength, but it taxes largely the energies of the mind, the imagination and the memory, till at times one feels completely overworked.

As we have seen here all we care about seeing, we have concluded to go on to Dresden to-night, though in general we avoid night traveling, if possible, as we want to see as much of the country as we can.

LETTER LXXIII.

Dresden.—Hotel Bellevue.—Currency.—Japanese Palace.—Bridge over the Elbe.—Historical Museum.—Table d'hote.—Bruhl Terrace.—Dog-carts.—Romish Church.—English Church.

DRESDEN, Sept. 17th.

MY VERY DEAR F:

Behold us, at last, in this capital of the kingdom of Saxony, a beautiful city of ninety thousand inhabitants, situated on both sides of the river Elbe, in the midst of a charming country. Below and above the city, the banks of the river display many scenes of loveliness, hills covered with vineyards, and dotted with country seats.

We are at the Hotel Bellevue, having on one side the river, and on the other a pretty park with winding walks, and a little pond in the centre, across which small boats are constantly darting, while in front of the hotel is an open square, bounded on one side by the theatre and the Romish church, with the royal palace in the rear. Many of the houses in Dresden are very handsome, and the palaces and public buildings are on a magnificent scale, but they all have a dull and dingy look, and there is ever a smokiness in the air, as in London or Liverpool, or other places where large quantities of coal are burnt.

Just as we were becoming accustomed to "florins" and "kreutzers," the currency has changed, and we are now among "thalers" and "groschen," thirty groschen making a thaler, which is about seventy-five cents of our money. For a little while, I could not "get the hang" of this new money, but now it comes quite easily.

Our first exploit here in the way of sight-seeing, was to visit the "Japanese Palace," on the other side of the river. We crossed over by a stone bridge of immense length and strength, built of solid arches, so as to be able to resist the force of the current, which is very strong. Besides the current, it has other impediments to fight against, for in the Spring, when the snow and the ice begin to melt, the river has often been known to rise sixteen feet in one day. This bridge was built with money raised in a peculiar way; by the sale of dispensations from the Pope, for the use of butter and eggs during Lent. A very small toll is demanded for horses and carriages, while foot passengers go free, those going over taking the right hand side, which tends to diminish confusion.

The "Japanese Palace" is so called from the figures and ornaments in porcelain with which it is decked out, and contains a collection of china and porcelain from all parts of the world, a cabinet of antiquities, and the royal library, but we confined our attention entirely to the first two. The collection of porcelain and china occupies twenty rooms, and contains more than sixty thousand pieces, the catalogue of which fills five large volumes. They date from the earliest period of the manufacture of china, down to the present day, and you may readily imagine one could find there many beautiful specimens of every period. The keeper, an important, consequential sort of a personage, showed us one cup and saucer made in Japan, of transparent china, which was more than seventeen hundred years old! What a tale they could tell, if a tongue were given to them.

The ware from Italy and from Sevres is very beautiful, every article being of different design. There were some magnificent vases, also, and the bust of a female, the head covered with a veil of china, made to imitate lace, a wonderful thing, and, by some, considered the gem of the collection.

In the cabinet of antiquities we found some fine busts and statues, but far inferior to the galleries of Italy, and not to be compared with that at Munich. It, however, is well worth seeing, though I must confess I was quite as much interested in looking out on the beautiful gardens surrounding the palace.

Then we came back to this part of the town, and went to the Historical Museum, where we saw so many things, my head really aches in trying to remember them. This is contained in what is called the Zwinger, which consists of a portico running around a square, and designed by Augustus II. as the entrance to an immense palace, which has never been built.

The collection of ancient armor here is said to be the largest and the richest in the world. For my part, I thought that at Vienna could not be surpassed, but this goes before it. Some of the suits of armor are elaborately carved, while two or three are of silver, gilded over. All sorts of weapons of warfare that were ever heard of are here collected, and historical relics from all parts of the world. There was a beautiful cabinet, enamelled and inlaid with ivory, presented by John Frederic to Martin Luther, and the drinking cup of the great reformer, which I think if some of our temperance advocates at home could see, they would think his principles of abstinence were not on a par with his Protestantism.

The cuirass belonging to Augustus the Strong weighs one hundred pounds, and as for his cap, I tried to raise it, but gave up the attempt, as quite beyond my strength, and we saw a horse-shoe which he broke in two with his fingers, preserved as a relic, to show he merited the appellation of "Strong."

Hilts of swords, stocks of guns, elaborately wrought in gold and silver, and inlaid with ivory and precious stones, a harness of gold, set with rubies, and others of silver, inlaid with pearls and turquoises; the little, old-fashioned looking hat worn by Peter the Great, and a wooden bowl turned by his own imperial hands; a saddle of red velvet, once belonging to Napoleon, the boots he wore at the battle of Dresden, and the satin shoes he had on at the time of his coronation; a Turkish tent and collection of arms, taken at the siege of Vienna, each in its turn claimed due attention from us, and elicited many expressions of admiration.

When I had gone through with these objects of interest, I declared I would see nothing more that day, for I was really wearied with admiring, so we took a turn through some of the principal streets, where I saw handsome shops, and beautiful engravings in almost every window.

There are two *tables d'hote* here, the first at one o'clock, the other at five. As we do not breakfast till nine, the one o'clock dinner comes rather too early for us, so we take the later one at five. The dinner at one o'clock is cheaper by about thirty cents, but then, on the other hand, if we dined at that early hour, we should require a supper, which would more than balance the difference in the price of the dinners.

After dinner, we walked along the banks of the Elbe, on what is called the Bruhl terrace, made from the gardens of the minister of that name, after his palace was destroyed during the "Seven Years' War." Broad walks, shaded with lofty trees, pretty views of the Elbe and the opposite banks, groups of gay people flitting in and out among the trees, make this garden a delightful place of promenade. We stopped at a café to get some ices, and were rather surprised to find that as we come north, they are getting dearer and dearer.

One of the most striking peculiarities of Dresden, is the number of little carts drawn by dogs, and it is surprising to see what loads these poor creatures draw. To-day, we saw one dragging along a cart, with a ton of coal in it. Although, as you know, I have no great partiality for dogs, while I think it is well to have them put to some good use, I cannot bear to see them so harshly treated. But there is one thing in this that gives me comfort; I should feel quite safe in eating sausages here, knowing dog's flesh was not liable to be one of the ingredients, since dogs must be too valuable, as beasts of burden, to be killed for food.

This morning, we went to the Romish church, where we heard magnificent music, an oratorio being performed by a large choir and a number of musical instruments besides the organ. There was quite a new feature in this church; the men were all seated on one side, the women on the other. A private gallery connects this church with the palace, but there were none of the royal family present this morning, the court being now at one of the summer palaces.

This afternoon, we attended the service of the English church, held in a small chapel, at a long distance from our hotel. It was quite decked out with flowers and wreaths, and over the altar was a picture of our Saviour, and on one side of that, the portrait of Martin Luther, and on the other, one of John Huss. Flowers, and paintings, and candles, decorate all the Protestant churches in Germany, of whatever name, and the English follow the received fashion.

After dinner, we took a quiet walk in the pretty park in front of our hotel, and the remainder of the evening I have spent in chatting with you, and thus have given you a pretty full account of our first two days in Dresden.

LETTER LXXIV.

Picture Gallery.—Royal Palace.—Green Vaults.—Pleasant Surprise.—Cabinet of Minerals.—Environs of Dresden.—Plauen.—Tharand.—New Town.

DRESDEN, Sept. 19th.

MY DEAR FRIEND:

I must confess I was rather disappointed yesterday morning, in finding it was raining fast, for we were intending to make an excursion to some of the beautiful environs of Dresden, for which pleasant weather was very desirable. We devoted the morning to the Picture Gallery, the best collection of paintings in all Germany, that is, of the old masters. Here is the famous "Madonna di San Sisto" of Raphael, considered by many connoisseurs equal to any of the works of that painter in Italy, and for which nearly forty thousand dollars were paid. Here, too, is the celebrated "Night" of Coreggio, in which all the light that falls upon the figures in the group, comes from the body of the infant Saviour. Time would fail me to give even a list of the renowned masters whose works compose this collection; suffice it to say, it is probably the best gallery in the world, out of Italy. In every room, artists were engaged in copying pictures, and in many instances, their copies were of great merit. The Germans, as a nation, have much enthusiasm for art, and added to that enthusiasm and reverence, they unite perseverance with energy, and thus a great many of them become artists, in the true and noble sense of the word.

In the afternoon, we went through the rooms in the royal palace, known by the name of "the Green Vaults," and here we saw articles of such priceless value and brilliancy as quite to dazzle our eyes and bewilder our imaginations. The collection of jewels and precious stones, of gold and silver, is said to be the most costly in the world. Could you have listened to our exclamations, as we passed from one dazzling article to another, and then could you have had a peep yourself at the tempting array, I am sure you would have said with us, that it was nearer the realization of gorgeous tales of Eastern life than any thing you had ever before imagined.

I scarcely know where to begin in my description of this magnificent collection, which fills eight large rooms, so I will give, in a desultory manner, the names of some of the most prominent objects. The carvings in bronze and ivory are inimitable; among these is a vase on which is represented the fall of Lucifer and the wicked angels, composed of a group of eighty-five figures, the whole cut out of one piece of ivory not a foot and a half high! Next in order, came Florentine mosaics, composed of precious and costly stones; shells and ostrich eggs carved and engraved in a thousand forms; a large cabinet, all of amber; a chimney-piece of Dresden china, of priceless value; an immense collection of gold and silver plate, among which were eight vessels of solid gold, and large wine-coolers of silver gilt. As for articles cut in agate, chalcedony, lapis-lazuli, onyx, jasper, rock-crystal, &c., they were innumerable, among which was an onyx cameo, and two goblets, composed entirely of precious stones, and valued at six thousand dollars each! The largest pearl in the world is in this collection, and as for sapphires, emeralds, rubies, brilliants and diamonds, there really seemed no end to them, and their dazzling brilliancy defies description.

Then there were some things very curious and unique, such as a golden egg, which, when opened, showed a minature chicken; this, in turn, contained a ring, which when touched in a peculiar manner, sprung open, displaying another ring and a small minature. This certainly is an egg worth having. Then there was a set of figures in pure gold, enamelled, to the number of one hundred and thirty-eight, representing "the court of the Grand Mogul," wherein the Emperor Aurengzebe is seen seated upon his throne, surrounded by his guard and attendants, each in appropriate costume. This was executed by Dinglinger, court jeweller at Dresden about 1720, and termed the Saxon Benevenuto Cellini. He was employed upon it eight years, and the whole cost of it was about fifty-nine thousand dollars!

Chains, ear-rings, bracelets, jewels, sword-hilts, studded with diamonds, gems of all kinds and every hue, were there in such abundance, that the wonder to me was, where they all came from. It is said a prominent object of the revolutionists in 1849, was to obtain possession of the treasures of the Green Vaults, and I am inclined to think the mob would have made sad havoc of them, if it had once had them in its power.

A nice old man, a little pompous, showed us round these apartments, and allowed us to look and admire to our hearts' content. He seemed mightily pleased, when I told him there was nothing more in the world now for us to see, and therefore we might as well go home to America.

As we were going down to dinner, yesterday, whom should we meet but our fellow-companion in the Desert, Mr. R.? To say which was the most surprised at this unexpected meeting, would be exceedingly difficult, and the way we talked over, during the evening, our mutual adventures, since we parted on the Bosphorus, was not slow.

This morning we went to the cabinet of minerals, where I was exceedingly interested. I had no idea before that Saxony was so rich in minerals. I knew the silver mines at Freiberg were very extensive, for in the space of fifty years, it is said, more than two thousand tons of silver have been obtained from those mines, but I was disappointed in the specimens of silver ore in this collection, for they were not so large, or so good as I supposed they would be, from such valuable mines in the neighborhood. There was one piece from another mine, taken from a block of pure silver, which was originally of such large size, that it served for a dinner table for the Elector of Saxony, when he visited the mine. A rude engraving represents the scene, the royal personage seated in the mine at his table of solid silver.

Notwithstanding the drops of rain that occasionally fell, and the dark clouds which hovered over us, we resolved to drive out into the country, that we might know, at least, something about the environs of Dresden, of whose beauty we had heard so much. We went out to Plauen, a small village composed of picturesque looking houses, like those we used to see in some parts of Switzerland; the wood-work forming the frame being left in sight, and the spaces between, lathed and plastered. The appearance is like dark lines drawn in various directions across the entire surface. We rode through a narrow glen, along the bank of the Weisseritz, while high hills arose on either side, some covered with trees and bushes, others rocky and bare. Occasionally the glen widened, and we saw pretty meadows and neat cottages, and then the rocks disappeared and wooded hills were on both sides of us. It was almost as grand as the Tyrol.

Then we came to the village of Tharand, which has some mineral springs, enough to make it entitled to the name of a "watering place," and to be much visited in the summer by the inhabitants of Dresden. It is delightfully situated in an open glade, where three valleys meet, two of them watered by little streams that give great beauty to the scene.

We left the carriage and climbed up to the top of a hill, where stands a ruined monastery, and from which we obtained a delightful view of the lovely vale beneath us, and the forest clad hills around us. It was, indeed, a charming spot, and I only wished we had hours, instead of minutes, to spend there.

On passing through a toll-gate, on our way out, the keeper being quite too indolent, or too fearful of the weather, to come out of his house, thrust through the window a bag, fastened to the end of a long pole, precisely like what I used to see years ago carried about in the churches in New Jersey for contributions.

And now I have finished my chronicles of Dresden, for to-morrow we must bid adieu to this beautiful city, favored abode both by nature and art. Oh, I forgot to say, that yesterday we walked over to the "new town" on the opposite bank of the river. We went up a long street, with a double row of trees in the centre, and handsome houses on either side. There is a fine equestrian statue of Augustus II., where this street opens upon the river.

And now good bye.

LETTER LXXV.

Departure from Dresden.—Tetzel's Box.—Obelisk.—Hill of the Cross.—Berlin.—British Hotel.—Linden Trees.—Street of Palaces.—Brandenburg Gate.—Park.—Monument of Frederick the Great.—Streets.—Berlin Iron.—Potsdam.—Royal Palace.—Sans-souci.—Windmill.—New Palace.—Antique Temple.—Charlottenkof.—Russian Colony.—Burial Place of Frederick the Great.—Voltaire's Residence.

BERLIN, Sept. 21st.

MY DEAR P.:

On Wednesday morning we were called at the early hour of five o'clock, so that we were obliged to light the candles to see to dress. Perhaps it was not "tough" getting up at that unseasonable hour, and starting for the railway station in the grey light of the morning. But we must either do this, or arrive at Berlin at nine in the evening, and I don't know which is the most forlorn, starting off before sunrise, or arriving after dark.

The country, for the greater part of the way between Dresden and here, is exceedingly poor and uninteresting. It has, however, a few stirring historical associations, which served to keep one awake during the journey of six hours. In the town of Jutterbog, for instance, in one of the churches, there is the very box of which the monk Tetzel, the antagonist of Luther, was robbed in a forest near by. It was full of gold, the price of the indulgences Tetzel had sold, and the most singular part of the whole story is, that the robber was one of the very men to whom Tetzel had sold an indulgence for any sins he might commit.

Further on, an obelisk, with a cross carved on it, is

erected to commemorate the victory over the French by the Prussians, August 23d, 1813. The French were commanded by Oudinot, the Prussians by Bulow.

Just before arriving here, we passed a little hill, called the Kreutzberg, "hill of the cross," so named from a Gothic cross of iron, one hundred and sixty feet high, erected upon its summit, to commemorate the recovery of the independence of Prussia, from the French.

This city is, as you doubtless know, the capital of the kingdom of Prussia. It is situated on the river Spree, in the midst of a wide plain, such poor land, that it can never be carried to a great extent of cultivation, but it was the will of Frederick the Great, that his capital should flourish, in spite of the obstacles nature had placed against it, and that iron will conquered, and Berlin now covers an extent of land twelve miles in circumference, and contains four hundred and eighteen thousand inhabitants.

As we entered the city our carriage was stopped by a police officer, who inquired if we had "any thing subject to duty?" We told him "no," and after pinching the carpet bag, and knocking his knuckles against my writing desk, he motioned for the carriage to drive on, without even asking for our keys, an act of forbearance very pleasant to us, for the delay occasioned by unstrapping and unlocking trunks and bags, and then locking and strapping them again, is not very pleasant, particularly in the rain, for you may be interested in knowing we arrived here in a heavy shower.

We came to the "British Hotel," but when we went down to dinner at three o'clock, the fashionable dinner hour in Berlin, and found ourselves surrounded by a party of Germans, there being no one but ourselves and an English gentleman whom we met at Dresden, speaking the English language, I concluded it was an "hotel" without the "British."

After dinner, the rain having ceased, we went out for a walk for general observation, preliminary to taking a more particular survey. This hotel is in the street called "Unter den Linden," from a double row of linden trees, railed off for a promenade along the centre, having on each side a wide-carriage road. I cannot say much for the sidewalks of Berlin: the strip of flag-stones in the centre is very narrow, while the round stones on either side, are villainous in the extreme.

But the buidings that line this street are splendid. It may well be called a street of palaces, and I scarcely know a finer one in any part of Europe, that has been favored with our presence. At one end, is the Brandenburg gate, said to have been a copy of the Propylæum at Athens, though on a larger scale even than that. On the top, it is surmounted by a triumphal car, bearing the goddess of Victory, who holds aloft an eagle and an iron cross, added by the Prussians, after her return from Paris, whither she was carried by the French. Extending a long distance beyond this gate, is an immense park, thrown open to the public, adorned with large trees, and sheltered walks, and open glades, the last being the play-ground of the city. Along these walks, at every hour of the day, you may meet groups of children and babies "in arms," attended by their careful nurses or tender mothers, and as I looked upon their ruddy faces and fat little figures, I thought how much better they seemed to thrive under such discipline, than to be shut up in close nurseries, as is too often the case with children in our country. When will our countrymen and countrywomen learn true wisdom in relation to life out of doors?

But to return to the street, from which I started. At the other extremity of it, is a collection of magnificent edifices, among which are the palace of the Prince of Prussia, the Royal Palace, a collossal building, the Museum, having a beautiful colonnade, the Guardhouse, with a portico in front, the University, an immense structure, the Opera House, the Arsenal, heavy, yet grand, the Academy of Arts, and I can't tell how many more, on a similar scale of magnificence and architecture.

Directly in front of the palace of the prince of Prussia on the one hand, and the University on the other, is a monument of Frederick the Great, said by some to be the grandest monument in all Europe. It consists of a pedestal of granite twenty-five feet in height, having on each side, groups in bronze of the great military chieftains of the seven years' war, on foot and on horse, all the size of life, and said to be capital portraits. And besides these, the portraits of several of Frederick's great statesmen are introduced, and his favorite musical composer, Graun. Of these life-like figures, all represented in the costumes and with the arms of the time, there are thirty-one, thus making this monument of immense importance, in a historical point of view. Beneath these figures are two tablets bearing the names of eighty of the most distinguished soldiers of Frederick's time. On the third side, are the names of sixteen statesmen, artists and scientific men, while on the fourth, is the simple inscription, "To Frederick the Great, Frederick William III., 1850; completed by Frederick William IV., 1851."

Above the figures there is at each corner a female statue representing the cardinal virtues, Prudence, Justice, Fortitude and Temperance, and between them are bas-reliefs, illustrating different periods in the life of the great Frederick.

Surmounting all, is the equestrian statue, seventeen feet three inches in height, and the monarch is represented in the clothes he was accustomed to wear, with the exception that a mantle of ermine is thrown over his shoulders. The very queue is given, the three-cornered hat, and even the stick which he was wont to carry.

And while I am on the subject of statues, I might as well say here, that there are several others in Berlin, but none on so magnificent a scale as that of the great Frederick. Among them is a bronze statue of Blucher, an equestrian statue of the great Elector, Frederick William, also in bronze, and marble statues of Generals Bulow and Scharnhorst.

The streets of Berlin are wide, and cross each other at right angles, and the uniformity of the houses in many of the streets, and their general air of cleanness and neatness remind me somewhat of Philadelphia. The shops are brilliant, and have furnished me with food for gazing for several hours. The iron-work of Berlin is very beautiful; I think I have once before alluded to the origin of the ornaments of this kind, but it may bear repetition. At the time of the war between France and Prussia, the ladies, in their zeal for their country, gave their jewels towards furnishing funds for the expenses of the State. To all those that contributed in this manner, ornaments in Berlin iron were given in return, bearing this inscription, "I gave gold for iron," not in English however, but in German.

This morning we were refreshed with letters from home, which were only fourteen days in coming here, seeming thus to annihilate time and space. We have made an excursion to Potsdam to-day, about fifteen miles from here, our English friend accompanying us. It is called the Prussian Versailles, and is quite a large town, containing forty thousand inhabitants, but as we went there merely to see the palaces, I shall confine myself entirely to them, or to that part of them which particularly interested us, as being associated with the memory of Frederick the Great.

And to accomplish seeing these with the least possible fatigue, we took a carriage by the hour, and under the guidance of a respectable "valet de place," commenced the duties of sight-seeing with a good deal of interest and enthusiasm. And first we went to the "Residenz" or royal palace, where we saw only the apartments once occupied by the great Frederick, which remain very nearly in their former state. The large saloon is a very splendid room, liberally adorned with statues and ornaments in solid silver, the frames of the chairs and sofas being also silvered over.

In a small room there is a table, made to ascend and descend through a trap-door in the floor, and here Frederick often dined with a friend, while the dinner was served without the presence of servants.

His writing-table, blotted with ink, his piano, music-stand, and a piece of music composed by himself, and written out with his own hand, the green shade he used to wear, the books he once read, all in turn were eagerly scrutinized by us.

At a little distance from the town commence the gardens of Sans Souci, (meaning without anxiety or care) which extend for miles around. Avenues, lined with lofty trees, closely shorn lawns, bordered with luxuriant hedges, ponds, fountains and statues, are seen in abundance in this stately garden. The palace itself we could not enter, as the royal family is at present residing there.

It is not a large building, and stands at the top of a series of terraces, on which grow, under glass, the fruits of warmer climates. It was built by Frederick himself, in 1745, and the gardens were laid out under his own eyes. In a sheltered nook are the graves of his favorite dogs, and of the horse that carried him through the greater part of his battles. In his will he declared his wish to be buried beside them, but his wishes, undisputed in life, were not attended to after death, and his remains repose in another spot.

The celebrated wind-mill of Sans Souci came in for a share of our observation, and for fear you may not know the history of it, I shall relate it to you. This mill is only separated from the garden of Sans Souci by a road, and Frederick wanted to pull it down that the ground on which it stood might be included in his garden, but the bluff old miller refused to give it up, and affairs were carried to such a length that a law suit ensued, which was decided in favor of the miller, and against the sovereign. The mill was small, and Frederick, after losing the case, had the magnanimity to build a larger one on the site of the old one. Within a few years, the descendant of that very miller, having met with reverses, decided he must give up his mill, and he offered to sell it to the late king, who refused to take it, saying that the mill now belonged to history, and was therefore a kind of Prussian monument, showing that the rights of the people could not be overthrown, even by a king, and he gave the miller money sufficient to release him from his embarrassment, and to enable him to keep the cherished mill.

Some of the fountains in the garden were playing; one of them throws up a stream of water one hundred and thirty feet high. The machinery which makes these waters play, is in the town, in a building representing a Turkish mosque.

In another part of the garden stands the new palace, an immense edifice of brick, erected by Frederick at the end of the seven years' war, between 1763 and 1769, to show his enemies that his finances were by no means exhausted. "They say" it contains seventy-two apartments, but we had neither time, strength or inclination to go through them, particularly as there is said to be nothing remarkable about them, except the one called the "marble hall," and this we visited. The walls are lined with marbles, with large tablets, faced with every variety of shell and minerals. Some of the minerals were splendid specimens.

In a building known by the name of "the antique temple," in the rear of this palace, is a recumbent statue of the beautiful Louisa, late queen of Prussia. She is represented asleep, her arms crossed peacefully on her breast. It is most beautiful, though I cannot say the attitude exactly pleases me, but the face is exquisite. The expression of repose is perfect. It was done by Rauch, the Prussian sculptor, and is said to have cost him fifteen years of thought and study. In still another part of the garden of Sans Souci, there is a villa, built by the present king when prince of Prussia, called Charlottenhof, in the style of a house in Pompeii, the size and arrangement of the rooms, following as nearly as possible, the Pompeiian plan. The bath-room is fitted up precisely like those found in ancient Pompeii. The beautiful fountains, the statues and bronzes, and an antique altar, came from Herculaneum and Pompeii, and were presents from the king of Naples.

At a short distance from Potsdam lies a little village called the Russian colony. It consists of eleven houses, built in true Russian style, and very much resembling Swiss houses with wooden galleries. It was built by the late king for a party of Russians, sent here as a present from the Emperor of Russia. There is a beautiful little church, having one large dome and two smaller ones, an imitation of the Kremlin at Moscow.

Coming back to the town, we went into the church of the garrison, a plain, unpretending church, but having great interest for us, and for all the world, for under the pulpit in a little chapel lie the mortal remains of Frederick the Great. They are enshrined in a plain metal sarcophagus, once having on top of it Frederick's sword, but this was carried away by Napoleon, and all traces of it are lost. And now over the entrance to the tomb wave the standards, and appear the eagles taken from the French armies by the Prussians.

I believe I have now told you all that interested us in Potsdam, though I find, on looking over it, I have not said any thing about Voltaire. Opposite the royal palace in the town, is the house he occupied when he played "toady" to Frederick the Great.

It was evening when we came, and long past the dinner hour at the hotel, so we went to a nice café and got our dinner, and then came back to our room, for I must "own up" to being somewhat tired after the fatigue and excitement of the day, and this must be my apology for the abrupt termination of this epistle.

LETTER LXXVI.

Chamber of Art.—Picture Gallery.—Sculpture Gallery.—New Museum.—Zoological Collection.—Porcelain Manufactory.—Pleasant Meeting.

BERLIN, Sept. 22.

MY DEAR F:

We have devoted to-day to the "lions" of Berlin, going first to the Chamber of Art, at present in the attic story of the royal palace, though soon to be removed to rooms in the new museum, which, it is to be hoped, will be a little more easy of access than the present chambers, for steeper stairs I never went up than those leading to it.

Of the "thousand and one" things collected there, I was the most pleased with those connected with associations of the great Frederick, or that had some particular historical reference. And first, as to the great monarch. Behold a wax figure of him, wearing the very uniform he had on the day of his death, the coat looking the worse for wear, the scabbard of his sword mended with sealing-wax by his own hands, and his shirt-sleeves trimmed with very dirty looking lace.

His cane, his flute, and even his pocket handkerchief are here, the last torn and bearing several patches. We were shown his watch, which he always wound up himself, and which, neglected the last day of his life, by a singular coincidence stopped at the very moment of his death, and still points to the hour of his departure from this mortal life, twenty minutes past two. There is a cast of his face taken just after his death, and the bullet is shown that wounded him in the battle of Rossbach in 1760.

And now let me think what else I saw. Oh, all the stars and orders given to Buonaparte by the different sovereigns of Europe, the black eagle of Prussia being conspicuous among them. These were taken by the Prussians as trophies, after the battle of Waterloo, and were found, it is said, in Napoleon's own carriage, which he left in such a hurry that he forgot his hat, which is also shown here. I can well imagine the eagerness with which the Prussians seized upon every thing belonging to the great despoiler of their country.

Then we saw the "orders" that had been given the great Blucher, and the chair of Gustavus Adolphus, and the pipes of the father of Frederick the Great, who established a smoking club that held its meetings in a house we saw at Potsdam.

We no longer wondered that Buonaparte called Murat a dandy, if he had many dresses as fantastic looking as the one we saw, all trimmed off with gold lace and shining with finery.

The model of a wind-mill made by Peter the Great, while working as a ship-carpenter in Holland, we all stopped to look at, for every thing connected with the name of Russia has more than usual interest just now.

Luther must have been rich in beer-mugs, for we saw another of his in this collection, and of a goodly size, too. I looked with great interest on the drinking cup of the renowned Baron Trenck, engraved on the outside by himself, while in a dark prison.

One of the "extraordinary" things that was shown was a stone, a species of "giode," which on being broken open, was found impressed with the figure of a black eagle, the coat of arms of Prussia. The cicerone looked indignant when I said "if it had been found in Austria, I suppose the eagle would have had two heads," for you know a double headed eagle is the badge of Austria.

We saw, too, some immense topazes, the largest in the world, which makes the fourth or fifth time we have seen "the largest topaz known." Then came exquisite carvings in wood and ivory, cabinets in amber, rare specimens of old china, ancient paintings, weapons, &c., and curiosities from different parts of the world, altogether too numerous to be mentioned here.

In the rear of this palace are some houses and shops, glittering with every thing attractive, at which I took a glance, while J. went on to the post-office with letters.

Next we went to the picture and sculpture gallery, inferior to those at Munich, but still containing many beautiful things. I must say I was sorry to see a few paintings, that for modesty's sake I think would have been far better left out. After a while one becomes accustomed to naked figures, and looks upon them with less and less reluctance, and whether this is a proof of "educated refinement" or not, I leave for others to decide. I would be the last to wish, from any prudish notions, to have beautiful pictures excluded from public or private galleries, because the figures were more or less after the fashion of Adam and Eve before the fall, but I would raise my voice here and elsewhere against having pictures exhibited that a daughter would blush to look at in the presence of her father, or a wife before her husband. No beauty of form or expression of face, no rich coloring or extrinsic charm, ought to cover the heinousness of such an offence, for it strikes at the root of all that is pure and lovely in the human character. A picture which from so-called "prudish motives," a scion of the house of Orleans, in that country too, where of all the world there is the least of what could be termed "prudery," or what others might even call modesty, refused to have in his collection, was "luckily" purchased by Frederick the Great, and now stands in a prominent position in the picture gallery of Berlin, and I say shame on the gallery that admits so indecent a picture within its collection. How out of keeping is it among Holy Families and Crucifixions, and pictures of young and innocent children, and pleasant family groups, and beautiful scenes of nature! Is there not pure food enough in the ideal and real world for the artist, without touching on subjects that should be forbidden to the thoughts, to say nothing of the eyes?

The entrance to the Sculpture Gallery is through an imposing circular hall, around which hang some antique tapestries, worked from designs by Raphael, and originally belonging to Henry VIII. of England. Among the works of art to be found in this gallery, I shall merely mention one, in bronze, called "the Boy Praying," found, it is said, in the bed of the Tiber. The child is standing, but his hands are raised and his head thrown back in an attitude of devotion, while the face is expressive of supplication, mingled with a look of holy calmness and meekness. The face is that of a boy, but oh! of such a boy! I returned again and again to look at it.

I must not omit to say that before the entrance of this museum, is an immense basin of polished granite, twenty-two feet in diameter. The block from which it was formed was found about thirty miles from Berlin. The fineness of the grain is equal to any marble.

In the rear of this building, is the new museum, one of the most beautiful edifices, as far as regards the interior, in the world, the walls decorated with magnificent frescoes, and the ceilings panelled and adorned with gildings, and carvings, and gems of pictures.

We passed quickly by the collection of Roman, and Grecian, and Etruscan antiquities, and devoted all our time and attention to the collection brought from Egypt, for you can easily fancy how full of interest this would be to us, coming, as we so recently have, from that land, cradle of the arts and sciences. Here we looked upon mummies, and figures, and urns, and vases, and coins, brought by Leipsius from temples and tombs we visited and found emptied of their rich contents, because brought away by the hand of the despoiler. Murray says an actual temple has been brought from Philæ here, the parts wanted being restored and painted as in the original, but I saw very little that looked like an ancient temple, and very much doubt whether a great part of it was ever at Philæ. If he had said it was a capital imitation of an Egyptian temple, he would not have erred, for it certainly is an admirable copy, and would give one an excellent idea of the form and manner of the temples in that country. Next, we went to the Zoological collection in the University, one of the best collections of stuffed birds and animals in the world, to say nothing of thousands of insects, snakes and fishes preserved in spirits, which imparted rather a "rummy" smell to the gallery.

After dinner, we took a long walk to the royal manufactory of porcelain. On our way, I saw a man run across the street, and slap J. on the shoulder. For a second, I stood bewildered, all my old fears of Austrian police, and strangers seized on slight pretences, coming back with renewed force, but I looked again, and saw the parties shaking hands very cordially, and then I found it was Mr. L., whom we met last winter up the Nile, and who parted from us at Cairo. You must travel long in a foreign land, before you can appreciate the pleasantness of these unexpected meetings. Mr. L. accompanied us to the manufactory and back, and perhaps our tongues did not run fast on the way!

We saw most beautiful specimens of porcelain at the manufactory, dinner sets and tea sets that would make one's eyes shine. The transparencies were very beautiful. You remember there was, at one time, a great rage for them at home, but within the last few years they seem to have been lain by. They are "all the go" here; you cannot pass a house, even one of moderate pretension, without seeing one or more of these transparencies hanging at the windows.

The streets of Berlin are so very level that you may walk miles, without ascending or descending a foot, and the houses are mostly of brick, stuccoed. Carriage hire is very cheap here, three of us, yesterday, going to the railway station, a long distance from our hotel, for twenty-five cents of our money.

I have written this letter at different intervals to-day, and in rather a disconnected manner, and I am not sure but you may think it dull. Indeed, I fancy all my letters, lately, have been dry and prosy, for to tell the plain truth, I am rather tired of writing descriptions. I must confess I should like to sit down and write a long gossipping letter, but would it "pay"? (for the postage, I mean.)

LETTER LXXVII.

Charlottenburg.—Louisa of Prussia.—The late King.—The Spree.—English Chapel.—Disappointment.—Cathedral.—Difference between Protestant and Catholic Countries.

BERLIN, Sept. 24th.

MY DEAR F.:

I sent you two such long letters yesterday, that there is little left for me to write about to-day, and to-morrow we are off. We made a delightful little excursion yesterday to Charlottenburg, about three miles from here, the road lying through the great park at first, and afterwards through a long, straggling street, lined with gardens and country houses.

Beyond the village, there is a large palace, built by Frederick I., who married Sophia Charlotte, daughter of George I. of England, (hence the name, Charlottenburg.) We did not enter the palace, for, as I believe I have told you before, we have forsworn palaces, unless they have some special historical interest, but we walked through the grounds, which are prettily laid out, and made very charming by the meandering of the Spree.

Within this garden, is the most beautiful little Doric temple imaginable, and within the temple lie buried the beautiful, the interesting Louisa of Prussia, and the late King, her husband. Contrary to royal etiquette, I name the Queen first, because I am more interested in her than in her husband. The Queen lies in the same attitude here as at Potsdam, only there she is represented as asleep, here, as dead. Both statues are by the same sculptor, and I don't know which I like best. In both, there is the same look of calm repose about the mouth, and the soft shutting of the eyes; in the first, the expression of the face is of one who quietly and sweetly sleeps, while that of the other speaks of a soul gently passed away. A subdued light, from a window of colored glass, falls upon the exquisite face, and the fair hands, folded in the sleep of death, and beside her, upon a similar sarcophagus of marble, reposes the form of her husband, wrapped in his "martial cloak." His face is calm and quiet, and seems to say, "life's troubles and cares are over, and I am now at rest." What a magic power the sculptor has! Out of a block of marble, he makes a figure, so instinct with life, that it almost seems to breathe, to move.

After dinner, we took a long walk on the other side of the Spree, passing through streets lined with nice houses, the lower stories of which were shops, presenting a brilliant display of handsome goods. Perhaps it would not sound well for my reputation at home, to say I have been on "a spree," since I have been here, but I can say I have been on *the* Spree several times.

We came back to our hotel by a new way, and passed

through a square, on one side of which was an immense theatre, having a large church on either hand. Rather a novelty, to see churches and a theatre side by side! We have not visited any of the churches of Berlin, because we were told that, with the exception of a few monuments, and some very commonplace pictures, there was nothing in them to see.

All day to-day, there has been a pouring rain, but we were determined not to lose our church for the weather, so we took a carriage, or drosky, as they are called here. When any one at the hotel wants a carriage, the porter steps to the door and sends forth a loud, prolonged whistle, and in a minute, a carriage is at your service. At all hours of the day, these whistles are heard from the different hotels in this street.

Judge of our disappointment on arriving at the English chapel, to find there was no service, the clergyman being absent from the city! We thought we would not spend Sunday without attending some church, so we told the coachman to drive us to the Cathedral, where Murray says the "Berlin choir" sing Mendelssohn's Psalms so well that they should be heard by all lovers of sacred music, but when we arrived at the church, prayers were over, and a clergyman, in a black gown, was preaching to a quiet and attentive audience. Every seat was filled, and after standing up as long as I was able, I stole softly out into the passage way, and sat down upon the stairs leading up into the gallery, and there I opened my Prayer Book and Bible, and read the Psalms and lessons for the day. At length the sermon was over; there was a general stir in the congregation, and the minister came down from the pulpit and went within the chancel rails, where, although it was a Protestant church, two immense candles were burning upon the altar, over which hung some pictures. There, standing up with his back to the altar, and his face to the congregation, he read two or three prayers from a book, among which I could distinguish one for the royal family and the Lord's prayer. Then the organ struck up, and I said to myself, "Now comes the music." The choir sang something, I don't know what, but it was nothing remarkable, and in a few minutes the service was over.

We returned to the hotel, and I have not been out of my room since, except to go down to dinner. J. went to another church this afternoon, but I cannot say I fancy these services in unknown tongues, so I staid at home, and have spent the hour in writing to you. If there is one time, more than another, when the heart of the traveller turns fondly to his home, it is on Sunday, and when I cannot go to church, I sit down and commune with the dear ones at home. Will you say this is wrong?

As we went down to dinner to-day, the waiter handed us a play-bill, saying there was a great opera to-night, and asking us if we would like to go! We have now seen both Catholic and Protestant countries, and truth compels me to say, there seems but little difference in the manner the Sunday is kept by the two religions, or if there is a difference, I shall be obliged to confess that the Protestants seem to give up more of the Lord's day to pleasure, than the Catholics. The shops, except those for cigars and tobacco, are closed, it is true, but men, women and children betake themselves to gardens, and different places of resort, and end the day by dancing at some public place, or going to the theatre. I do not say this in condemnation, but merely to show that there is no apparent difference between the two religions.

And now, good bye.

LETTER LXXVIII.

Wittenberg.—Church.—Burial place of Luther and Melancthon.—House of Melancthon.—Statue of Luther.—University.—Oak Tree.—Church where Luther preached.—Railway Carriages.—Smoking.—Dessau.—Birthplace of Mendelssohn.—Halle.—Interesting Day.—Historical Associations.—Jena.—Weimar.—Erfurt.—Eisenach.—Castle of Wartburg.—Reminiscences of Luther.—Exquisite View.—Sebastian Bach.

FRANKFORT-ON-THE-MAINE, Sept. 27th.

MY DEAR F.:

I give you fair warning this is going to be a "tremendous" letter, so make up your minds accordingly.

We left Berlin on the morning of the 25th, and for two days we have been running about after Martin Luther, visiting two or three places particularly associated with his memory. Our first stopping place was at Wittenberg, which has been called the Protestant Mecca, so many thousands of Protestants going there every year to pay their respects to the place, which may be called the cradle of the Reformation. When we left Berlin, it was with the expectation of having about four hours for Wittenberg, which would be amply sufficient for viewing the celebrities of the town, but when we arrived at the station, we found no train left earlier than half past eight in the evening, which was giving us at least five hours too much. But there was no alternative; it was either to stop or to go on, though, in fact, we had no alternative at all, as the train had gone on, before we knew we should be obliged to stop so long at Wittenberg.

However, we determined to make the best of it, so leaving our luggage at the station, we walked to the town, about a half mile distant, and going to the London Hotel, ordered dinner at four o'clock, and then strolled out to see the town, under the guidance of a man who could speak no English and only a little French. However, with helping himself out pretty frequently with German, he got along quite nicely, doubtless to his own satisfaction, judging from the price he demanded for his services, but of that more hereafter.

Nearly opposite to our hotel, was the church in which Luther and Melancthon sleep their last sleep, and not far from them, are the tombs of Frederick "the Wise," and John "the Steadfast," Electors of Saxony, and friends not only of Luther himself, but of the Reformation also. The monument of Frederick is of bronze, and is a beautiful piece of work, by Peter Vischer.

Against the doors of this church, not the present ones, for they were burnt by the French, Luther hung up his celebrated theses, containing ninety-five propositions or arguments against the doctrines of the Romish church, and these arguments he offered to prove against all opposers.

If you could have walked through the town, over those horrible round stones with which the streets are paved, in new boots, as I did, I am sure you would have wondered how my thoughts could have been as much with Luther as they were. I think the stones were worse than those of Jerusalem, and they were bad enough, in all conscience.

We passed by the house in which Melancthon lived

while at Wittenberg, and saw two or three other houses of the time of Luther, and picturesque old houses they were, too, with their little narrow windows and high roofs.

In the market place, is a bronze statue, by Schadow, of Luther, under a canopy of cast-iron, erected in 1822, and on one side of the pedestal are the words, (in German,) "If it be God's work, it will endure; if man's, it will perish," and on another side, "A strong tower is our God."

Next, we went to the old University, once one of the most famous in Germany, now united with that at Halle. It was at this University Shakespeare tells us Hamlet studied, and here Luther was Professor of Theology and Philosophy. His room in the old building, where he lived after his marriage, remains almost entirely in its original state, and you may judge the feelings and emotions of our hearts, as we entered Luther's room. There stood the very table at which he was accustomed to sit and write; there was his high-backed wooden chair; there, on a raised platform, was the bench he occupied when delivering some of his lectures, and there stood the huge stove, made after his own directions, and adorned with statues in bas-relief of the four Evangelists. Against the window of small panes of glass, was the chair where his wife used to sit, occasionally looking out, I've no doubt, to see what was going on below. Nor must I omit to mention a curious old portrait of Luther, by Cranach, nor his drinking mug, as usual of goodly proportions. I was anxious to bring away a small relic from the room, so the guide cut off a snip from the table, and took a half-broken peg, which formerly helped to sustain the portrait of the great reformer, and gave them to me, with many injunctions to secrecy, so, therefore, you must not tell!

Peter the Great once visited this chamber, and wrote his name in chalk over the door, but whether it was "Peter" or "Czar" we could not decide. To preserve the royal autograph, a glass case has been put over it.

Just beyond the gate of the town, is an oak tree, planted on the site of the one under which, on December 10th, 1520, Luther committed the daring act of burning the Papal bull issued against him and the doctrines he promulgated.

Back again, over the round stones, we hobbled, to another church, where our guide left us, saying it was not his province to show us that. And how much do you think he wanted for his services, that had not occupied him two hours? Why, no less a sum than one thaler, seventy-five cents, which is the usual pay for a whole day's services. It was no use to grumble; he only shrugged his shoulders, and said it was his price. Perhaps the round stones had something to do with this exorbitance, or the wooden peg; if the latter, I have nothing more to say on the subject.

In this last church is a bronze font of very beautiful workmanship, by Vischer, and at this font, both Luther and Melancthon were in the habit of baptising. In the old pulpit, since taken down, Luther used to preach, and there is a singular painting by Cranach, in which he is represented preaching, his wife and young son being the two most prominent individuals in the congregation. She seems to be listening to him with the greatest possible attention, a goodly example, which should be followed by all "preachers'" wives, who should set, in this respect, a pattern for the rest of the congregation!

There are other pictures here by Cranach, one representing the Lord's Supper, wherein the artist appears as a servant, and another, the Sacrament of Baptism, where Melancthon is officiating as the priest.

We finished the sights of Wittenberg, which is but a small town on the Elbe, of about seven thousand inhabitants, and it was not two o'clock! What should be done with the remaining six hours? Had it not been for those excruciating stones, I might have walked around for an hour or two longer, but I could better endure doing nothing than encounter those pavements. It was excessively stupid in me leaving my writing desk at the station; with that I could have defied ennui for any length of time. Fortunately, in a little bag I had with me, were three handkerchiefs to be hemmed, and to these I addressed myself with considerable zest. And when I raised my eyes from my work, directly before me rose the church in which reposed the mortal remains of the fiery, earnest Luther, and the gentle, loving Melancthon. Then, in due time, came dinner, and a very good dinner we had, and at reasonable charges, and afterwards, in the deepening twilight, we strolled to the station, where we had to wait about an hour and a half in a room in which, at one time, I counted no less than seventeen cigars under full smoke. Perhaps this was not a trial to my eyes and nose, but it was too cold for me to wait outside. Fortunately a train soon stopped on its way to Berlin, and the smokers all departed, and I eagerly threw open doors and windows, hoping soon to be rid of the noxious vapors.

At last our train came along, and we found ourselves in a carriage with three gentlemen, one asleep in a corner, and two with lighted cigars at their lips. Have

I told you that the railway carriages are not large "cars," as at home, but divided off into small apartments, as it were, furnished with nicely stuffed seats, even in the second class ? In fact, the greater part of the second class carriages here are nicer than our first class at home. As there is no prohibition against smoking, to avoid being shut up with a number of smokers, we have generally signified to the conductor our wish to be alone, or where there would be no cigars, and a small fee has helped him wonderfully to understand our poor German lingo, and thus far we have contrived to have a carriage to ourselves. But when the train came along on Monday evening, there were so many passengers we were obliged to be put into a carriage with the three gentlemen I have already mentioned.

No sooner did we seat ourselves, than J. let down the window on his side, and I the one on mine. This excited a rebellion at once, for the Germans are dreadfully afraid of the air. And this is a mystery I cannot account for; so much as they live in the open air, spending hours in gardens and parks, yet put them in a diligence or railway carriage, and venture to open a window, and they will look at you with as much indignation and horror as though you were on the point of committing some deadly sin. On that evening, the sound of the falling window roused my opposite neighbor from his sleep, and he and the two others began a tirade, of which the long and short of the matter seemed to be, that they wanted the windows closed. I muttered away in broken German, something about cigars, but J. came out boldly in his mother tongue, with the assertion that so long as there were lighted cigars in the carriage, he must have a window opened, or suffer. Either the German or the English produced an effect, for one cigar was instantly thrown away, whereupon I closed the window near me. The other passenger, I cannot now call him a gentleman, kept puffing away at his, with unabated vigor. However, by degrees, it dwindled away, and I flattered myself after that was gone, he would go to sleep, but, would you believe it? no sooner was that used up, than he deliberately lit another, and so on, till he had smoked three cigars! And all the time, I knew the cool, fresh air was very annoying to him, yet he was too "spunky" to give up, and we could not breathe in such an atmosphere, if the window had been closed.

Fortunately, in about two hours, we arrived at Halle, and just as we were getting out of the carriage, I found out the young smoker, for he could not have been more than twenty, understood English! Well, I hope he profited by our remarks about his smoking.

Oh! I must not forget to say that between Wittenberg and Halle, we passed through Dessau, the birthplace of Mendelssohn, whose strains of surpassing sweetness and melody have so often enchanted our ears.

We drove through street after street of the old town of Halle, until we reached the hotel of "the Crown Prince," (for the German hotels are famous for high sounding names,) where we arrived little after eleven o'clock. We lighted a candle, long enough to see to undress by, went to bed, were called at half past six, at seven had our breakfast, and at eight o'clock were once more moving along on the railroad. And that is all we know of Halle, except that we saw some quaint looking houses, as we drove to the station, and had a glimpse of the University, one of the most renowned in Germany. Hotel keepers must make money on their candles, for, although ours was not lit a half hour, we were charged full price for it.

Yesterday was one of the most interesting days we have had for a long time. Every step was full of beauty, or of historical and thrilling associations. The country was varied and lovely; now we were amid beautiful meadows and vineyards, and now we were among hills and by quickly rushing streams.

Soon after leaving Halle, we passed near the spot where Frederick the Great gained one of his victories over the French and Austrians, in 1757. Next, we reached the town where the dead body of Gustavus Adolphus was brought, after the battle of Lutzen, in 1632, and also where Napoleon slept the night after the memorable battle of Leipsic.

In that neighborhood the country was exquisitely beautiful, hills rising around us, covered with vineyards, the impetuous Saale running through the valley, along which towns and villages were clustered in picturesque confusion.

Farther on, we had on our left the battle-field of Jena, where Napoleon's "star" shone out so brilliantly, and the Prussians were so disastrously defeated. Then, again, there was something exceedingly attractive in the manner in which we passed from the possessions of one king to those of another. At one time the black and white colors of Prussia marked the stations and the crossings; at another the crown of Saxony appeared, and not long after the green and yellow (or green and white, I've forgotten which) of the Grand Duchy of Weimar varied the scene. Then came Prussia again, and afterwards the dominions of the Duke of Saxe-Coburg, after which we once more entered Saxony. And although we thus passed from one nation to another, neither our passports nor our keys were demanded.

Of Weimar we could see but little from the railroad; it is the residence of the Grand Duke of Saxe-Weimar, and when Schiller and Goethe, Herder and Wieland, and other men of science and literature lived there, it was called "the Athens of the North." There, Goethe, worshipped as a genius of the first order by the Germans, died in 1832, and till recently his house, exactly as he left it, has been shown to strangers, and thousands flocked to see the room in which he had written so many beautiful things.

Not far from Weimar we came to Erfurt, associated in our minds with memories of Luther. There, in the Augustine convent, he passed many years of his life, entering it as a monk in 1505, in consequence of a vow he made just after the shock caused by the sudden death of an intimate friend, who was struck by lightning while standing at his side.

About here the country assumed a different aspect, dark forests rising around us, called by the old and well-known name of the forest of Thuringia. And side by side with the forest trees there were lovely meadows, and pretty glens, and sheltered nooks, and old-fashioned looking houses and villages, that gave their own charm to the landscape.

The dominions of the Duke of Saxe-Coburg cover about as much ground as one of our counties at home, so it did not take long to traverse these, and we were soon at Eisenach, where we were to stop three or four hours, giving us ample time to visit the castle of Wartburg, situated on a lofty eminence over-topping the village. It was at this castle, as doubtless you know, that Luther was kept in custody for nearly a year, by his friends though, and not by his foes. Perhaps you may have heard the story a hundred times, yet I must venture to repeat it to make my own narrative clear. On returning from the Diet at Worms, Luther was seized by a party of armed men, in the forest of Thuringia, and led away prisoner to the castle of Wartburg, where he remained from May, 1521, to March, 1522. For a long time no one knew what had become of the "bold Reformer," and Luther himself was ignorant for a while of the cause of his seizure, till at length it came out that the whole plan was matured by the Elector of Saxony, with the view of keeping him out of the dangers that threatened him.

I don't know when I have enjoyed a walk so much as I did that yesterday up to the old castle. We had ample time before us, so there was no need of being in a hurry, the weather was perfect, and the country beautiful. Just as we were leaving the station, a man came up and offered to be our guide; he could not speak one word of English, and was quite as ignorant of French, but all the information we wanted was concerning the path, and that he could give us by his actions, which in this case would "speak louder than words." If the walk had been ever so dull it would have been enlivened by him, for when he could not make us understand by words, he would resort to gestures, and when he got into one of his gesticulating moods, it was "as good as going to a play," as A. used to say, to see him. For my part I have not laughed so much in a long time, and once when the ascent was very steep he came up to me and offered his arm with such a quizzical air and look, it was as much as my self-control could accomplish to keep from laughing in his face.

Eisenach is a very neat, thriving town of ten thousand inhabitants, and I was surprised to see so many nice looking houses and prettily arranged shops. To be sure, the paving-stones were rather sharp, but we soon left the town behind us, and began to ascend the hill, along winding paths, under lofty trees, the dead leaves rustling under our feet and producing that pleasant sound I love so much to hear. Up and up we went, crossing little glades and sheltered nooks, and winding in and out among the trees, stopping now and then to get a peep at the charming valley below.

After more than an hour's walk, for we took it leisurely, we reached the top of the hill, and went at once within the castle, which dates back as far as the twelfth century. I shall not tell you now of its long arched passages, nor its antique suits of armor, but proceed at once to the chamber which Luther, as "Junker Georg," inhabited. His chair and bedstead are among "the things that were," having been carried away in piecemeals by visitors, but his table is there still, and is now surrounded by a strong iron band to prevent its being whittled up. On the wall is still shown the spot where he threw his inkstand at the head of the devil, who he thought was tempting him to evil. As I saw here another of his big drinking cups, I could not help wondering whether this apparition of the evil one was just after dinner or not.

No description can do justice to the loveliness of the view from this old castle. Masses of forest trees, relieved by meadows of the richest green, gently swelling hills and sunny vales, peaceful villages and a wide spreading country, fertile and bright, made up a charming prospect. No wonder Luther called this spot his Patmos ; no wonder his strong feelings and vivid imagination were acted upon by scenes like these. Solitude, in a region of such beauty, could not be solitude, and even imprisonment might be borne here with less repining than usual.

At a little distance from the castle is a recess in a rock, overgrown with luxuriant moss, and this still goes by the name of "Luther's seat." Here, it is said, he used to sit, and meditate, and pray, and a more beautiful spot for meditation and prayer I have not seen in a long time.

We came down by a different path from the one we went up, passing through a narrow defile, rocks towering above our heads. Occasionally we caught glimpses of the fine old castle above us, and of the enchanting valley beneath. At one place, where the rocks rose precipitously to a considerable height, our guide pointed to a white stone gleaming out from the trees below, and then by his gestures explained to us that a man fell from those rocks into the vale beneath, and was buried in that little inclosure. Solemn as the subject was, for my life I could not help laughing, to see him act this out.

As I wanted to make two or three purchases in the town, we walked again through some of the streets, which were remarkably clean. The women we met had on short calico cloaks ruffled round, and it looked just as though they had thrown the skirt of a flounced dress over their shoulders.

Sebastian Bach, the great musician was born in this town. We had a nice dinner at the station, and before dark started for Cassel. But I cannot finish the account of this journey to-night, for I am too tired, so will leave the remainder for to-morrow, and send this off as it is.

LETTER LXXIX.

Cassel.—Hessian Troops.—Slow Train.—Broom-sellers.—Frankfort-on-the-Maine.—Hotel de Russie.—Old Town.—New Tówn.—The Jews.—Rothschilds' House.—Suburbs.—Zeil.—Town House.—Statue of Goethe.—Museum.—Dannecker's Ariadne.—Cemetery.—Mirrors in Windows.

FRANKFORT, Sept. 28.

MY DEAREST F:

My last letter left off in the midst of the account of our journey here, and without any circumlocution, I will now take up the thread of my narrative. The distance from Eisenach to Cassel was sixty-six miles, but we were enabled to see very little of the country, on account of night coming on so soon after our departure from Eisenach. We were sorry to lose any part of this interesting and beautiful country, but we could not arrange it so as to arrive at Wiesbaden on Saturday, unless we went some part of the way by night, and we preferred losing the sight of this part of the country to any other. Had we known as much day before yesterday as we knew yesterday, we might have stopped at Eisenach all night, and even then reached here in season last evening.

We arrived at Cassel about nine o'clock, and went to

the "Hotel of the king of Prussia," for all the German hotels that are not "golden" or some other kind of "ships" or "stags" or "eagles," are named for some distinguished individual. It was too late of course to go out that evening to make any observations: in fact we had had quite enough of sight-seeing for one day, but the next morning we were out in good season. Our hotel was on one side of an oval "place," in the centre of which was a remarkable echo, as we had a good opportunity of proving, for just as we were hesitating about screaming out to try the echo, some boys at play set up a loud halloo, which reverberated in grand style from the houses around.

Cassel is the capital of the dominions of Hesse-Cassel, and is divided into what is called the old and the new town, in the old town the streets being narrow, and the houses having high, peaked roofs, while in the new, every thing bears a different aspect, for the streets are wide and the houses handsome. The gardens around the town are lovely, but do you know where the money came from to pay for all this loveliness? Well, then, I will tell you. You remember the part which the Hessian troops bore in the war of our Revolution? They came from this very province of Hesse-Cassel, and the Elector, Frederick II., received twenty-two million dollars from the king of Great Britain, for the twelve thousand troops sent to America to fight his battles.

The town is full of barracks and soldiers, and every time I passed a tall grenadier at his station, I wanted to say, "I suppose you are a descendant of the men who fought against my country."

We left Cassel at half past eleven, and although it

is only one hundred and twenty-five miles here, we were ten hours getting over the road, having the misfortune of being again in the slow train. It actually seemed to me, that sometimes when we stopped at a station, we were never going to move on again, while there really seemed nothing to cause such delay, the men connected with the road standing around with their hands in their pockets, and it is my real conviction that we made those long stoppages merely to pass away the time. And then there was another evil connected with this train; passengers not often coming by it, there was no provision made for their accommodation at the stations, and at some of them it was impossible to get any thing to eat, and had it not been for an accidental slice of bread, and a German sausage, strongly flavored with garlic, we should have arrived here in a famishing condition.

Notwithstanding all these drawbacks we had a good many enjoyments, for the weather was pleasant, and the country delightful, though not so full of historical associations as that we passed through the day before. We saw old castles and towers, and venerable looking churches, and pretty villages, and thriving towns, and rich meadows, and gently rolling hills, and quickly flowing streams, and a thousand other things, that tend to make up the elements of a beautiful landscape.

From this part of the country come the personages known in our country and in England as the German broom-sellers, but we saw none of them on the road. They were probably singing elsewhere their song of "buy a broom."

Notwithstanding all our precautions to avoid arriving here after dark, it was nine o'clock before we entered the city, so we could see nothing of the country round it. We came to the Hotel de Russie, a splendid hotel, although at present its name may go somewhat against it.

Frankfort is as you know, one of the free towns of Germany, and therefore has its own independent government. It lies on the Maine, and has seventy thousand inhabitants, a tenth of which are Jews. Like Cassel, it is divided into an old and a new town, and no two towns in different countries, could be more dissimilar than these two. In the new town the houses are handsome, the shops brilliant, the streets wide and clean, while in the old town every thing is just the opposite, the streets being so narrow that the projecting gables of the houses seem to meet, the shops are dark little booths filled with old clothes, &c., and the paving-stones are so covered with mud and dirt that one is obliged to mind carefully his steps. The Jews mostly reside in this quarter, and at one time were compelled to live entirely within it, and they were not allowed to pass in or out after a certain hour in the evening, but during the bombardment of the town by the French in 1796, the gates of the Jews' quarter were thrown down, and they have never been replaced since, and the Jews now can live in any part of the city they choose. In the old quarter of the Jews' we saw the house in which the Rothschilds were born, and where their mother recently died at an advanced age of one hundred and three years (I think.) It is one of the most old-fashioned looking houses I ever saw, the eaves projecting far over the other part, giving it a dark and gloomy appearance. The suburbs of Frankfort are beautiful, the streets lined with trees, and each house standing within a garden prettily laid out. Along the quay too, are handsome houses, and the street called the Zeil, in which is our hotel, is lined with palace like buildings.

The Cathedral was undergoing repairs, and we could not gain admission, but we were told we could go to the top of the spire, and have a fine view of the country around, but I must confess I did not feel equal to the exertion of mounting up so many stairs, and for once I declined the prospect of an elevation in life.

Not far from the Cathedral, is the Town House, where once took place the ceremonies attending the election of the Emperors, and the banquets after their coronation, and in the great hall, are the portraits of all the Emperors elected here. In front of this building is a fountain, which, at the time of an election of a new Emperor, was made to run with wine.

We saw the house in which Luther resided while in Frankfort, and also the one where Goethe was born. There is a bronze statue of Goethe in one of the streets, by Schwanthaler of Munich, and worthy of the name of that artist.

Although I am sick of museums, I was tempted into the one here, by being told I should see many "rare specimens, not to be found in any other museum in Europe," which, by the way, is said of every collection, I believe. However, the museum here is really a very valuable one, having a collection of stuffed animals, birds, &c., brought from Egypt, Nubia and Abyssinia, by the "enterprising" traveller, (all travellers are "enterprising," I believe,) Ruppell, who was a native of Frankfort. The cabinet of minerals is good, though not to be compared with the one in Vienna.

In a garden belonging to a citizen of Frankfort, is the

statue of Ariadne, by Dannecker, a German artist. She is represented riding on a panther, and the face, though beautifully chiselled, has a hard look about the mouth, but perhaps in keeping with the character of the person, for a woman who could ride a panther through a forest, without the slightest apology for clothes on her, ought to have nerve and resolution, I should think. However, whether Ariadne ever did exist, and whether she ever rode a panther, are questions for poets and sculptors to settle, not for me. By connoisseurs, this statue is called a splendid work of art, and the owner of it paid about nine thousand dollars for it. I should think he was in a fair way of getting his money back, however, as every body pays a fee for seeing it.

After we were tired walking round, we drove through the environs of the town, and stopped at the new cemetery, a labyrinth of flower-decked graves and crosses, the Protestants here using crosses, as well as the Romanists. Here, the Prince of Hesse Cassel has built a mausoleum, a perfect little gem of Gothic architecture.

At the entrance to this cemetery is a house, in which the bodies are placed for a little while, to avoid all possibility of premature interments. The corpse is laid on a bier, and attached to each finger is a small cord, communicating with a bell, so that the slightest pulsation causes the bell to ring. In an ante-chamber, persons are on the watch, a warm bath and a bed are always ready, and a physician, with a box of restorative medicines, at hand, so that if at any time the bell is heard, every measure may be promptly taken to restore life. I can assure you it was with solemn feelings we walked through these passages, lined with biers, the little cords hanging over them, and although there were no bodies there then, I shuddered, for fear I should hear a bell ring. How awful must a night watch be there! And yet what an excellent arrangement it is to avoid premature burials.

The country around Frankfort is very beautiful, backed by the range of the Taunus mountains, and watered by the Maine. I should really like to see more of it, but there is no time. While, at times, I tire of museums, and cabinets, and naked people, whether in pictures or in statues, I never grow weary of beautiful scenes, but turn from one to the other with ever increasing and fresh delight.

In this city, as well as in many others we have visited lately, attached to the windows of many houses, are little looking-glasses on the outside, thus enabling persons within, unseen themselves, to see all that is going on in the streets below. Although this evidently betrays the curiosity of the persons using the mirrors, is it not better than stretching one's neck out of the window, if one really must see the passers-by?

At five we dined, and after dinner we took another stroll through the Zeil, but in nearly all these German towns, the shops are closed early in the evening, and the people are off to cafés, theatres and gardens, so there is not much to be seen in the streets, which is well for me, as thus there is not a great deal to tempt me out after dark, and I have, therefore, so much the more time for writing.

To-morrow morning we are again on the move. To pack and to unpack, to go and to come, to see and to record what is seen, to enjoy, and then to communicate our enjoyments to others, this now sums up the history of our days. May their record be as interesting to you as to us! And I can assure you this is wishing you a great deal.

LETTER LXXX.

Heidelberg. — University. — Church of the Holy Ghost. — St. Peter's Church.—Jerome of Prague.—Olimpia Morata.—Ruins of the Old Castle. — Wolf-spring. — Mannheim.—The Rhine.—Worms.—Wiesbaden.—Kursaal.—Taste for Flowers.

WIESBADEN, Sept. 30th.

MY DEAR M.:

Here we are, at this quiet little watering place, quiet just now, because the season is nearly over; but in the summer, I am told, it is full of bustle and English people. We came, however, for quiet and rest, for I am at present a little weary, going about so constantly as we have done, ever since our landing at Trieste. But two or three days of rest, and a mineral bath, will quite restore me, I dare say. I do not think I shall drink the waters, for I am somewhat afraid of their effect. And now to go back a day or two.

We left Frankfort yesterday morning, by railroad, for Heidelberg, distant fifty miles, and through the most delightful country imaginable, but I have already said so much about scenery, I fancy you must be quite tired of my monotonous descriptions, and I will therefore merely say, that our road lay through a valley, luxuriant with vineyards and vegetation, while in the distance were towering hills, many of them crowned with ruined castles and fortresses.

Heidelberg lies on the Neckar, in a long, narrow

valley between the river and the mountains, the principal street running parallel with the river, and extending about three miles in length. It is celebrated for its University, one of the oldest in Germany, having at present about seven hundred students. We passed by the church of the Holy Ghost, where many of the Electors and Counts Palatine are buried. The Protestants and Romanists claim an equal division of this church, and a partition wall is thrown up in the interior, and the services of the two religions, so essentially different, are thus carried on beneath one roof.

On the door of the old church of St. Peter, Jerome of Prague attached his "theses" against the Papal religion, and large congregations assembled in the church-yard to hear him explain the doctrines of the Reformed faith, as well as to denounce the corruptions of the Romish church. Here, too, the celebrated Olimpia Morata is buried, she who combined, in a peculiar manner, beauty, and intelligence, and accomplishments, far beyond the generality of her sex, at that time. Born in the sunny clime of Italy, she was obliged to flee from her native land, on account of her religious sentiments, and, after many wanderings, came to live in Heidelberg, where she gave lectures, on various subjects, to as enlightened an audience as could be found any where in Europe.

The chief object of interest in Heidelberg, to every traveller, is the ruins of the old castle, formerly the residence of the Electors Palatine, but now the most extensive and beautiful ruin in all Germany. It was built in different ages, and in different styles, and this materially adds to its picturesque appearance, and the ruined turrets and battlements overgrown with ivy, the richly carved window frames and niches, the suite of magnificent apartments, once occupied by the beautiful Elizabeth Stuart, and the grounds laid out in exquisite taste, constantly appeal to the eye and the imagination of the lover of the beautiful, and to those who delight in historical associations. And then the views from this elevated position are charming in the extreme. Below, lies the old town, belted on the one hand by the "green, green Neckar," and on the other by wooded hills, and beyond, stretches a lovely country, varied with meadows and vineyards, mountains and forests, and far away, you catch glimpses of the Rhine. What an exquisite picture it was! I stood against the ruined battlements, shining with the glittering leaves of the ivy dotted over with little white blossoms, among which the humming, buzzing bees were flying, and I looked now on the majestic ruins around me, and now on the lovely landscape, stretching far away, and I thought earth had few scenes more enchanting than this. On such days, when the air is so pure, and every thing around is so lovely, I think what a luxury it is to breathe such air and to behold such scenes, and then my thoughts fly quickly to those at home, who, less favored than we, have long sighed in vain to visit foreign lands, and to revel amid those works of art not found at present in our own country.

About two miles from the castle, in a little nook, among the forest-clad hills, is the "Wolf-spring," so called from a pretty little spring that bubbles up from the ground, and because it is said the enchantress Jetta was here torn in pieces by a wolf. A great many trout are kept here in ponds and tanks, and while we were walking about, we ordered some to be cooked for us, which, with a mug of German beer, were quite acceptable to us, after our long ride.

As we wound round and round up the hills, and then down again, back to the railroad, we had charming views of the valleys, watered by the winding and rapid Neckar, and of the green hills beyond. In fact, the country all around Heidelberg is exceedingly beautiful, and I should think one might spend weeks there, without exhausting the delightful walks and drives.

Little more than a half hour on the railroad brought us to Mannheim, a town of about twenty-four thousand inhabitants. We drove through the town, along wide streets crossing each other at right angles, till we came to the quay on the Rhine, where we stopped at the Hotel de l'Europe, to be ready for the steamer this morning. As I stood at my window last evening, looking out upon the moonlit river, I grew quite "sentimental," at the thought of all that had transpired in the thirteen years that have elapsed since I last saw that mighty stream. What changes in thought, and feeling, and action, have taken place, both in the old world and the new! How the years come and go, and what traces they leave behind of their rapid march!

At seven o'clock this morning, we were on board the steamer, but we had scarcely started, when a dense fog came up, and after getting aground two or three times, we were forced to drop anchor, and wait till the mist had passed away. Our sail of five hours to Mayence was any thing but interesting; the banks were low, while the distant hills were enveloped in mists, that totally concealed them from our view. Occasionally we had glimpses of pretty scenes, but they were few and far between. We saw Worms, famous for that Diet, in

1521, before which Luther appeared to proclaim his adhesion to the doctrines of the Reformation, declared at that very session of the Diet to be heretical. You have, of course, read his declaration, when besought by his friends not to appear at this Diet, "that he would go to Worms, even though there were as many devils within its walls, as there were tiles on its houses." A dangerous place it must have proved, if this comparison had been true, for the roof of every house is covered with tiles.

Arriving at Mayence, we did not stop to visit its "lions," but proceeded directly to this place. Finding no train coming out for two hours, we took a carriage here, a nice, quiet drive of about an hour and a half, through a pleasant country of vineyards and orchards, with occasional glimpses of the Rhine, to vary the scene.

Wiesbaden is the capital of the Duchy of Nassau, and lies in a pretty valley, within an amphitheatre of hills. It is a larger town than I expected to see, having about fourteen thousand inhabitants. At least two-thirds of the houses are hotels, bath houses, boarding houses, &c., for its hot mineral springs attract a great many visitors here every year. So many English have come here the last few years, it has become quite an English colony, and the waiters in all the hotels, and almost every petty tradesman, speak our language. We are at the Rose Hotel,, and as soon as we had become settled in our room, (an operation that takes from five minutes to an hour, according to the distance we have come, and to the length of time we are to stay,) we strolled out to see what there was to be seen. At the upper end of the town, are villas, and gardens, and parks, forming delightful promenades, which were full of people, every body seeming intent, like ourselves, on enjoying this beautiful weather. On one side of a square, planted with noble trees, is the Kursaal, which contains rooms for eating, reading, dancing and gambling, and is, therefore, I need not say, the principal place of resort for the generality of visitors. Two other sides of the square are lined with colonnades, filled with little shops or booths, containing pretty wares from different parts of the world. Back of the Kursaal, is an extensive garden, or park, prettily laid out in winding walks, with o'erarching trees, and parterres of flowers. Roses were in full bloom, and delicate, lovely flowers scattered about in rich profusion, and although hundreds were walking in the garden, not a flower was disturbed. Judging from the quantity of flowers seen every where, I should say the Germans are excessively fond of them; every cottage that has an inch of ground attached to it, has its flower bed, and where there is no land for cultivating flowers, every window will have a half dozen flower-pots. I like to see this, for, as a general thing, where there are flowers, there is to be found a species of intellectual refinement and cultivation. In Germany, music, and flowers, and paintings, seem to go hand in hand, and the artist-soul finds every where something to fill it with lofty aspirations.

During the summer, an excellent band plays in this garden every afternoon, but to-morrow is the last day of the "season," and after that, they play here no more. How much better is music thus, in the open air, than in a confined hall, as at our watering-places at home.

But I have written quite enough for one day, so I will stop for a while.

LETTER LXXXI.

Quiet Sunday.—Lutheran Service.—English Service.—Gardens.—Music. Platte.—Donkey Riding.—Mineral Bath.—Concert.—Kursaal.—Law against Gambling.

WIESBADEN, Oct. 1st.

MY DEAR P:

One year ago this day, we sailed from New York, and how much we have seen and enjoyed in that year, so much that at times it seems a dream. This day has been the most like Sunday of any we have had for a long time. To be sure, we are in a very quiet part of the town, and for any noise we hear in the street or in the hotel, we might readily fancy ourselves in a country village at home. We have been to church all day, in a chapel in one of the palaces of the Duke of Nassau. It is first used for Lutheran worship, and when that is over, divine service after the order of the English church is celebrated. When we got there this morning, the Lutheran service was not over; the Lord's Supper was being celebrated, the men going first to the altar, the women afterwards, each one kneeling at one side of the chancel, and receiving the bread from one priest, and then passing round to the other side, and taking the wine from another, each bowing reverently the head on receiving the elements. No woman went up with her bonnet on, each one leaving it on the seat as she went out. All seemed devout and solemn, and the service, though simple, was exceedingly impressive. The priests wore bands and a black gown. The English congregation was large, and the service exceedingly interesting, for it is such a comfort to attend your own church in a foreign land.

After service this afternoon, we walked for an hour in the gardens back of the Kursaal, where the band was playing most delightfully. As we strolled along some of the distant walks, the strains of Beethoven and Von Weber came floating on the air, mingled with the breath of the flowers and the fragrance of the pines. Among the groups around us, there was not one face we had ever seen before, but the " dear, familiar strains" carried us far away from foreign faces and scenes, and made us think of home and of distant friends, till the tears came gushing to our eyes.

Oct. 2d. This morning we took a donkey ride to the "Platte," a hunting seat of the Duke of Nassau, about four miles off among the hills. Our path lay through the forests, the wind softly sighing through the branches, and the dead leaves rustling under our feet. How did this simple act of mounting a donkey call up, as with the mighty wand of an enchanter, the scenes of the past, bringing before me every ride I ever took on a donkey, from my first trembling attempt at Alexandria, to that last memorable one from Hebron to Jerusalem! This morning I was not in Germany, but in Egypt and Syria, and our faithful Hassan was by my side. Had I happened to have met a camel, the illusion would have been complete, and I should have been startled to find myself, on my return, at Wiesbaden, instead of Cairo, or on the banks of the Nile.

This hunting seat stands thirteen hundred feet above the level of the river, and commands an extensive view, but unfortunately for us there was a golden haze in the air which effectually prevented us from seeing any thing at a distance. The house is very nicely furnished, most of the furniture being framed in buck-horn.

To-day I have taken a mineral bath, and drank some of the water; the former I liked much better than the latter, which springs up from the ground, at a temperature so near boiling, that one has to wait awhile for it to cool before it can be drank. The taste of it has been compared to weak chicken broth, but I must say it is a kind of broth I should not care about taking often.

This evening we have been to a concert, and I need not say how much I enjoyed it. Besides the instrumental music we had two of Handel's grand choruses given in a perfect manner. The concert over, we saw many of the audience wending their way towards the Kursaal, to witness the gambling operations going on there, and perhaps to take part in them. I believe not many strangers have been here three days without visiting the Kursaal, but I did not feel any inclination to go in, to see human nature under such an aspect as it must present at the gaming table. These tables are kept by a Frenchman, who pays forty-three thousand florins a year, nearly twenty thousand dollars, and it is said the public lose there every year more than one hundred and twenty-five thousand dollars. And this money comes from foreigners, for the Duke of Nassau, while he permits these gaming tables in his dominions does not allow one of his own subjects to frequent them otherwise than as spectators. The law is so stringent against the inhabitants of the province of Nassau gambling, that the first offence is punished with a fine, the second with imprisonment, the third banishment from the country.

A few miles inland from Wiesbaden, there are baths said to produce such an astonishing effect upon the skin and the complexion, that the bathers fall in love with themselves. You may be sure, with a complexion none of the clearest at the best, but now suffering under the effects of the scorching sun of the East, I have been strongly tempted to try these baths, but on mature reflection I came to the conclusion that I had no time to spare, even for the important purpose of taking care of my complexion, and so to-morrow we go back to the Rhine.

LETTER LXXXII.

The Rhine.—Legends.—Vintage.—Steinberg.—Johannisberg.—Sparkling Moselle.—Coblentz.—Ehrenbreitstein.—Royal Family.—Stolzenfels.—The Lahn.—Monument.—The Moselle.—The Rhine.—Seven Mountains.—Bonn.—Dinner.—Bill of Fare.

COLOGNE, Oct. 4th.

MY DEAREST F.:

It is too rainy this evening for me to take a stroll through the streets of this old town, so I sit down to chat with you. We came down the Rhine Tuesday as far as Coblentz, and it was a day full of interest to us, I can assure you. I made the acquaintance that morning, of an interesting English family, and they were as enthusiastic about every thing to be seen as we were. We took our seats among the luggage in the forward part of the boat, where we could have a good view at once of both banks of the river. Every tourist raves about the Rhine; every American who stands up for "his own country against the world," institutes a comparison between the Rhine and the Hudson, greatly to the disparagement of the former, of course, or his nationality would suffer. For myself I made up my mind to be disappointed, as I always do when I have heard so much of any place, but on the contrary, I was charmed, delighted at every step of our progress, and I don't know when I have had a day of more intense enjoyment than on Tuesday. And yet I do not intend to bore you with a long and rapturous description of the beauties of the Rhine. They have inspired the pen of hundreds of tourists, and the pencil of thousands of artists. They have been delineated in dozens of panoramas, which have been shown from one end of the world to the other, and as for comparison between the Hudson and the Rhine I should say the two rivers were as dissimilar as Mount Washington and Mont Blanc.

One charm of the Rhine is its variety; here, the river is wide, and runs between meadows, beautiful as a lawn in an English park; there, you see gently swelling hills, covered to the very top with the luxuriant vine; here again, the river is narrow and rushes along between almost precipitous banks, covered with dark forest trees, and farther on the trees disappear, and the mountains are "rock ribbed" and craggy. And then there is such a number of castles, a few entire, the greater part in ruins, and attached to each is some traditionary legend; here of seven fair young maidens, who having infatuated half the knights of the country, but without favoring any, were changed into seven rocks, which often endangered the navigation of the river, as much as the hearts of the cruel ones did the knights of old, and there the legend tells us of another beauteous fair one, who was beloved by two brothers, the fate of which is not made clear, for one guide-book says the two brothers fought, till, I believe, they killed each other like the Kilkenny cats, while another declares the brothers went to the wars, (I don't know what wars) where one was slain, while the other, covered with glory, returned to claim his bride. But it would take pages, merely to glance at these legends, so I will say nothing further about them, particularly as they are more or less traditionary, and this is the difference between the Rhine and the Danube; there, the associations are historical, here, more or less fabulous. And yet one meets all along the Rhine, remnants of true antiquity, marks left by the Romans of their wealth and grandeur, when they possessed this land and called it a part of their empire.

The Germans look upon this river with as much veneration as the Egyptians do upon the Nile, or the ancient Israelites did upon the Jordan, and often speak of it as "father Rhine," or "king Rhine." And it is a noble river, nearly a thousand miles in length, and having some of the most beautiful scenery the world can present.

The vintage of the Rhine is famous all the world over, and I have thought a few remarks in relation to it might not be uninteresting to you, "temperance folks" though you may be. All through Germany, the vine is planted in rows along the ground, running up a pole, as beans do with us. When the hills are steep, the earth is terraced up, and every where the vine is tended with the most vigilant care. The first celebrated vineyard after leaving Mayence, is that of the Steinberg, belonging to the Duke of Nassau. . By some it is considered of equal value with the Johannisberg, and it is said the culture of it requires even greater care and expense. It consists of one hundred acres, and the wine from it is held in such estimation, that in 1836 a cask of it containing about six hundred bottles, was sold for twenty-five hundred dollars.

Next comes the Johannisberg vineyard, the property of Prince Metternich, though like the other, once belonging to monks. The vineyard covers about seventy acres, and no trees are allowed upon it, for fear of depriving the vines of the rays of the sun. The grapes are kept on the vine till they are more than ripe, and every grape that falls to the ground, is picked up with a fork made for that purpose. In good years the vineyard produces about thirteen hundred bottles, and the wine has been sold as high as five dollars and a half a bottle, wholesale price, the purchasers generally being royal personages. Near Coblentz a wine is made, called "the sparkling Moselle," said to be equal in flavor to Champagne, while the price of it is much lower.

We arrived at Coblentz between two and three o'clock Tuesday afternoon, and immediately took a carriage and started off to see the town and the country around. Coblentz is an old town, and lies at the junction of the Rhine and the Moselle, and from its situation was called Confluentes by the Romans. The country around is surpassingly lovely, watered by the two rivers, which wind along among fertile fields and flourishing vineyards. The water of the Moselle is blue, that of the Rhine green, and each retains its own color for a long time after they join, till at last the "blue Moselle" is lost in the green Rhine.

We crossed the Rhine by a bridge of boats, and went up to the fortress of Ehrenbreitstein, whose frowning ramparts had been seen from a long distance. It is called the Gibraltar of the Rhine, and is one of the strongest fortresses in Europe. While we were waiting for an officer to accompany us around the ramparts (for no one can visit the fort without the surveillance of a guard, for fear drawings may be taken of the plan of the fortifications) I amused myself with seeing the soldiers drill.

Ehrenbreitstein (I assure you it requires an effort to write the word) stands on a rock about five hundred feet above the level of the river; it is defended by four hundred pieces of cannon, and has magazines capable of containing food for eight thousand men for ten years, and cisterns, which can hold water enough for three years.

But the warlike appearance of this fort had not half the charm for me as the beautiful landscape, seen from that elevated position. The town below us, the lovely valley of the Moselle, the castle crowned hills of the Rhine, the sunny slopes covered with vineyards, the meadows green and bright, the villages dotted here and there, church spires peeping from the trees in every direction, all formed a scene of exquisite beauty. We counted no less than twenty-two towns and villages scattered over the country.

As we recrossed the bridge of boats, we met a royal turn-out, and had the honor of seeing the Prince of Prussia and his wife, and the young prince their son, heir apparent to the throne, and bearing the royal name, Frederick William.

We then drove along the banks of the Rhine to the castle of Stolzenfels, where we had another magnificent view of the charming country around. We were told the castle contained some fine paintings and suits of armor, and moreover had the honor of being occupied by her majesty, Queen Victoria, in 1845, but none of these things were sufficient to tempt us to exchange the splendid view from without for the prospect within. Opposite Stolzenfels the river Lahn empties into the Rhine, and opens before us a lovely valley, fit to be chosen for a scene in Eden. And this, I should say, is another delightful characteristic of the scenery along the Rhine, the succession of valleys constantly opening before you, now showing a peaceful vale, very green, and fresh, and bright, and now allowing you to peep up a narrow glen, deeply shaded by trees.

Not till the thickly gathering shades of evening prevented us from seeing any more, did we return to our hotel and allow ourselves time for dinner. The next morning we took a walk around the town. The only thing I saw approaching to costume was that the young girls wore a sizeable dagger through the braids of their hair.

I have been in cleaner towns than Coblentz, and more pleasant smelling ones too, but notwithstanding these drawbacks, I rather enjoyed a walk through the streets. The houses are so antique, the churches are so rich in historical associations, and ever and anon come such lovely glimpses of the country beyond, that your interest is constantly kept up. In the square, in front of the old church of St. Castor, (I'm sure I don't know what saint that is) there is a monument, erected by the French in 1812, to commemorate the invasion of Russia by the French, bearing an inscription to that effect. When the tables were turned, and the Russians came here, their commander caused the following to be engraved in French under the original inscription: "Seen and approved by us, the Russian Commandant of the town of Coblentz, January 1st, 1814." Rather spicy that.

The bridge built over the Moselle commands a charming view of the valley of that river. On one side of the bridge is the house where Prince Metternich was born, and on the other, is the old Town Hall, the original castle of the Electors of Treves, an ancient building, erected in 1280.

At noon we went on board the steamer, and came on to this city. As a general thing, the scenery is not so fine between here and Coblentz, as between Coblentz and Mayence. The banks are lower, and the country more monotonous, but still abounding in pretty scenes, and picturesque looking towns and villages, many of which existed in the time of the Romans. About twenty miles from here, however, is a cluster of mountains known by the name of "the seven mountains," one of which, Drachenfels, has been immortalized by Byron. Here the scenery is remarkably grand, every turn disclosing "some fresher beauty varying round," while almost every summit is crowned by a castle.

At Bonn, not far from Cologne, is a celebrated University, founded in 1818 by the King of Prussia. Here Prince Albert was a student, but a higher honor belongs to the town, that of having given birth to Beethoven.

We dined on board the steamer, and as I have never given you the " bill of fare" of a German table d'hote, I will make up for that omission now. First came soup, rather weak, then boiled beef, from which the goodness had been all extracted, by having been boiled for the soup. This beef was served up with potatoes and pickled beets, and after that came boiled bacon, with peas mashed fine, and that peculiar combination of cabbage and some sort of dressing known as " sauer-kraut." These having disappeared, fresh fish came on, attended by potatoes and mutton chops, and followed by a pudding with sweet sauce. Do not think however that dinner was over, for after that, roast hare, salad and stewed plums made their appearance, and for all these different dishes you were allowed but one knife and fork, for if you put them on your plate to be carried away, they were coolly taken off and laid on the table by your side. Last of all came the fruit, grapes and pears, almonds and raisins. Those who talk about Americans " bolting" their food, should see Germans eat. Knife and fork are used indiscriminately, and the food disappears in a marvelously short time.

I can't write any more now, but must leave the story of this renowned city untold till to-morrow.

LETTER LXXXIII.

Cologne.—Bad Smell.—Eau de Cologne.—Church of Santa Maria.—St. Peter's Church.—Rubens.—Marie de Medici.—Cathedral.—St. Ursula.—Town Hall.—Deutz.

COLOGNE, Oct. 5th.

MY DEAR F.:

To-day we have devoted to this city, and a quaint old place it is, some of its streets being scarcely wider than those of an Eastern town. A few of the streets have a narrow side-walk, about a foot and a half wide, but as the steps of the houses intrude on that small space, our progress was marked by a succession of dodges, first on to the walk, then back into the street, and so on, in a variety by no means pleasing, as the streets are none of the cleanest. And here, once for all, I must say, that for unpleasant odor I think Cologne can compete with any place we have ever been in. I don't wonder some of the inhabitants were led to making "Eau de Cologne," to compensate somewhat for the noxious smells of the town. At present there are no less than twenty-four manufacturers of it here, and I believe all claim to be descendants of "Jean Maria Farina," the original inventor. As I could not buy of all, without ruining my purse, and overloading my trunk, I selected one of the "veritable" establishments, and bought a box containing six bottles, which, if it perform safely the voyage across the Atlantic, I shall be happy to distribute among you, according to your respective merits.

Cologne is the largest and wealthiest city on the Rhine, and has a population of one hundred thousand.

It is said to have been founded by the Romans under Marcus Agrippa, and to have been named by Agrippina, mother of Nero, Colonia Agrippina. In time, the latter part of the name was dropped, and the former changed into Cologne. Even now, the city shows many marks of its ancient origin, fragments of walls and of gateways being met in different parts of the town. The church of "Santa Maria in Capitolio" is said to occupy the site of the capitol of the Roman city, and to be nearly a thousand years old. After having looked at this as long as we cared to, we proceeded to St. Peter's church. Here is the font in which Rubens was baptized, and here is the painting by that artist, of the Crucifixion of St. Peter, with his head downwards, according to the tradition concerning the manner of his death. The painting hanging over the altar, however, is a copy of that by Rubens, though for a fee of fifteen groschen (thirty-seven and a half cents) the sexton will turn it round and show the original picture, but the expression of the face and the figure of St. Peter was so painful to me I had no disposition to look at it farther. I could not help noticing the difference in the manner of the sexton on approaching the altar, and in coming away from it. When he passed it in going behind to turn the picture, he knelt very devoutly, but when he found he was not to have his accustomed fee, he quite forgot to bow the knee as he returned, and his face bore any thing but a look of pious resignation at his disappointment.

In the very house where Rubens was born in 1577, died Marie de Medici in 1672. Her heart is buried in the Cathedral here, but her other remains were carried to France.

And now what shall I tell you of the glorious old Cathedral of Cologne, begun more than six hundred years ago, but never yet finished ? Indeed for hundreds of years it remained untouched, and was fast assuming the appearance of a ruin, until within the last few years, when a new impulse was given to the work of completing the edifice, and the King of Prussia has offered to give between thirty and forty thousand thalers a year towards the funds necessary, until it is finished. It is supposed more than three million dollars will be required for its completion.

Thus far it is a noble specimen of Gothic architecture, more than five hundred feet long, two hundred and thirty wide, and the height of the nave is one hundred and seventy feet. The pillars dividing the nave from the aisles are of great size and beauty, and the effect of the interior, even in its present unfinished state, is exceedingly grand and imposing.

The choir is large enough to form a church of itself, and has some of the most beautiful windows of stained glass I have ever seen. Within this church is the famous shrine of "the three Kings of Cologne," or the magi who went with gifts of "gold, frankincense and myrrh" to the infant Saviour. I know not whether it is pretended Cologne, at that time, stood in "the East," and that these kings went from here, or whether, by some miraculous agency, the good people of Cologne got possession of their mortal remains, but this I know, the skulls of the so-called kings of Cologne are shown, in a shrine, elaborately adorned with jewels and precious stones to the amount of one million of dollars. To see this shrine, the sum of more than one dollar is demanded, but as I am never particularly fond of seeing skulls, even when offered to the sight gratuitously, you may be sure I did not care enough about seeing these, to pay such an exorbitant fee. We were quite willing, however, to pay a moderate fee to ascend to the gallery within the choir, where we could look down upon the edifice below, and go out upon the roof, from which we could form an excellent idea of the size and height of the church, when finished, and command a magnificent view, both of the city and the country around. The city sweeps around the bank of the river, or perhaps it would be more proper to say, the river sweeps around the city, in a semi-circular form, and from the number of spires and towers, this might be called the city of churches. The country around is very level, and the Rhine flows peacefully along among green fields, while at a distance up the river, "the seven mountains" are distinctly seen.

How many times, the last few days, have I repeated the words of Byron,

"Adieu to thee, fair Rhine! a vain adieu!
There can be no farewell to scenes like thine;
The mind is colored by thy every hue;
And if reluctantly the eyes resign
Their cherished gaze upon thee, lovely Rhine!
'Tis with the thankful glance of parting praise.
More mighty spots may rise—more glaring shine,
But none unite in one attaching maze
The brilliant, fair and soft, the glories of old days."

How true it is, though we say "adieu," there really is no "farewell," to certain scenes, for they leave a lasting impress upon the mind. And thus it will be with the beauties of the Rhine; forever are they passed away from my external vision, but fresh and fair they will long remain to the mind's eye. Gloriously beautiful scenes are presented by this fair earth of ours; would they were better appreciated every where by the eye, the heart, and the soul!

A church in Cologne that receives a great deal of attention from relic lovers, is that of St. Ursula. The legend informs us that Ursula was the daughter of an English king, who left her native land with a train of eleven thousand virgins, to make a pilgrimage to Rome. On their return from Rome, they were all murdered at Cologne by the savage Huns, and their bones having been carefully preserved, are exhibited in the church which bears the name of St. Ursula. But as I said before, I am not particularly fond of seeing bones, so we did not see the far-famed relics of St. Ursula and her eleven thousand virgins.

The old Town Hall is an interesting building, not only from the style of its architecture, but for the events that have taken place within its walls. I like these old Gothic buildings, for they appeal strongly to my love of the picturesque and the beautiful.

Having walked about for several hours, we drove round the city, to get a good general view. We went over the bridge of boats, fourteen hundred feet long, that connects this city with Deutz, and from the opposite bank could command a view of all that part of the town that lies on the Rhine, extending three miles along the river, the time-honored walls of the Cathedral rising conspicuously over all. Returning to this side of the river, we made the complete circuit of the city, passing by innumerable fortifications. The country is very level, and seems to be one vast vegetable garden, and I am sure I can see no excuse for people starving in this neighborhood, or being even stinted for food.

LETTER LXXXIV.

Down the Rhine.—Rain.—Arnhem.—Amsterdam.—Peculiar Features of Holland.—Windmills.—Amsterdam.—Quaintness.—Canals.—Head-dress.—Museum.—Palace.—Pleasant Meeting.

AMSTERDAM, Oct. 7th.

MY DEAR FRIENDS:

How we pass "from one nation to another, from one kingdom to another people." We often breakfast in the dominions of one king, and dine in those of another, and we pass so quietly from one to the other, no fuss being made about passports or luggage, that it is only from our maps we know we have made the transit.

We were called at quarter before five on Friday morning, to take the steamer down the Rhine, and a dark morning it was, too, while the rain fell in torrents. Fortunately, we had passed the finest scenery on the Rhine, and therefore we bore the rain with more equanimity than we could have mustered, had we been amid grand or lovely views. We were in the steamer thirteen hours, all which time there was literally nothing to be seen, but the rapid river, with its low banks dammed up in many places, to prevent inundation. I was obliged to stay in the cabin nearly all the time, as the rain fell incessantly. There were few passengers, and nothing to amuse me; still with books and maps, with sewing and sleeping, I contrived to pass the day, and perhaps its quiet, after all, was not an unpleasant change, succeeding, as it did, so many days spent in constant sight-seeing.

We arrived at Arnhem at seven o'clock, but it was quite too wet for me to go out. I could see the town was lit with gas, as we went from the boat to the hotel. We left Arnhem by railroad, this morning at seven, and arrived here about ten, the distance being fifty-eight miles. That unfortunate rain followed us, so that we had to catch glimpses of the surrounding country as we could. Canals intersected the country in every direction, while countless windmills spread out their broad arms on every side. These windmills answer a double purpose, for they not only grind corn, but they act as pumps, many of them having water wheels attached to them, by which water is raised into the canals, thus keeping the low land dry and fit for cultivation.

Undoubtedly you have not forgotten what your geography tells you, that Holland does not lie, like other countries, above the surface of the sea, but below it, the lowest ground being twenty-four feet below high-water mark, and even thirty, when the tide is driven high by the winds. Such a country can be preserved from the inroads of the sea, only by the most untiring diligence and industry, so that the Dutch have, from necessity, been obliged to be so constantly on the alert as to well merit the appellation of "the most industrious people in the world."

And now behold us in our quarters at the "Hotel des Pays-Bas," where we were refreshed by a comfortable breakfast, and cheered by letters from home, that we found awaiting us at the banker's. Now we are off to see the lions, and the result of my observations I will give you this evening.

Evening. I scarcely know what to tell you of this strange city, so unlike is it to the generality of cities we have visited. Canals intersect the streets in every direction; in fact, it is all streets and canals, canals and streets, each street having a canal in front and in the rear, the canals bordered with trees, the houses being of brick, many of them in quaint styles of architecture. In fact, every thing about Amsterdam is quaint and odd. I don't know two words that better express the characteristics of Amsterdam, than quaintness and oddity. Some travellers think it like Venice, but the chief similarity between the two cities seems to me, that both are intersected by canals, in short, made up of canals, if one may so speak. I have not time, however, to enter into the points of similarity, or difference between the two cities, so hasten on. As I said before, every thing in Amsterdam is quaint. It strikes you with a feeling of freshness, perfectly delightful to the hackneyed traveller. The canals, with their queer looking barges, the succession of bridges spanning the canals, the streets, one so like another, that it is difficult at times to tell where you are, the neat, fresh looking servant girls, in their nicely fitting caps with quilled borders, the singular costumes, the cleanliness seen in every thing, these, and a thousand other things, new and strange, meet you, and challenge your admiration, at every step. One kind of head-dress, peculiar to Holland, I must mention more particularly, it is so utterly unlike any thing I have seen before. Around the head is a wide fillet of gold, having on each temple a large rosette, also of gold; over this is worn a cap of lace, often of the very richest quality. I saw one of these head-dresses that was worth five thousand dollars. It was a sort of heir-loom in the family, and was worn as a part of every-day attire, both in the house and the streets. I must confess these head-dresses of gold and of fine lace, seemed rather incongruous with wooden shoes, as I saw them more than once to-day.

Amsterdam is situated at the confluence of the river Amstel with an arm of the Zuyder Zee. It has about two hundred and twenty-five thousand inhabitants, of whom one-tenth are Jews. The whole city is founded upon piles, and this caused Erasmus to say, "he had at length reached a city whose inhabitants, like crows, lived on the top of trees."

Our first visit was to the Museum, or Picture Gallery, where we found a rich collection of paintings, most of them of the Dutch and Flemish schools, and almost every one a masterpiece in its way. With the historical pictures, I was particularly well pleased, not only for being gems of art, but for the light they threw upon varied passages in the history of the Dutch nation.

Next, we turned our steps towards the Palace, a large edifice of stone, standing upon nearly fourteen thousand piles, driven seventy feet deep into the ground. Formerly, it was used as a sort of state house, latterly, as a residence for the royal family. In the centre of the building is a magnificent hall, lined with white marble, one hundred and twenty feet long, fifty-seven wide, and one hundred high. It is adorned with the most exquisite bas-reliefs. Interested as I was in the different rooms in this palace, and the historical associations that clustered around each, nothing pleased me more than the charming view from the roof, taking in the quaint city, with its picturesque gables, the wide canals, with their avenues of green trees, the surrounding country, with its fresh looking meadows, intersected in every direction with canals, and dotted with windmills, and at a distance, the waters of the Zuyder Zee sparkling, gleaming in the sunlight, all forming a picture of varied beauties, exceedingly delightful and refreshing to the eye.

On our way home, we met, to our great delight, a party of Americans, whom we last saw in Cairo, mounting their camels for a journey across the Short Desert to Jerusalem. How pleasant such meetings are in a foreign land, none know but those who have experienced them.

And now I must say good night.

LETTER LXXXV.

English Church.—Orphan House.—Ship Canal.—Broek.—Excessive Cleanliness.—Toll.—Civility.—Streets of Amsterdam.—Incident.

AMSTERDAM, Oct. 9th.

MY DEAR P:

Yesterday we had the pleasure of attending the service of the Church of England in a plain, unpretending chapel, but the service was not without its interest to us, you may be well assured. In foreign lands, surrounded by every thing strange and wondrous, nothing comes to our hearts with a greater feeling of home, than the familiar words of our church service. Wherever we hear these words, whether amid the refinements of Europe, the vast deserts of Asia, or on the banks of the storied Nile, we are at home. In the brotherhood of the church, we are linked together as the members of one large family, with one common interest, bound with a tie of no ordinary strength.

On our way to church, we saw a procession of boys in a singular costume, one-half of their jackets being black, the other red. I thought they belonged to a State Prison, was therefore agreeably surprised to find they were members of an orphan house. In fact, Amsterdam is celebrated for the number and variety of its charitable institutions. There is said to be a great many poor people in this city. Many of these live in the cellars of the houses, not only under ground, but under water. I peeped into quite a number of these cellars, as I passed along, and invariably found them remarkably clean and neat, very different in that respect from the abodes of the poorer class in England, Ireland, or even in our own favored republic.

A great many of the inhabitants of Amsterdam, too, live in boats, like the Chinese, and here, too, you see the usual Dutch thrift and cleanliness. If, according to good old Jeremy Taylor, "cleanliness is next to godliness," how very nearly approaching to piety must the Dutch be.

And where do you think we have been to-day? To Broek, (pronounced Brook,) known by the enviable appellation, or unenviable, (as different persons might view it,) of "the cleanest village in the world." We drove there, it being but a few miles distant, our road lying the first part of the way along the grand ship canal of North Holland, one of the greatest undertakings of the kind ever executed. I should like, if I had time, to enter into details concerning this canal, as well as of the others that go so far towards making up the distinctive features of Holland, but the number at the top of this page warns me that the time ought to be near when this Budget should be closed, and so I must hasten on to Broek, "the cleanest village in the world." It has about eight hundred inhabitants, many of them retired merchants and tradesmen, landed proprietors or small farmers.

For fear of disturbing the excessive cleanliness of the place, no horse is allowed to pass through the streets, so we left our carriage at a small inn on the outskirts, and walked through the village. I said no horse was allowed to pass through the streets; I meant no horse attached to a carriage; in fact, the streets are scarcely wide enough to admit the passage of a wheeled vehicle. If a man enters the village on horseback, he must dismount, and lead his horse through the streets at a foot pace! No one can smoke without a stopper on his pipe, for fear of the ashes settling on any thing! The streets, narrow lanes, or passages rather, are paved with bricks or small stones, arranged in divers patterns. And these are kept just as clean as the nicest parlor floor. The slightest appearance of a weed or a tuft of grass in the interstices of these stones, would throw the inhabitants of Broek into an agony. For my part, I must confess every thing looked too precise to please my eye.

The houses are mostly of wood, in fantastic styles of architecture, every house dazzling the eye with the freshness of its paint. Indeed, some housekeepers are said to keep a painter in their employ the year round, that the same freshness of aspect may be preserved at all seasons. This, I think, must be worse than the annual infliction of painters and whitewashers at home. The gardens are prettily laid out, and adorned with flowers of every hue.

But you should go into one of the dairies! Every thing was so exceedingly sweet and clean. Even the stables were models of neatness, the floors of tiles, nicely polished, the walls of partitions of boards as smooth and neat as possible. Over each stall was a hook in the ceiling, which instantly attracted my attention. "What is that for?" I asked. "Why, when the cattle are within doors, their tails are fastened up to these hooks, that they may not run any risk of soiling their sleek, nicely washed sides, by brushing against them!" I thought that went ahead of every thing I had ever heard of in the way of cleanliness.

In passing along the road, to-day, whenever we came to a toll-gate, which was pretty often, the keeper thrust out a wooden box to receive the toll, evidently thinking it quite too much trouble to come out after it. The people we met along the roadside and the canals, seemed polite and civil, the men invariably touching their hats to us. And yet have I not sometimes heard the Dutch spoken of as "boors?"

This evening, we took a long walk through the streets of Amsterdam. The gable roofs and turreted chimneys give the houses a very picturesque look. The display of goods in some of the shops would do credit to Paris. The streets are so much alike, one has to be very careful, else he will lose his way. In fact, a friend of ours, a few weeks since, got so completely bewildered here, that he wandered about the streets till long after midnight, trying in vain to find his hotel, the name of which he had entirely forgotten. And he never could exactly remember, when telling about it afterwards, whether it was Amsterdam or Rotterdam where he lost his way; he only knew that it was a town that ended with a "dam."

I would we could stay longer in this interesting city, but our motto is "onward."

LETTER LXXXVI.

Haarlem.—Environs.—Village of the Washerwomen.—Method of draining the Lake.—Nurseries.—Large Organ.—State House.—Leyden.—The Hague.—Museum.—Gallery of Paintings.—Royal Library.—Scheveningen.—Bosch.

THE HAGUE, Oct. 11th.

MY DEAR F.:

On we go with a "perfect rush;" here to-day, gone to-morrow. Ever on and on, the restless tide of life is hurrying man, till at last the end is reached, and the goal attained.

We left Amsterdam yesterday morning, and came on as far as Haarlem, about twelve miles, through a flat country, of course, intersected in all directions with canals; but few trees or cultivated fields, most of the land being used for grazing, and we saw large herds of cattle and flocks of sheep.

We had the misfortune of arriving at Haarlem in a pouring rain, and as we had had no breakfast, our first care was to look out for the wants of the "outer man." So we drove to the Hotel, bearing the name and the insignia of "the Golden Lion," and there we met a nice landlady, who not only furnished us a good breakfast in short order, but also gave us every requisite information relative to the sights of Haarlem.

As we were anxious to see the means employed for draining the lake of Haarlem, which a few years ago covered quite an extent of country, we drove out three or four miles from the town, passing at first very pretty gardens and country seats, each house having some motto over the door, which our guide interpreted to us. One signified " a little quiet;" another, " sweet rest;" a third, " having worked diligently I now take my comfort," while a fourth had " summer comfort," and so on, through an endless variety. The grounds were tastefully laid out, and were radiant with flowers of every hue.

We went through a small village called " the village of the washerwomen," every house having a large green meadow behind it, covered with linen bleaching in the rain and mist. The guide said a great deal of money was made there, and I did not wonder at it, if they all charged at the rate our washerwoman in Amsterdam did.

Arriving on the borders of a canal, we left our carriage and were rowed across in a little boat, which was so wet we could not sit down at all, but fortunately the distance across was not great. The rain continued to pour, and I could not but think the burning sands of Egypt, and the fervid sun of Syria, were better than this climate.

In a building of immense strength and thickness, is one of the engines used in pumping water from the lake. This engine is of five hundred horse power, and works eight pumps, each of them seventy-three inches in diameter. At one stroke of the engine, sixty-four tons of water can be pumped up, which is carried off into the canal by means of sluices. Notwithstanding the work which this engine performed, aided by two others stationed at opposite sides of the lake, it required four years of almost constant pumping to drain the lake, but at last it was done, and there are now more than forty-five thousand acres, which were once covered by the waters of the lake. This is divided into lots and sold, and when all are sold, the owners of the land will be obliged to keep it properly drained, and the engines therefore will be given over to them. Government will then receive back what it has spent for draining the land, and the land thus redeemed and cultivated will furnish a constant revenue in addition, by means of the proper taxes.

One canal connects with another, and when one gets too full, the sluices are opened, and the surplus water let off, and thus, on and on, through the endless canals with which Holland is supplied. This requires the most vigilant care and watchfulness, for one foot of water too much, or left one minute too long, may cause the destruction of millions of property, and hundreds of lives.

On our way back, we visited one of the celebrated nurseries of Haarlem, from which many of the most renowned gardens in Europe procure their seeds. Do you remember reading in the newspapers several years ago, of the great tulip mania that raged in Holland? At that time nearly three thousand dollars were given for one tulip root. Indeed, for a long time, speculations were carried on in buying and selling tulip roots, as one would speculate in funds or stocks, till at last government interfered, and put a stop to this species of gambling.

You are doubtless aware that one of the largest organs in the world is in Haarlem. We were so fortunate as to visit the town on one of the days the organ is shown off gratuitously; otherwise we must have paid five dollars, or have had the other alternative of going away without hearing it. For an hour the organist discoursed to us most eloquent music, though I am told he makes a greater display and dash on those days he is particularly paid for playing. Some of my musical friends at home may be interested in knowing that this organ was made in 1738 by Christian Muller, of Amsterdam, and that it has five thousand pipes (the largest of which are thirty-two feet in length, and fifteen inches in diameter,) sixty stops and three rows of keys.

One thing in the church annoyed me exceedingly; the people coming in and walking round, while the organist was playing, seeming to use the church as a place for promenade and for meeting their friends. The men kept their hats on, except when they met an acquaintance, and then, oh! strange inconsistency! they lifted the hat quite from the head, thus treating man with more ceremony and reverence than God.

The Dutch claim the invention of printing for a citizen of Haarlem, named Coster, and in the State House here are shown specimens of the blocks or wooden types which were invented and used by him. Two or three rare books are shown, one printed in 1428, and another in 1440, and two or three autographs of Coster, and some medals, and for exhibiting these few articles the keeper had the audacity to demand one florin, (about 40 cents.) They prize their antiquities high here in Holland.

We found Haarlem a neat, pretty town, the houses of dark colored brick, the streets intersected by canals and bordered with trees. The environs are delightfully varied with gardens and country seats, but these of course could not be seen to good advantage by us in a drenching rain. In historical associations Haarlem is exceedingly rich, having suffered a terrible siege from the Spaniards in 1572–3, during which period the citizens maintained an heroic defence, the very women even bearing arms under Kenan Hasselaer, whose portrait we saw in the State House. In two or three of the houses in the town, we saw cannon balls imbedded in the walls, relics of that same siege.

We had a nice dinner, our landlady who speaks English very well, waiting on us herself, and then the rain having ceased, we walked to the station, where we had left our luggage in the morning. Many wealthy merchants doing business in Amsterdam reside in Haarlem, and their carriages and liveried attendants dashed by us on the way to the railroad, to meet their respective masters and owners.

We left Haarlem at little after five o'clock, and for the first four or five miles after leaving the town, the country was very pretty, but after that the land was less rich and fertile. Every meadow was bounded by canals, and almost every house was surrounded by water. The sunset was magnificent, giving promise of fair weather to-day, a promise, like many others, unfulfilled.

It was near dark when we arrived at Leyden, and we could see nothing of that town, but we know it is famous for its University, and for having endured a terrific siege by the Spaniards in 1553–4. It was the birth-place, too, of Rembrandt, Jan Steen, Gerard Douw, Mieris, and some other painters of the Dutch school.

We arrived here at half past six o'clock, and came to the Hotel de L'Europe, but as we did not have our room till we had been here nearly two hours, I could not settle down to any thing. Besides, I must confess, going about in the rain at Haarlem, made me not a little dull and sleepy.

In spite of the rain we have been out sight-seeing to-day, for we have no time to spare in waiting for fine weather.

This town is at present the residence of the King of Holland, and has about sixty-four thousand inhabitants. The houses are not so picturesque looking as those of Amsterdam, but look more like the brick and stone houses of our own land. Many of the streets and the canals are bordered with trees, and the parks and gardens that surround the town are very beautiful, so much so I regretted exceedingly the weather would not permit me to see more of them.

Although I had said I would visit no more museums, I was tempted to break my resolution here, because I was told there was such an admirable collection of Chinese and Japanese articles, so different from most of the museums we have visited. The Dutch being till lately the only European nation admitted into Japan, of course have had excellent opportunities for collecting curiosities from that country, and the collection here is exceedingly rich. If I should attempt to go into details, I should fill a small sized volume, so I will merely say, we saw enough to give us an insight into the manners and customs, both warlike and domestic, of that nation.

The Chinese articles were very beautiful, among which I shall merely mention specimens of carvings in ivory and porcelain ware, exceedingly rich and rare.

In another part of the museum is a large number of historical relics, and here too I was exceedingly interested, because they all, more or less, bore reference to the history of this country. Shall I give you a list of a few things that interested me particularly? Articles belonging to the renowned Admirals, Tromp and De Ruyter and Piet Hein; the dress William, Prince of Orange, wore the day he was assassinated in Delft; a model of the cabin where Peter the Great lived while learning the trade of a ship-builder in Zaardam, and a variety of beautiful vessels in ivory and silver, elaborately carved.

Next we went to the Gallery of Paintings, almost exclusively composed of works of the Dutch school, and here we saw some of the master-pieces of Berchem and Cuyp, of Douw and Van Dijk, of Mieris and Ostade, of Potter and Rembrandt, of Steen, Teniers and Wouverman, and a host of others, whose names are not so well known on the other side of the Atlantic as on this. Like the pictures of the German school, the Dutch masters charm me by their faithful delineation of every day life; life in the cottage and in the fields, and woods and meadows, cattle and horses, men and women and little children are portrayed with that trueness to nature which attracts even the most uninitiated in the mysteries of art.

We crossed a pretty little park, and came to the Royal Library, where is a collection of one hundred thousand volumes, neatly arranged. But these did not detain us long, for we went on to look at the manuscripts, among which are the prayer-books of Catherine de Medici, and the unfortunate Catherine of Aragon, a book beautifully written and elaborately adorned with pictures in the fifteenth century, another in the sixth or seventh, and a Bible published in 1682, bearing on a blank leaf the words, "This book was given to the king and I at our crownation. Marie R;" which was more interesting from the fact that the Bible was given to King William and to Mary, than from the grammatical construction of the sentence.

Here too, is a rich collection of coins and medals and cameos, to the number of fifty thousand, and we spent some time in looking at them, though the full study of them with all their historical bearings, would well employ years.

Still on we went in the pouring rain, to see a private collection of paintings, all of the Dutch school, and all gems, not a common one among them. The walls of three rooms were covered with these priceless works of art, and I must say I envied the possessor of them.

As it did not rain quite so fast when we came out, we ordered a carriage and drove to the village of Scheveningen, which lies directly on the sea shore. It contains about six thousand inhabitants, all more or less engaged in the fisheries. We overtook numbers of men and women who had been here to sell their fish, going home with empty wagons drawn by dogs, sometimes three abreast. The women wore very short clothes, immense wooden shoes, and bonnets that can be compared to nothing under the sun, unless it be a coal hod.

The waves dashed in upon the sandy shore with a sullen roar which made me shudder, when I thought that in one month from to-day, I should have to tempt the fury of the ocean. From this spot Charles II. embarked for England at the time of the Restoration, and here too the Prince of Orange landed in 1813, several months before the overthrow of Buonaparte.

After we came back, we drove through the Bosch, a

beautiful wood with noble forest trees, and pretty sheets of water, and green glades, where a large number of deer were frolicking around.

When we had seen all these things, it was time to return for our dinner, which was at half past four. After dinner I had intended walking out again, but the elements were against me, so I took my pen and scribbled this letter. And this is all I have to tell you about the Hague, so adieu.

LETTER LXXXVII.

Ryswick.—Delft.—Schiedam.—Rotterdam.—Statue of Erasmus.—Church of St. Lawrence.—Organ.—Country Houses.—Dort.—The Schelde.—Arrival in Antwerp.—Loss of the Arctic.—Decline of Antwerp.—The Cathedral.—The Spire.—Chime of Bells.—Magnificent View.—Interior of the Church.—Paintings by Rubens.—St. Paul's Church.—St. Jacques' Church.—Docks.—Rubens.—Hotel de Ville.—Exchange.—Costumes.

Antwerp, Oct. 14th.

My dear P.:

We left the Hague on Thursday morning, and little more than half an hour on the railroad brought us to Rotterdam, through rather a pretty country, varied with villages, and farm houses, and meadows, green and bright, on which sheep and cattle were browsing. The first village was Ryswick, where, in 1697, was signed the treaty of peace between England, France, Germany, Holland and Spain. Next, we came to Delft, a quaint looking town, famous in olden time for its pottery, and for having been the scene, in 1584, of the murder of William I., Prince of Orange, by Balthazar Gerards. A little farther on, we reached Schiedam, known the world over, for its distilleries of gin, of which there are two hundred in that small town of not more than twelve thousand inhabitants. So much grain is used in the distilleries, that it is said thirty thousand pigs are fed on what is left, after the spirituous matter has been extracted. So they must carry on quite a trade there in pork, as well as in gin.

Arriving at Rotterdam, we took a carriage, and made the complete circuit of the city, where, though we saw not many things to admire, we found quite a number to interest us. Rotterdam lies on the Maas, (or, as we should call it, the Meuse,) and on the Rotte, and from a large dyke or dam erected at the junction of the two rivers, derives its name of Rotterdam. It is the second city in Holland, having a population of more than eighty thousand, and although it is twenty-four miles from the sea, by means of the Maas, which is navigable up to the very town, it carries on great shipping transactions with all parts of the world. Its trade alone with Batavia is immense, eighty large ships being constantly employed in it.

Our hotel, the "New Bath Hotel," was on the Maas, and directly before our window, large ships were unloading their cargoes. Like Amsterdam, the mixture of land and water, of streets and canals, of houses and ships, gives it a strange charm. We drove through a labyrinth of streets and crossed an immense number of canals, many of them bordered with trees, and lined with substantial houses of dark colored brick.

On a wide bridge, which is used as a market place, stands the bronze statue of Erasmus, who was born in Rotterdam, in 1467, in a small house which we afterwards saw. It has an inscription in Latin, which, as I translate it, means, "This is a small house, but great, because Erasmus was born in it."

In the church of St. Lawrence, are some fine monuments of the old Dutch Admirals, and an immense organ, larger than that at Haarlem, and said by some to be superior to it in tone. But this we had no opportunity of finding out for ourselves, for although the organist will at any time play an hour, for the sum of five dollars, our purse was not quite heavy enough to pay a fee of that size, even to gratify our love of music. Perhaps we felt more indifferent than we otherwise should, having just had so good an opportunity to hear the surpassingly sweet tones of the one at Haarlem.

The Rotterdam organ is ninety feet high, (only think, twice as high as the interior of St. Stephen's church,) and has ninety stops, and six thousand five hundred pipes, the largest of which is thirty-two feet long, and seventeen inches in diameter. What a baby the most of our organs at home are, compared with this giant!

We passed by the Exchange, and the Town Hall, and two or three other public buildings quite noble in appearance. The quay along the river Maas has many handsome houses. All around the city, are the country houses of the wealthy citizens, each with its canal covered with green slime before the door, spanned by a little bridge, thrown across, or drawn back, at the pleasure of the owner; thus one could live quite secluded from his neighbors, if he chose. Almost every garden had a little summer house in one corner, where the "good man" retires to smoke his pipe. I should think he would need the smell of his pipe, or some other fragrance, to triumph over the noxious odors exhaled by the stagnant canals around him.

After dinner, we walked out, and as I like to stroll along, and stop at nearly every shop window, I do not care about being followed, or preceded, rather, by a guide, so we dispensed with his services in the evening. We found the shops in the principal streets well lighted, but no great variety of goods was displayed, red bandannas, pipes and women's caps being the principal commodities. In the interminable labyrinth of streets, and canals, and drawbridges, we entirely lost our direction, and were obliged to take a hackney coach back to the hotel. And thus ended our visit to Rotterdam, for yesterday morning we took a steamer for this place, where we arrived quite late in the evening, after an uninteresting sail of nearly ten hours. The banks of the river, or rivers, rather, were low and flat, and the several arms of the sea, flowing between the islands of Zealand, that we crossed, were often so wide we could scarcely see the land on either side. Fortunately for us, the weather was good, for in storms, we are told, these estuaries make rather rough sailing.

The only place in which I was interested, was the old town of Dort, where, in 1618–19, was held that assembly of divines, known as the "Synod of Dort." During six months, they sat one hundred and fifty-two times, almost entirely engaged in discussing the subject of "election" and "free grace." Ship building, to a large extent, is carried on in this neighborhood, and immense rafts come down here from the upper Rhine.

It was quite too late, when we entered the Schelde, to see any thing of its banks, and our passage from the kingdom of the Netherlands into that of Belgium, was literally made in the dark. We received the customary visit from the revenue officers, and although their examination was quite strict, they made us pay nothing for duties, even allowing my cologne to pass free.

We came to the Hotel St. Antoine, and though I eagerly went to the windows, and strained my eyes to get a peep of the Cathedral, there was nothing to be seen but the little park in front of the hotel, with its row of gas lights, while beyond, a dark mass loomed up against the sky, which my instinct told me was the far-famed Cathedral of Antwerp.

The first news we heard this morning, was the destruction of the Arctic. You may imagine the shock it gave us, not only because we have to make that very voyage across the ocean which has proved so fatal to her, but because in that same ship we made our last passage across the Atlantic. It is just one year and two days since we bade adieu to her and her gallant commander. How vividly comes up that parting scene! As the small steamer, that was carrying us to the shore, left the Arctic, "three times three" cheers were given for "the noble ship Arctic," the passengers all standing and waving their hats or handkerchiefs, with great enthusiasm. Capt. Luce stood beside me; now he has found a watery grave, and the "noble Arctic" lies in the bosom of the great deep!* Wherever I have been to-day, whatever I have seen, that sinking ship, with her hundreds of souls hurried into eternity, has been before my eyes. God grant their fate may not be ours! From many loving, praying hearts at home, earnest prayers are going up for our preservation on the great deep, and I trust those prayers will be answered.

And now let me tell you a little about this city, which,

---

* The first news was that Capt. Luce was drowned.

at present, contains ninety thousand inhabitants, though, in the sixteeenth century, it is said to have had a population of two hundred thousand. It would be an interesting subject of inquiry, to investigate the causes which have led to the decline of so many European cities, but at present, that is far beyond my reach, and so I will content myself with merely saying, that Antwerp has greatly declined from her former prosperity. Every year, immense numbers are leaving this part of the country for the New World, and during the last year, from this port alone, twenty-two thousand sailed for the United States.

Of course, our first visit was to the Cathedral; to reach this, we merely had to cross the little park in front of our hotel, now nearly stripped of its leaves. In the centre of the park, is a colossal statue of Rubens, who lived here for a long time, and died here. The Cathedral was commenced in the thirteenth century, and it is said to have taken eighty-four years in its erection. It is five hundred feet long, and two hundred and fifty wide, and the interior is divided into a nave and side aisles, by six rows of large pillars, thus giving four side aisles, an unusual number, the generality of churches having only two.

Besides two or three small towers, it has one of the loftiest spires in the world, rising to a height of nearly four hundred and four feet, more than twice as high as the steeple of the First Baptist meeting house in your own city. This lofty spire is adorned with such delicate Gothic arches, and fairy-like tracery and fretwork, that Charles V. used to say it deserved to be kept in a show-case, and Napoleon said it reminded him of Mechlin lace, so exquisite was the finish of every part.

Before we had fatigued ourselves with walking about, we ascended to the top of this spire, by no less than six hundred and sixteen steps, which made me pant and groan somewhat, before we reached the summit. The man who went up with us, says, some days in summer, when there have been many visitants, he has been up twenty-five times. No wonder he asks a franc, and even more, every time he goes up.

Half way up the tower, is a chime of forty bells, which plays a regular tune at the striking of each hour, and at the quarter and half hours, a short strain, and at every seven minutes and a half, utters a few pleasing notes. Even now, while I write, there come, stealing out upon the air, strains of the softest, sweetest harmony, and I sit with my pen raised in my hand, for fear one delicious note will escape my ear.

The face of the clock in this tower is thirty feet in diameter. You can readily imagine that from so elevated a spot as the summit of this spire, we should get a magnificent view, and the city below us, and the country around, lay spread out like a map. The pointed and red-tiled roofs of the city, varied here and there by a venerable church, the windings of the Schelde, the green, level meadows, and clumps of many tinted trees, the villages, dotted at intervals over the plain, the tower of the Cathedral of Mechlin, looming up against the sky, the canals stretching far away in the distance, all tended to form an exquisite scene. A soft haze was in the air, which prevented us from seeing very far, but the guide told us, in clear weather, he could see Brussels, thirty miles distant.

And now for the riches of the interior of the church. The seats in the choir are new, and elaborately sculptured, and the pulpit is almost an edifice of itself, carved to represent the four quarters of the globe, with their natural productions of trees, shrubs and birds. But that which has brought the greatest renown to the church, are the paintings of Rubens, among which, the most celebrated are the "Descent from the Cross," and the "Elevation of the Cross." No one, who looks at these paintings, can help acknowledging that they are indeed masterpieces of art. Rubens' forte is the delineation of strong, fierce passions, and brilliancy of coloring, and in these he is inimitable, but all his female figures are gross and unrefined. The face of the Virgin, soft, yet beaming with life and intellect, the deep, mournful eyes, speaking of a soul baptised in sorrow and suffering, these are for Raphael, not for Rubens. Raphael's pictures touch my heart; Rubens' excite my admiration; the first depicts the heart, the soul; the other the body. In these two paintings, Rubens' Christ is sublime; nothing can exceed the expression of the figure, so full of mortal agony, tempered with heavenly peace and resignation.

In the Museum here, are several other paintings by Rubens, some of which I like quite as well as those in the Cathedral. In the crucifixion of Christ between the two thieves, an executioner is seen piercing the side of the Saviour, while another, with a bar of iron, is breaking the limbs of one of the malefactors, who, in his agony, has wrenched one of his feet from the cross. Of the thousand crucifixions I have seen, there has never been one before like this, and although I turned away from it, at first, with shuddering, I went back more than once to get another view.

There is an admirable collection, in the Museum, of

paintings of the old Flemish school, and a few by artists of a later date, which seems to show that the mantle of Rubens and the Van Eycks has fallen upon some of their successors.

Next, we went to St. Paul's church, where, on an artificial eminence against the walls of the church, is a representation of Calvary, to me perfectly horrible to behold, and in the church are some admirable as well as curious paintings.

Then, we turned our steps towards St. Jacques' church, which has twenty side chapels and eighteen altar-pieces, rich in sculpture and fine marbles. In this church, Rubens is buried, and the little chapel in which his body lies, was designed by himself. Over the altar, hangs a Holy Family, painted by the great artist, in the short space of sixteen days. In this picture, he has given his own portrait, as St. George, those of his two wives, as Martha and Mary Magdalen, while his father is represented as St. Jerome, his grandfather as Time, and his own son as an angel, thus making it an historical, as well as an ideal picture.

By this time, I was quite tired, so we took a carriage and drove around the city. We found the docks and basins filled with vessels, from all parts of the world, and the quay along the Schelde presented a lively scene, there were so many vessels loading and unloading. Doubtless you are aware that Napoleon was very anxious to make this city the greatest seaport of the north of Europe, and it is said the works carried on here, under his instructions, to promote that object, cost ten millions of dollars, but at the peace of 1814, the dock-yards were obliged to be demolished, according to one of the articles in that treaty, though the two basins were suffered to remain. They are lined with large, substantial warehouses, and the whole aspect of the neighborhood is bustling and active.

The country around Antwerp is very pretty, having gardens and handsome houses, and roads bordered with trees, and public parks. Some of the streets of this city present an ancient and picturesque appearance, many of the houses having gable ends rising like steps. The more modern part has handsome houses, and fine public buildings.

Of course, we stopped to see the house in which Rubens died, and we have now visited the place of his birth, the scene of many of his labors, the spot where he died, and where his mortal remains repose. His works and his name will never die.

The Hotel de Ville, which was built in 1581, is a noble building, and near it is the house where Charles V. lived, while in Antwerp. The Exchange, built in 1531, is a magnificent edifice, around the inner court of which runs a kind of cloister, supported by beautiful columns. This court, formerly open at the top, has recently been covered with a roof of glass, like the late Crystal Palace of London.

We stopped at Mr. Baillie's warehouse, not so much to see his Antwerp silks, as his fine collection of paintings. I saw silks there that cost eight dollars a yard, but then, eight yards are sufficient for a dress. He tried to tempt me to buy, but my purse assisted me in resisting the temptation.

Sunday, 15*th*. This morning, we attended the English chapel, but this afternoon there was no service. The shops are open here to-day, and every body seems to be in the street. Wooden shoes and calico dresses jostle silks and satins. Many of the women wear caps, with large round lappets, trimmed with wide lace, and sometimes, surmounting this cap, is seen the most antique looking bonnet imaginable, resembling those Shaker bonnets we call "scoops," attached to which are immense streamers of wide ribbon. Again, many wear cloaks of black cloth, with hoods to them, lined with black silk, and these they throw over their heads, giving them quite a nun-like air. Others wear rich wide scarfs of black silk, the ends trimmed with heavy fringe.

As twilight came on this evening, I stood at the window, and saw the delicate tracery of the spire of the Cathedral, standing out like a picture, against the sky, and, floating on the air, came the rich notes of the bells. One particular note sent my thoughts far away, across the broad, deep ocean, and I sighed to think of the distance that still separates me from those I love, but the sigh was chased by a smile, at the idea that in six short weeks from this evening, I may hope to be in your midst.

The weather is so cold, we have been obliged to-day to have a fire in our room, for there is no nice public parlor to sit in, as in the hotels at home. I sit here writing to you; J. is reading, and in the grate a bright fire of sea-coal is burning. Do we not look cosy? Do you not wish you could take a nearer peep at us? Oh! do I not wish it?

LETTER LXXXVIII.

Ghent.—Church of St. Bavon.—St. Michael's Church.—The Belfry.—Prison.—Incident.—Town Hall.—Friday Market.—Quaint Houses.—Ruins.—Nunnery.—Bruges.—Hospital of St. John.—Church of Notre Dame.—Cathedral.—Town Hall.—Palace of Justice.—The Halls.—Chime of Bells.—Belgian Officers.

GHENT, Oct. 17th.

MY DEAR FRIENDS:

We left Antwerp yesterday morning, and came on here by railroad, through a level country, exceedingly rich and well cultivated. We devoted the greater part of yesterday to the "lions" of this old town, which lies upon two rivers, the Schelde and the Lys, and contains one hundred and three thousand inhabitants, within a circumference of nearly eight miles. Like the greater part of Flemish towns, it has fallen from its high estate, for in the time of Charles V., it was said to be the largest city in all Europe. Its trade and manufactures were very extensive, there being, in the fourteenth century, no less than forty thousand weavers here. Though its manufactures are by no means so large as formerly, it may be called the Manchester of Belgium.

And now I will tell you, in a succinct manner, what we have seen here worthy of note. Our first visit was to the Cathedral of St. Bavon, a new saint to me, but perhaps as worthy of canonization as many others that bear the title. It is an old church, founded in the tenth century, though not finished till the sixteenth. Rich paintings, sculptured tombs, the walls of the choir and transepts lined with black marble, with railings of white and variegated marble, all tend to make it an interesting object of observation. In front of the high altar, are four immense candlesticks of copper, once belonging to Charles I. of England, and still bearing the English arms. It is supposed they were sold during the time of Cromwell, though how they came here, we are not told.

There are twenty-four chapels in the side aisles, each containing valuable paintings by Cawer, Jansens, Porbus, De Crayer, Vander Meiren, Vander Heuvel, Honthorst, Roose, Vennius, Rubens, and the brothers Hubert and John Van Eyck. Those by Rubens are not his masterpieces, and I have not time to particularize the merits of the other artists, save to notice an extraordinary picture by the Van Eycks, "the Adoration of the Spotless Lamb," taken from the Revelation of St. John. There are more than three hundred heads in this picture, and each one is as highly finished as though it formed a separate miniature. It was painted in 1432, and yet the colors are as perfect as though put on yesterday. It is truly a splendid picture, and well worth coming to Ghent to see. In one of the chapels is the font in which Charles V. was baptised, who, perhaps you may remember, was born in this city, Feb. 24, 1500.

Although the weather was unfavorable, a few drops of rain occasionally falling, we went up to the top of the tower, by more than five hundred steps; it was so very misty, however, we could see but little beyond the immediate city, the distant country being shrouded in obscurity.

In St. Michael's church, are some magnificent paintings, of early and modern date. Here is the celebrated Crucifixion by Vandyck, for which he was paid the sum of three hundred dollars! The corporation of the church have lately refused forty thousand for it, offered them by some gallery in England! Side by side with this, is a modern painting, by a Belgian artist, whose name, I am sorry to say, I have forgotten. It represents the miraculous finding of the cross, to which I think I alluded in one of my letters from Jerusalem, and the figure of the Empress Helena in it, is a portrait of the beautiful and unfortunate Josephine of France.

There is a fine pulpit in this church, adorned with exquisite carvings, in wood and marble, the work of another Belgian artist, I think of the name of Franck.

The Tower, called the Belfry, is one of the most ancient in the city, dating as far back as the twelfth century. It was originally used as a watch-tower, and contained the alarm bell, the stroke of which was sufficient, at any time, to call the turbulent citizens to arms. In the rear of this tower, is a prison, and while we were stopping to admire its antique doorway, an officer came up with a prisoner. Just as the door was opened, the man, quick as lightning, kicked off his wooden shoes, and darted down the street, the officer in full hue and cry after him, calling on those in the street to stop him, but nobody heeded the call. A great crowd collected at the corner of the street, and soon the runaway appeared between two officers, each holding him by a cord twisted so tightly around the wrist, that the poor man's hands were actually livid.

The Town Hall is a splendid specimen of ancient architecture, having been commenced in the fifteenth century; it is elaborately adorned with carvings and Gothic arches.

In the large square, called the "Friday Market," the inauguration of the Counts of Flanders formerly took place. Here, Jacques Van Artevelde, in 1340, headed a band of weavers, against an opposite faction, when such a furious battle ensued, that fifteen hundred dead bodies were left on the square. Here, in 1381, Philip Van Artevelde was made "Protector" of Ghent, and here, in later days, under the cruel Duke of Alva, the terrible fires of the Inquisition were lighted, which were quenched only in blood. Oh! what scenes of dread and horror has this square witnessed!

Near the Fish Market, is an old gateway, built in 868, which formerly led to the castle of the Counts of Flanders, in which Queen Philippa, wife of Edward III. of England, gave birth to that son called "John of Gaunt," after this city.

Rich historical associations cluster around this ancient city, and make it exceedingly interesting. Here, in 1477, Mary of Burgundy was married to the Grand Duke Maximilian, and by this event, that part of Europe called the "Low Countries," was annexed to the dominions of Austria.

Many of the houses in Ghent are exceedingly picturesque, having gables rising in steps, like those I saw in Antwerp. On one of the canals, stands a fine old house of this description, bearing the date of 1513. On the gable are carved the insignia of the craft of watermen. The windows are pointed, thus presenting quite an ecclesiastical appearance.

We drove to the ruin of an old abbey, which the female cicerone told us was on the site of the oldest Christian church in Europe, but perhaps she meant in this part of Europe. In a court-yard, were found, in digging down into the earth, some very ancient tombs, but as I stood in the wet grass, looking at them, the rain pouring down upon me, I thought I was in a fair way of soon reaching my own, so I was glad to give up sight-seeing, and come home.

After dinner, we went to a chapel connected with a nunnery, to see the sisterhood at their evening prayers. The church was but dimly lighted, and all I could see, was hundreds of kneeling figures, shrouded in black, with immense white handkerchiefs of stiffened muslin, thrown over their heads. There was some chanting by female voices, but nothing very remarkable about it, and the priest muttered over his part, and one of the sisters went round with a plate to take pay for the chairs which were used, and the hard expression of her face, seen in the dim light, and the clinking of the copper coins, detracted a great deal from the impressiveness of the scene.

Most of these nuns live in separate houses; they teach the poor children, and nurse the sick, but are bound by no vows, each being at liberty to return to the world, whenever she pleases. Many of these sisters are from rich and noble families of Belgium. We went into one of the houses; every thing was neat and clean, but I had not much opportunity to look around, the "sister" being so very anxious to sell us little articles made by the children, the profits of which were for the poor, she said. These houses compose a large village by themselves, and are enclosed within walls, the gates of which are shut at seven o'clock in the evening.

To-day, we have been to Bruges, another old Flemish town, of about fifty thousand inhabitants, one-third of which are said to be paupers. In the fourteenth century, the commerce of the whole world was centred in this city; privileged companies of merchants, from seventeen different nations, were doing business here, and twenty foreign ministers were residing here. Now, there is but little commerce or manufactures going on; its streets and canals seem almost deserted, and the stones of many of the streets are overgrown with grass. But it is a rare old town, and far richer in picturesque houses than Ghent. Our first visit was to the Hospital of St. John, in the chapter-house of which hang some celebrated paintings by Hans Hemling, who came here as a patient, in 1477, and remained eight years, coming here "blessed," our guide said, (meaning "wounded," not "canonized,") his mixture of French words being thrown in in a very judicious way, to help out his imperfect English. These pictures Hemling painted and gave to the Hospital, in token of his gratitude for services rendered to him. They are admirably done, and as yet bear no marks of age, although nearly four hundred years old.

In this room is a shrine of wood, made like a little church, in which the arm of St. Ursula once reposed. On the outside of this shrine, are paintings representing scenes in the life of St. Ursula and the eleven thousand virgins of Cologne, to which subject I have already referred, in my letter from that city. In one of these little pictures are seventy figures, each one executed with the most exquisite finish. Ah! he was a rare old painter, that Hans Hemling!

Our next pause was at the church of Notre Dame, where are many beautiful paintings, and rich carvings in wood. There is a statue of the Virgin Mary and infant Jesus, said to have been done by Michael Angelo. The child is perfectly beautiful, but I do not like the face of the mother; it has a hard, cross, pouting look. It is not known how this statue ever found its way here, but the tradition is, that a vessel, bearing it to England, was wrecked on the coast of Flanders. The report is, that Horace Walpole once offered nearly fifteen thousand dollars for this group.

In a side chapel, (but concealed from view by large wooden screens, so that we were obliged to pay a franc extra for seeing them,) are the monuments of Charles the Bold and Mary of Burgundy. Around the sides are the coats of arms and the various titles of those sovereigns, and on the top of each, a full length statue of copper, richly gilt, and beautifully wrought.

The Cathedral is an immense edifice of brick, not handsome certainly, externally, but beautiful within, with its rich collection of old pictures.

The Town Hall is a beautiful edifice, in the Gothic style, built in 1377, and adorned with niches in front, in which were formerly statues of the Counts of Flanders, but in the visit of the French revolutionists here, they were all thrown down, being considered as "representatives of tyrants."

Near this, is the Palace of Justice, in which there is a magnificent fireplace, of black marble, surrounded by carvings in wood, and adorned with full length statues of Charles V., Mary and Maximilian, Charles the Bold and Margaret of York, besides having rich bas-reliefs in white marble. This fireplace is eight feet high and ten wide, according to our own measurement.

On one side of "the Grand Place," is a building called the "Halls," of brick, commenced in 1291. It has a beautiful Gothic tower, to the top of which we went, (by four hundred and two steps,) to get the view, which was very fine. The land around Bruges is exceedingly level, but rich as a garden, and cultivated to the very utmost, and fields and woods, canals and villages, and the distant sea, and the town of Ostend, formed a pretty picture. In this tower is a chime of bells, considered the finest in Europe. Permit me to copy this little account of them, that I bought on the spot. "They consist of forty-eight bells, the largest of which weighs eleven thousand three hundred and eighty-nine pounds, and the smallest, twelve pounds; the weight of the whole forty-eight is fifty-five thousand one hundred and sixty-six pounds, and they cost sixty thousand dollars. They are played by one hundred and forty hammers. The weights moving the drum, by means of which the chimes are made to play every hour, are four thousand pounds. The drum is made of copper; it weighs nineteen thousand nine hundred and sixty-six pounds, and serves to vary and regulate the chimes."

The machinery is very intricate and complicated, at least to one who is no more of a mathematician than I am, and difficult as it was for me to understand it, it would be altogether too much trouble to attempt to explain it to another. It was all very wonderful, and I looked at it with perfect amazement. The face of the clock is nineteen feet in diameter, and each of the figures is three feet in height.

On another side of the "Grand Place" is the house where Charles II. lived while an exile from England, and near it is the site of the building that was the prison of the Emperor Maximilian, shut up here by his own subjects, till he swore to grant certain conditions which they required.

We rested ourselves, after this long promenade and gazing about, with a good dinner at the "Hotel du

Commerce," and then walked through some of the principal streets to the railway station, and came back to Ghent. Just as we had, as the tourists say, "done up" Bruges

> "The sky with clouds was overcast,
> The rain began to fall,"

but we were thankful it did not begin to come down before.

From here to Bruges it is about twenty-nine miles, and there is not a hill in the whole distance, but the country is exceedingly pretty, varied with meadows bordered with hedges, and woods, and streams, and neat villages, with their red-tiled roofs.

There, I have written this long letter without rising from my chair, and I must say my fingers ache, so I will not add another word. But I must tell you however, that at the dinner table here yesterday, there were about thirty Belgian officers, and to our great surprise not one of them took any wine, a remarkable instance of abstinence for these countries. An English gentleman, noticing this circumstance, said to the waiter after dinner, "how happens it those officers take no wine? Why the officers in our army not only take their bottle of wine every day at dinner, but keep their horses and carriages too." "Oh, sir," answered the waiter, with an expressive shrug of the shoulders, "it is different here; not one of these officers could afford to keep a dog even." So then it seems "it is their poverty, not their will," that makes them temperate. They dine here daily at four o'clock, and pay by the month, which may be an interesting fact to you, for it seemed so to our "valet de place," who told it to us with a great deal of gusto.

LETTER LXXXIX.

Rain.—Mechlin.—Vilvorde.—Arrival at Brussels.—Fish.—Place-Royal —Statue of Godfrey of Bouillon.—Arcade.—The Park.—Rue Royale. Gallery of Pictures.—The Cathedral.—Funeral Ceremony.—Lace Manufactory.—The Grande Place.—Hotel de Ville.—Incident.—The House of the King.

BRUSSELS, Oct. 20th.

MY DEAREST F.:

We have already been here nearly three days, and yet I have scarcely any thing to tell you of this city, to which I have looked forward with a great deal of pleasure for many months. With the exception of a few hours, it has rained ever since our arrival here, or rather I should say, ever since our departure from Bruges on Tuesday. We left Ghent in such a rain on Wednesday that we did not think it advisable to stop at Mechlin, 'though it was an old town I was very anxious to see, but I really cannot stand sight-seeing in a soaking rain; it produces too damp an effect upon one's enthusiasm, to say nothing of one's clothes.

The country between Ghent and Brussels is very pretty, level, but well-wooded, well-watered and cultivated to the utmost. The houses are of brick, generally one story in height, and look clean and comfortable. We passed by Mechlin, known for its lace, though if you called it Mechlin here no one but those speaking the Flemish language would understand you, for in French it is Malines, and French is the predominant language now, and the money is reckoned by francs, so we are quite at home in that currency.

The next place of interest was Vilvorde, where Tindal, translator of the Bible into the English language, was strangled at the stake in 1536 as a heretic, and afterwards burnt outside the town.

There are pretty gardens, and parks, and country-seats between Vilvorde and this city, and I should think the drives around here would be delightful, but hitherto we have had no opportunity of testing this. Arriving at the station, we soon found ourselves with a dozen others in a large omnibus, the top fairly loaded with luggage, and just as we entered the precincts of the city, we were stopped by a custom-house officer, who wanted to know if we had any fish. You may be sure the question took us all by surprise, and the exclamation, "fish!" "du poisson!" resounded on all sides. At last the mystery came out, the city people were afraid of the country folks smuggling fish into the town, and thus depriving them of a part of their lawful revenues.

After duly pinching all the carpet bags inside the omnibus, the officer went on top, though how he could know what was in those huge trunks I could not tell, as he had not demanded a single key. One lady expressing this difficulty, a gentleman, in broken English, answered "why when he feels the smell," and here he made an expressive gesture with his nose, "of a fish, then he come down and make cry for the keys." A large basket puzzled the officer, and down he came with it, to demand what was in it. He was told in French and in English, "books," and replying "bookos," which I know not whether he meant for English, French or Flemish, he ordered it to be carried back, and on we came to the Hotel de L'Europe, situated on a square called Place Royal, surrounded by handsome houses. In the centre of the square is an equestrian statue in bronze, of Godfrey of Bouillon holding in one hand a partially furled banner, which at first sight I took to be an umbrella half closed by the wind. Perhaps the dismal weather had something to do with this illusion, but I cannot go to the window, and look at the statue without catching myself saying "it does look like an umbrella."

A straggling sunbeam burst out yesterday afternoon and immediately I threw down my pen, and rushed forth to get a breath of fresh air, and a glimpse of this city called "Paris on a small scale." I actually had not walked down one steep street (you must remember a hill is quite a curiosity to us, not having seen one for two weeks,) before the weather warned me I should soon have to turn back, but I was willing to brave it a little for the sake of peeping into the windows full of beautiful things, every third or fourth window splendidly decked out with laces, this city being famous, as you all know, for the manufacture of such commodities. Then we came to a handsome arcade or long street, with a roof of glass, and on either side were shops filled with every thing handsome and tempting. Here, walking back and forth, occasionally stepping into a shop to inquire the price of an article, or to venture on a slight purchase, I was quite protected from the weather.

This morning we intended going to Waterloo, but the weather was by no means clear; however we thought it quite safe to venture out within the limits of the city, though we had not gone far before the rain began to come down again in right earnest. But I was determined not to give up and come home till I had seen a little of the city. There is a very pretty Park here, with walks shaded by o'er-arching trees, now almost stripped of their leaves. It is surrounded by Palaces and handsome houses, and must form a delightful promenade in pleasant weather, but rather a dreary one just now, I must confess, with the wind blowing as cold and bleak as in December with us.

Brussels is the capital of Belgium, and the king's palace fronts this park. The king is at present away; in fact we do not seem to be at the right season any where for seeing crowned heads, the royal personages not having yet returned from their summer tour. But after all, "crowned heads," particularly without the crowns, look very much like other heads.

On one side of the park is "Rue Royale," a street three miles in length, and adorned with handsome houses, in one of which it is said the Duchess of Richmond gave the grand ball to the Duke of Wellington just before the battle of Waterloo, when, as Byron says, "all went merry as a marriage bell."

In this street we stopped to visit a private gallery of pictures, a beautiful collection, mostly of the old Dutch and Flemish school, in which one does not see so many naked figures as in the Italian school, but cottage and village groups, choice bits of landscapes, cattle, "as natural as life," and noble looking portraits of men and women in deep, stiff ruffles, or large collars of point lace.

Our next destination was to the Cathedral, an imposing Gothic church, with two magnificent square towers in front. The interior is rich in monuments and windows of beautifully stained glass, the latter being more than three hundred years old. The pulpit is an immense piece of wood carving, representing Adam and Eve driven out of Paradise, the figures as large as life. In all these Flemish churches there seems to be such a taste for elaborately carved pulpits, and I must confess I should like it on one account, for if I was not interested in the minister, I could look at the pulpit.

There was a funeral service in the church while we were there, and occasionally the organ burst forth with a strain of rich melody, and a trumpet added its stirring notes. One of the officiating priests had a magnificent voice, which now and then came out clear and full, but there was a great deal of form and ceremony that I could not understand. At a certain part of the service, one of the priests, standing on the steps of the altar before the coffin, held something in his hand like a gilt plate, which all the men in the church went up and kissed, and the quickness with which the priest held it to the lips of one, wiped it on a napkin, and then had it ready for the next one, was a marvel. Each man, as he passed the coffin, carried a lighted candle, which he held in his hand till he had kissed the plate, and then gave it up for the next comer, and thus candles and kisses passed in quick succession. Our guide told us afterwards that what I thought was a plate, was a little coffer inclosing a famous relic. I should have liked to have seen the end of the ceremony, but we had not the time to spare.

Near the church was a lace manufactory, and we went in to see the process. Some of the lace made here is very expensive, and is said to be worth its weight in gold. There is no foundation or web on which the work is placed, but each thread or mesh is formed at the time the figures are made. I don't know as I make this clear to you, but it is as well as I can explain it, without going into a long detail. Another kind is made in a different way; each leaf or sprig is worked by itself, and then caught together by the finest possible thread. Still another kind is woven by the hand, by means of an immense number of little spools, passed in and out and around a barricade of pins. I saw one collar that cost a woman sixty-five days' labor, and one small flower that another was five days in working. The work-women get from half a franc (about ten cents) to a franc and a half a day, and on this small pittance contrive to support themselves. There is a box at the door for those who become in time unable to work, but who has the charge of giving out this money I cannot say. It is a delicate way of asking those who visit the establishment to give something towards it, though truth compels me to add, there is not the slightest delicacy manifested in begging the visitors to buy the different laces exposed for sale in the show-room.

Passing through a number of streets composed of both antique and modern looking buildings, we came to what is called the "Grande Place," lined with picturesque old houses, each of which is a perfect study for an artist, and almost every one has interesting historical associations connected with it. On one side stands the "Hotel de Ville," or Town Hall, a perfect specimen of Gothic architecture, dating as far back as 1401. The tower, three hundred and sixty-four feet high, is of the most delicate fret-work, and deserves to be ranked by the side of the spires of Notre Dame at Antwerp, and St. Stephen's at Vienna. As the rain was coming down with respectable vigor, it was useless to attempt to go up into the tower to get the view of the country, so we contented ourselves with walking through a few of the rooms below, some of which had portraits of worthies long passed away, and the walls of two or three were lined with tapestries, illustrating events in the life of Charles V., &c. The female cicerone told us that monarch signed his abdication in the Gothic hall in this building, but others say it was in the Palace, which stood near our hotel, and which was burned down in 1733.

In one of the rooms in this hall all civil marriages take place, the parties afterwards going to a church and having the religious part of the ceremony performed. As we entered the room, a person in attendance there began to collect together some papers, upon which a dialogue ensued between him and our conductor which seemed to amuse both very much. As the saying is, " I smelt a rat," and thereupon I made a few inquiries, which elicited the following interesting story: The magistrate, or whatever his title may be, seeing a " likely looking" couple like us entering the room, supposed we came to get married, (he must have thought we were beginning life rather late in the day,) and on expressing his surprise at our coming on Friday, a day it seems that few knots are tied here, the cicerone told him we were strangers visiting the Hall. If he had been counting on a fee he must have felt a little disappointed at this overthrow of his hopes.

Opposite the Town Hall there is a large house built in heavy Gothic style, called " the house of the King." Here " the cruel Alva" lived, and it is said he used to stand at the window and look out upon executions in the square below, called forth by his insatiable thirst for blood.

On our way home we passed through the markets devoted to flowers, fruits and poultry, and stopped at the exhibition of paintings by modern Belgian artists, comprising a large collection, some of them very beautiful, and others not rising above mediocrity.

The gallery of old paintings was closed, so we could not judge of its merits, and as for zoological cabinets and museums, we have already seen so many, we are not ambitious of visiting any others, and the rain preventing us walking round or even taking a drive, we turned our steps homeward.

And now I will pause to take a little rest.

LETTER XC.

Changeable Weather.—Visit to Waterloo.—Sergeant Munday.—Field of Battle.—Brilliant Display.—More Rain.—Disappointment.

BRUSSELS, Oct. 21.

MY DEAR P.:

The sky was watched with great eagerness this morning, and it chose to assume various hues, so as one time to convince us the day would be fine, and at another to assure us that it would be folly to attempt to go to Waterloo. We were very anxious to visit that celebrated spot to-day, for on Monday we must go to Paris, and to come to Brussels without going to Waterloo, would be like seeing the play of Hamlet performed, with the part of Hamlet left out. At last all doubts were happily removed; the sun came out beautifully, and at ten o'clock we mounted on top of the coach, and found ourselves borne quickly through the streets by four good horses. At first I felt rather awkward in my elevated position, for I have not moved so high in the air since I was mounted on that tall camel between Akaba and Hebron.

The road is paved the whole distance from here to Waterloo (about ten miles,) but from the heavy rains that have fallen lately, it was not in the best possible condition, and for the first two or three miles my attention was quite absorbed in the efforts necessary to keep myself upright on the seat, and by that time, (I hope you will sympathize with me,) the sun went behind a cloud, or somewhere else, and the rain "began to fall," and I was obliged to descend from my elevated position, and betake myself to the inside of the coach, which I had all to myself.

I had an idea that the road from here to Waterloo ran nearly all the way through a forest, whereas we scarcely entered the forest at all, but went through villages and pretty meadows, some looking green and bright, while others, having been recently ploughed up and sown with winter grain, had a rich brown hue that contrasted beautifully with the green patches around.

Under the guidance of Sergeant Munday, himself an actor in the battle of Waterloo, we went all over the field, and saw the positions taken by different portions of the contending armies. And as I went back and forth, and looked over the gently undulating country, beautifully diversified with farm houses, and orchards, and fertile fields, I could not but contrast the scene of to-day, with that of years ago, when the earth was covered with the dying and the dead, and the air was loaded with the shrieks of the wounded. And as I listened to the details of that ever memorable day, my sympathies were not with the victors, but woman-like were with the conquered, and as I thought of him whose brilliant star set that day forever, I caught myself more than once exclaiming, "poor Napoleon."

I flatter not myself that I can do much in the way of enlightening you on the subject of this battle, for that could not be done in a few words. Hundreds and thousands of pages have been written about it, and every body that visits the field of Waterloo has something to add which he hopes will be edifying, and if I were to say much it would be only to repeat what has been said by wiser people than I am, about Napoleon's position, and Jerome Bonaparte's untimely move, and the daring of the French, and the opposing valor of the British, the bravery of the German legions, and the timely approach of the Prussians, and all this you have heard a thousand times.

Just as we reached the chateau of Hougoumont, the sun came out brightly, and although the grass was wet, I suffered no inconvenience from it, having come prepared for wet fields. About this chateau the hottest of the fight took place, and the walls of the orchard and of some of the out-buildings still remain, bearing to this day the marks of the hard firing going on at that time. The old house caught fire and burned nearly to the ground, and the chapel was sharing the same fate when the flames reached a crucifix that hung over the door, and suddenly stopped, which was considered a miracle by many.

We walked over the graves of hundreds, many of the dead having been buried just where they fell. Two or three monuments mark the spot where some noble commander died, but grass and grain grow over the greater part of the field, and trees wave their branches in the wind, the only monument that tells where hundreds are sleeping their last sleep.

The ground occupied by the contending armies did not extend more than a mile and a half from right to left, yet, on that small space of ground it is computed seventy-five thousand persons were killed and wounded. Oh! what a fearful slaughter (for I cannot call it by a softer name) was that! What bright hopes were quenched, what fond hearts made desolate! And for what? To crush the ambition of one nation and its leader, or to exalt another people to a higher eminence than they had before attained?

Of course we brought away a few relics from the field of Waterloo, two or three bullets and buttons, a cane cut from an old tree, and some chestnuts from the grounds of Hougoumont, from which we may yet raise Waterloo trees at home.

And thus we have visited the far famed field of Waterloo, and I have less interest than ever in war and its cruel results, and to my last breath would cry, "my voice is still for peace."

This evening the stars came out brightly, and we took a long walk through the brilliantly lit streets, and lightened our purses considerably.

Sunday 22. The bright stars last evening were false lights, for they ushered in a pour-down rain this morning, instead of the genial sun, as we fondly expected from the favorable auspices. I ventured out to-day merely to go to the English chapel, the weather being quite too unfavorable to tempt me to stay out longer than necessary. I feel very much disappointed in this visit to Brussels. I had anticipated so much pleasure, and these anticipations like many others have been much more pleasant than the reality. Yet travellers have to take their chance in all these things, and they must learn to make the most of the fine weather, as of every other blessing vouchsafed to them. And with this apt moral reflection I will leave you.

LETTER XCI.

At Home in Paris.—Examination of Luggage.—Hotel Bedford.—Familiar Sights and Sounds.—Cafè.—Champs Elyseès.—Madeleine.—Last Days in Paris.

PARIS, Oct. 27th.

MY DEAR F.:

I can't tell you what a feeling of home is given us in the sound of "Paris," in the consciousness we are once more in "dear delightful Paris," that city where we spent so many pleasant days thirteen years ago. And as I walk along the streets, and see so many familiar houses and even the very signs we saw then, I find it hard to realize that so many years have rolled away since we were here. And when you call to mind, that excepting Liverpool and London, Paris is the only place we have visited before, you can in a measure realize the truth of my assertion, that in this city we feel at home.

And now to review the past a little. We left Brussels on the morning of the 23d, our old enemy the rain pursuing us with relentless vigor. We were more than ten hours on the railroad, the distance being about 230 miles. I can say but little of the country through which we passed, the rain obliging us the most of the time to keep the windows closed. Had I time I should like to descant on the continental railroads, and show the many points wherein they excel those in our own country, but "time flies" and I must fly with it.

At Valenciennes, the frontier town, our light luggage that we had with us, such as carpet-bags, valises, &c., was examined, while that of the heavier artillery, trunks and boxes, was reserved till our entrance into this city. At Valenciennes it looked formidable, for the ladies were all taken into a separate room, where stood a fierce-looking woman, who told us in loud tones she should search the person of any one she suspected for a moment to be smuggling laces or any other contraband articles. Whether we were really very honest, or whether her suspicions were not excited, I know not. This one thing I do know, that nothing more was done than to look pretty closely into carpet-bags and baskets, and as each key was turned, and each trembling female allowed to pass on, all faces wore a brighter and less troubled look, and in due time we were seated once more in the cars, and the "iron horse" bore us swiftly on. The examination in Paris was equally light, as far as we were concerned, and in a little while after our arrival at the barrier, we were in comfortable quarters in Hotel Bedford.

Thus far, since our arrival in Paris, I have spent the most of my time, when it has been sufficiently pleasant, out of doors, lounging along the Boulevards, or in the gardens of the Tuilleries, exulting in my freedom from journalizing or letter writing, for as I wrote you so fully from Paris when I was here before, there remains but little for me now to add, unless indeed I repeat what I said then, and that my time is altogether too precious to allow me to do.

The shops along the Boulevards and the Rue Rivoli look as brilliant as ever. There is the same display of rich goods in the windows, and in the streets the same restless, moving throng of people. The ladies still hold up their dresses with that pretty grace, that it is impossible for any one but a French woman to attempt to practice.

Along Rue Rivoli, as well as in some other streets, we see important changes, proof that Napoleon III. is doing all in his power to beautify and improve his capital. And here I will just say, we shall not have the pleasure of seeing that monarch and his lovely wife, the court being at present out of the city.

This morning, we went to a café opposite the Tuileries, to breakfast, that we frequented very often when in Paris before. There were the same red books, containing the bills of fare, and for aught I knew, the same waiter that attended on our wants years ago. And to heighten the illusion, a regiment was reviewed right opposite our windows, and the band played the Marsellaise, just as in olden times.

Oct. 28th. Engaged a good deal of the time in that most feminine occupation, shopping, having commissions to execute for a "thousand and one friends" at home. We varied the scene this afternoon, by walking out to the Champs Elyseès, where was, as ever, a crowd intent on pleasure and amusements of different kinds. Nothing struck me more than the little carriages drawn by goats, while the reins would be held by a charming child, all life and animation, her nurse walking along by the side of the carriage. The weather was lovely, and I enjoyed the sunshine and the warm air fully as much as the children.

Passing by the Madeleine this morning, that beautiful church I have once described so fully to you, I saw that something unusual was going on, so I stepped in. The church was shrouded in black. Hundreds of candles were lighted in different parts of the edifice, which was filled to overflowing with people. The music was magnificent. Nothing could surpass it. In vain, I tried to find out who was the occupant of the coffin covered with a rich pall of black velvet, embroidered with gold. No one among the spectators seemed to know, and, of course, I did not like to ask any one whom I supposed to be the friends of the deceased. At last, the ceremonies were ended; the funeral cortège passed out, and as I saw the last mourning coach move on, I ventured to make one more inquiry, and this time of a venerable looking old lady. "I don't know, madame," was the reply, "but it is evidently somebody very genteel!" Oh! ye French people, "genteel" seems as talismanic a word to you, as it does to your neighbors across the Atlantic ocean!

Among the various items of business transacted the last few days, we have engaged our passage in the steamship Canada, which leaves Liverpool for Boston, Nov. 11th. How near that seems at hand! I sigh when I think this pleasant journey is drawing to a close, but I smile at the thought that its close will bring me once more to those I love best on earth.

31*st*. Our last walk in Paris has been taken, our last shopping done, and to-morrow we are off for England. Since I have been here, I have spent several hours each day out, wandering at my "own sweet will," wherever my inclinations prompted, and when in the hotel, busy writing, bringing this lengthened Budget to a close, so that when I go on board the steamer at Liverpool, I can feel at ease, with the consciousness that the work I placed before me, when I left home, was done. How well that work has been done, I must leave for you and for others to decide. The hours of labor it has cost me are now forgotten; there remains only the knowledge that those hours were spent for your pleasure, and that knowledge brings its own reward.

LETTER XCII.

Retrospect.—Leaving Paris.—Crossing the Channel.—Dover.—Arrival in London.—Occupations.—Novelty.—Review.

LONDON, Nov. 7th.

TO MY LOVED ONES AT HOME:

My first letter on board the Indus, off Gibraltar, commenced with this address; my last one must go to the same assembled household. Through all these months of travel, through all these varied scenes, my heart has ever turned "to my loved ones at home." Whatever of pleasure I have received in visiting strange lands, has been imparted to them, and if they have felt half the interest in reading these letters, that I have had in writing them, I am more than paid for the exertion they have cost me, for wearied out, as I often was in body and mind, it sometimes cost me quite an effort to sit down and write for hours, coolly reviewing all that I had seen, and selecting such things to write about as I knew you would like. And now this must be my last letter, for the next steamer after to-morrow's will take us instead of our letters. I linger over this letter with a loving interest, because it is the last I shall write from a foreign land. In the thirteen months that I have been absent from you, I dare not attempt to count the hundreds of written pages I have sent you. One little fact I must mention, because it would not otherwise be known to you. The paper on which these letters have been written, was bought in the United States, in London, at Assouan, (near the first cataract of the Nile,) in Constantinople, Athens, Vienna, Berlin, Brussels and Paris, so that you have had an opportunity thus of seeing paper from various quarters of the globe. But if I go on in this rambling way, I shall never reach the end of my last epistle, so I hasten on, or rather I must go backward for a few days.

On the morning of the first of November, we were called at the unseasonable hour of five. I should have been in a mood of bitter complaint, had I not known this was about the last time my slumbers would thus be invaded, so I bore it with unexampled equanimity. We bade adieu (I fear a final one) to Paris, and at seven were on our way to Calais, where we arrived without any incident worth relating, about half past two, having accomplished two hundred and thirty miles in that time.

We were obliged to go off to the steamer in small boats, an operation I by no means relished. Our departure from the French coast was signalized by the usual amount of noise and confusion incidental to a steamer getting under way. The passage across the channel was made in two hours, the water perfectly smooth, but it was so foggy we could not see the "white cliffs of Albion," till we were close upon them. Landing at Dover, we went through the usual formalities of the custom house, and then went to a hotel, where we had a late dinner and a comfortable night's lodging, and the next morning were whirled up to London, and soon found ourselves in excellent quarters, at Wood's Hotel, where, in addition to the substantials of this life, we were speedily regaled with letters from home, the last, probably, we shall receive.

And now you are ready to ask, "What have you been doing with yourself these five or six days you have been in London?" To which question I make an answer in three words, "Visiting, shopping and writing." As in our two former visits to London, we pretty well "did up" the celebrities of the place, there is nothing we particularly care to do in the way of sight-seeing, so that part of a traveller's duty is not very onerous to us just now. We have had great pleasure in renewing our acquaintance with some delightful people that came over with us from New York, in the Arctic, and with them we have spent many pleasant hours, lunching and dining with them whenever we liked, they having given us cordial invitations to spend as much time with them as possible. We have been once or twice, too, at Mr. A.'s house, where we have spent delightful hours talking over our mutual friends in Rhode Island. Shopping, being essentially a feminine pursuit, has, of course, engrossed some of my time, as there are always "last things" to attend to in that line. And as for writing, there is always sufficient of that commodity on hand to occupy any hours that might otherwise be unemployed. Thus, I have accounted for my time in London.

I cannot tell you how strangely it seemed, at first, to hear nothing but English spoken around us. Hearing, as we have done, ever since we left London, thirteen months ago, a medley of languages, French, Italian, Arabic, Syriac, Turkish, Greek, German, Dutch, and a variety of other idioms, we became almost unused to the sound of our mother tongue, except when spoken by ourselves, and for the first two or three mornings after our arrival here, I invariably commenced giving orders for the day to the waiter in French, and was not aware I was doing any thing out of the ordinary course, till I met his astonished gaze. You may think this affectation, but I believe every one who has been, for any length of time, in a foreign land, would bear me out in the assertion.

As I sit this evening before my bright fire, and listen to the whirl and noise of the streets, that whirl and noise which in London never seem to cease, it is difficult for me to realize how much I have seen, what lands I have visited, since I was in this great city before. The stormy passage of the Bay of Biscay; the beginning of our oriental life; Cairo, with its picturesque streets so full of novel sights and sounds; our sojourn on the sacred Nile; the tombs, temples and time-honored pyramids; the soft, lustrous African nights, the journey across the Desert, so fraught with interest; tent life; the sacred mountains; the rock-city Petra; the Holy Land, with all its thrilling, soul-moving associations; Constantinople the magnificent; classic Greece and its lovely isles; Austria, Prussia, Belgium, Holland, with their stores of riches, both in nature and art—all seem now to me as a dream, a lovely dream, and I say more than once, have I seen them all? Have I lived this chequered life? Have I heard these varied tongues? Have I walked the streets of Jerusalem, climbed the Mount of Olives, wept in the garden of Gethsemane, gazed upon the Sea of Galilee, in short, seen the land consecrated by the presence of Him, the God-man? It is so. Strange as it all seems, it is all true, it is not a vision.

My loved ones, adieu till I meet you all once more in my own native land.

NOTE.

Our voyage in the Canada was in due time over, and on the morning of the fifteenth day after leaving Liverpool, we landed in Boston, grateful to Him who had preserved us through all our wanderings, and for leaving unbroken the circle of our loved friends who were ready to welcome us home once more.

We were absent from the United States fourteen months, during which time we travelled nineteen thousand two hundred and fifty-eight miles, viz: thirteen thousand one hundred and eighty-three in steamers, one thousand eight hundred in our boat on the Nile, six hundred miles on camel, five hundred on horseback, in diligence and other carriages, three hundred and forty-five, and two thousand eight hundred and thirty miles by railroad. Of course, I could form no conception of the number of miles I rode on donkeys in Egypt, and in hackney coaches in Europe.

During this period, we slept sixty-two nights in steamers, seventy-two in our boat on the Nile, fifty-nine in a tent, two in a diligence, and two in railroad cars, avoiding, as much as possible, night travel on land, which is very exhausting to the strength of travellers.

The banking and posting arrangements were all settled by our banker, George Peabody, Esq., and through the constant exertions of that well-known house, not a solitary letter sent from us, or to us, from all quarters of the globe, failed to reach its destination in due time. Such are the facilities of mail transportation, I am convinced, if ordinary care is taken, there is no need of travellers ever having any trouble about their letters. In whatever part of the world we mailed a letter, it was always under cover to Mr. Peabody, in London, and all letters to us were sent to the same address, the banker having his directions, from time to time, where to forward our letters. By taking this little additional trouble and expense, we were saved all care and vexation about our letters, for any one who has travelled in foreign lands, will appreciate the blessing of regular letters from home.

www.ingramcontent.com/pod-product-compliance
Lightning Source LLC
LaVergne TN
LVHW020121110826
845151LV00001B/231

* 9 7 8 1 4 2 5 5 4 1 6 1 3 *